MOUNTAIN
DIALOGUES

Books by Frank Waters

Fiction

The Wild Earth's Nobility
Below Grass Roots
Dust within the Rock
People of the Valley
River Lady (with Houston Branch)
The Yogi of Cockroach Court
Diamond Head (with Houston Branch)
The Man Who Killed the Deer
The Woman at Otowi Crossing
Pike's Peak

Non-fiction

Midas of the Rockies
The Colorado (Rivers of America Series)
Masked Gods
The Earp Brothers of Tombstone
Book of the Hopi
Leon Gaspard
Pumpkin Seed Point
To Possess the Land
Mexico Mystique
Mountain Dialogues

MOUNTAIN

DIALOGUES

Frank Waters

SAGE BOOKS

SWALLOW PRESS
ATHENS, OHIO   CHICAGO

Sage/Swallow Press Books
are published by
Ohio University Press
Athens, Ohio

Library of Congress Cataloging in Publication Data

Waters, Frank, 1902–
  Mountain dialogues.

  I. Title.
PS3545. A82M6   813'.52   81-732
ISBN 0-8040-0361-0 (Swallow P.)   AACR2

TO BARBARA

CONTENTS

FOREWORD   ix

PART ONE
1.   The Living Land   3
2.   El Cuchillo Del Medio   11
3.   The Sacred Mountain   25
4.   Mountain and Plain   35
5.   Silence   49
6.   Water   56
7.   Air   64
8.   Spirits   72

PART TWO
1.   The Sacred Mountains of the World   83
2.   Ley Lines   95
3.   Movement   108
4.   The Hopi Prophecy   118
5.   The Circle of the Law Belt   136
6.   The Four-Fold Structure of Mind and Matter   149

PART THREE
1.   Jung and Maharshi—On the Nature and Meaning of Man   163
2.   Sierra Madre Outposts   194
3.   The East is Red   208
4.   America: A Footnote   229

Foreword

These brief essays on subjects seemingly nebulous and diverse as silence, spirits, movement, and the sacred mountains of the world, all seem to reecho one eternal theme—the inherent wholeness of man and his oneness with the entire universe.

Belief in this transcendent unity was undoubtedly common among all the great civilizations which preceded our own so far back in the prehistoric past that we often doubt their very existence. Today the hidden meanings of the few records they have left are breaking surface; and we are indebted to the many intuitive discoverers who are reconstructing, as if from the tips of icebergs, the great submerged continent of ancient man's apperception of one invisible and encompassing world beyond his senses. New and unfamiliar as its landmarks first seem, they yet strike a chord in our minds and hearts like something we have always known but forgotten; and their meanings are confirmed by our modern sciences.

We cannot doubt the influences of planetary and telluric forces upon us. Nor can we question the evidence that these cosmic energies are manifested alike in the forms of nature and in man's own psyche. Their imprints can be detected not only in the pattern of a leaf, but upon mankind's various religions and architecture, the shapes of civilizations. Even in the radiations distinct to a mountain, a separate locality, we feel the full forces of one harmonizing power.

Certainly my own home slope of the Sangre de Cristo Mountains has not been immune to the effects of these creative forces. Comparatively small and obscure as it is, it is part of the indivisible, universal organism. The two peaks behind me—El Cuchillo del Medio and the Sacred Mountain—have projected their dual, complementary influences for many years. In a way I can't explain, they have carried on a silent, curious dialogue which I seem to have overheard with my inner ear, and in which I have occasionally participated and interrupted. If I have interpreted their meanings too freely, and applied them to distant, wider fields, they still insist on the principle that everything which happens in the material world of visible things, in the suprasensible world of heaven, and in man, are synonymous. The ancient Chinese *I Ching,* the *Book of Changes,* is constructed on this trinity of the primal powers. The lower two lines in its hexagrams designate earth, the upper two lines heaven, and the middle two lines between them, man.

The present discussions hopefully suggest that these three dimensions of man's total experience are reconciled in the silent tongue of the one spirit that pervades them all. Our communication with the spirit of a place, with its constituent voices of a stream, a rock, a tree, confirms the truth that this interrelation is necessary for our continued existence as one species of organisms dependent like all others upon the same eternal powers that inform the universal whole.

PART ONE

1

The Living Land

A small girl in a group of other neighboring children came to see me some time ago with an enigma clutched in her somewhat scrubby hand. The visits of these Spanish-American children to the first Anglo-American living on our mountain road were not unusual. They enjoyed prowling through the house, asking questions about its unfamiliar gadgets. This little girl brought me instead a fistful of earth. "How does this dirt make our garden grow?" she asked simply.

Her question struck a responsive chord in me. In these days we seem to know everything about the planet Earth itself. But for some strange reason we know nothing about a mere handful of dirt whose miraculous fecundity makes our gardens, fields, and pastures grow.

My neighbors and I, more fortunate than big-city dwellers, see a great deal of earth from our homes along the steeply rising road from the small village of Arroyo Seco in northern New Mexico. Vast landscapes of it in every direction. Above us towers the Sangre de Cristo range in an enclosing semi-circle of forested mountains and snowy peaks. Below us, the land slopes westward through a sage plateau to the desert beyond, and extends far beyond that to the faint blue rise of the Rockies.

One would think that my young visitor would know better than to ask how the earth gives life to this immense plant kingdom of pine and sage, corn and wheat, and vegetable gardens. She comes from an earthy, hardy group of Spanish-Colonial ancestors who settled this remote mountain valley on a land grant made in 1716 by the will of His Majesty, the King of Spain. For more than two centuries they have lived solely from this earth, most of them on the same family *ranchitos*. They have lived within it, too, for their very homes are adobes fashioned from the earth.

Still her question demanded an answer. We spread out her handful of dirt on a newspaper laid across the coffee table. How variegated were its tiny particles, of all sizes, shapes, and colors. One thing we didn't see: whatever held them together in an invisible, creative unity that makes our vegetables grow. We wisely decided that it was the same mystery that somehow gave life to the colts, calves, and lambs in our pastures, all different but reflecting the creative powers of what we call Nature. Thank goodness, she was content with this. But I was left to seek a more conclusive answer.

Another visitor who used to come was Juan Concha, who had served several terms as the governor of Taos Pueblo, a horseback ride of an hour or so across the Indian Reservation extending south from the road. He was a little man, old, dark, and wrinkled. He would sit on the portál with me, waiting for supper, and watching the flanks of the Sangre de Cristos turn blood-red as their name in the flare of the sinking sun. For this range, the birthplace of his people, Old Juan held special reverence.

"Our Mother Earth. It borns us. Everything! Rocks, trees, grasses, corn. All them animals and birds. Us too."

How often, from so many Indians of other tribes, have I heard expressed this devout belief. To the Mayas, two thousand years ago in Yucatan, the earth was not dead, inorganic matter, but a living entity to which they were as intimately related as is it to the stellar universe.

The living land.

But we don't need for the moment to depend solely upon the ages-long belief of all Indian America. The earth itself assures us it is a living entity. Deep below surface one can hear its slow pulse, feel its vibrant rhythm. The great breathing mountains expand and contract. The vast sage desert undulates with almost imperceptible tides like the oceans. From the very beginning, throughout all its cataclysmic upthrusts and deep sea submergences, the planet Earth seems to have maintained an ordered rhythm.

Just how it was created no one knows. There have been many versions; the Planetesimal, Gaseous Tidal, and Gaseous Nebular hypotheses, and the Big Bang theory. All are variations of the modern belief that the planet was created by the Sun, the mysterious primal power, through the primary elements of fire, air, water, and earth. Our scientific myth of creation, uncertain of mechanistic details as it is, does not conflict in principle with the creation myths of Indian America which also assert in their own terminology the patrimony of our Father Sun.

What our earth, the planet, was like when born we don't know either, considering that the blessed event happened, according to current guess, about 4,700 million years ago. (Quite a good way back from the world creation date of October 26, 4004 B.C. at 9:00 a.m. exactly, the moment set by Archbishop Usher of Ireland in 1654. This date was then inserted as a marginal note in the King James version of the Bible, and adopted into scripture.) Whatever it was, this newborn child took its place in a family of nine revolving around the Father Sun of our solar system, one of many such systems in our galaxy, which is but one of many such galaxies in the illimitable universe. A tiny mote in cosmic space, but still to us a sizeable global speck. A great natal rock mysteriously imbued with life from its birth and which had a function to perform in the universe as it slowly matured through constant movement and change.

What this functional purpose was we can't define. Modern historical geology records only the slow physical evolution of Earth into the form we now know by reading the age and composition of successive layers of rock—a chronology of deep sea submergences, continental uplifts, colossal volcanic eruptions, glaciation, and erosion. One can view the static record of these changes in the paleographical maps of any standard textbook—an autobiography of the earth neatly divided into chapters entitled eras and epochs. What a pity we can't see the dramatic story of these mighty changes in a TV special, condensing the history of millions, billions of years into a dynamic moving picture of one hour, with time out for commercials.

Beginning perhaps 500 million years ago, there appeared the earliest forms of what we call life—the trilobites and brachipods, the first spokesmen of the evolving earth. Then came the succession of those great time-spans, the Age of Fishes, the Age of Amphibians, and the Age of Reptiles, which marked the rise to dominance of gigantic land creatures. Monstrous dinosaurs of many tons, standing twenty feet high and as long as sixty-five feet, with scientific names just as long and frightening. And yet some power beyond our comprehension obliterated forever the entire species of these lords of the earth, in order to clear the stage for the Age of Mammals and the appearance of that puny, cringing, and defenseless creature which would endure as man.

If, as Eastern sages assert, a mere stone possesses an unmanifest consciousness, we must believe that the living earth itself was endowed with a basic threshold of consciousness by the universal consciousness that gave it birth. The earliest trilobites and brachipods, too, must have possessed a dormant consciousness, and human life represented rises of consciousness to ever higher levels, being necessary accompaniments to the geological stages of the earth.

Undoubtedly the purely physical or geological record of the earth's long primordial past must be paralleled by a psychical record. The undying memory of man's own short and relatively recent primeval past is still preserved, according to C.G. Jung, as primeval images or archetypes in his collective unconscious. The psychical record of the life-forms that preceded him still lies in unplumbed depths beyond our present cognizance, but which eventually will be read as our expanding consciousness is gradually attuned to its spectrum.

As the archetypes of man's collective unconscious rise into consciousness which gives them form and meaning, so must the inherent consciousness of the earth itself have risen through the life-forms of its plant, animal, and human entities to give ever clearer voice and meaning to the universal consciousness informing from birth this great natal rock. Do we dare to suppose, then, that the human consciousness formulating these thoughts must also have derived from this living planetary rock?

Certainly the physical structure of man is akin to that of the earth. His body is composed of the same four living elements of our great global entity—earth, air, water, and fire. All are inter-related in one living whole. The earth pulsates in an almost imperceptible but ordered rhythm. Water in man and on earth moves in tune with the phases of the moon, as reflected by the tides of the sea, the rises of sap in trees, the female menstrual periods. Air circulates through both bodies, ascending over warm land areas and descending over cool areas, constituting the "breathing of the continents." And our common life energy of light and heat relates us to the sun.

How appallingly simple and complete it seems for a moment! A wholeness in which every part is interrelated in one vast body of universal Creation. How dependent we are upon each —the lofty pine and blade of grass at its foot, the deer and the eagle wheeling above it, mountain and man—all spokesmen who contribute their voices to the chorus of the living land. The top-soil layer of the earth's crust owes its fecundity to the worm. Still, I hesitate to move a pebble at my foot for fear of dis-turbing the equilibrium of the planet. Yet movement, constant cyclic change, is the immutable law of the whole. Only by it can the earth and its many forms of life fulfill their own functions and interact with every other planet, themselves evolving toward a common destiny.

What this might be has been conjectured by the sages of many time-honored religions, including those Native American philosophers in hairbraids living across the Reservation from me. What makes the question significant is that its answer may lie beyond the context of life on this planet, even beyond our comprehension. If so, our earth is but striving through mankind, its highest level of consciousness yet developed, to comprehend the purpose of its role in a universal order of creation. The earth is as dependent upon us as we are upon it.

Still the fecundity of a handful of dirt is as amazing to me as it was to my childish visitor. It seems to draw its life-giving power from the depths of the earth. The residents of an anthill metropolis subsist on the energy derived from a tiny area around it. Deer restrict themselves for generations to a small browsing area in the mountains. An elk herd migrates but a few miles back and forth between its summer and winter feeding grounds. My horses have subsisted for years on their small homeland of open pasture and tiny wilderness of chokecherry trees, wild rose bushes, and a variety of weeds and herbs. This is their world, small but self-sufficient, as our neighborhood has been for my Spanish-American neighbors.

Despite a common fecundity, every place on earth bespeaks its own rhythm of life. Each continent has its own spirit of place which it imparts to its distinctive species of plants and animals, its human races. So does every country, every locality. Even great cities impart their own special essence, apart from their architectural and cultural backgrounds. And within them, one runs into a *barrio*, a neighborhood, that seems to exude a sense of peace or evil without apparent cause. There is no accounting for the mysterious magnetism that draws and holds us to that one locality we know as our heart's home, whose karmic propensities or simple vibratory quality may coincide with our own.

Thus have I often wondered how I happened to choose this slope of the Sangre de Cristo Mountains for my own home. There was little to recommend it thirty years ago. Eight thousand feet high, the spot lay nine miles from the small, backward town of Taos and one mile above the tiny, old Spanish village of Arroyo Seco. The rutted dirt road was almost impassable several months of the year, deep in snow during the winter, and in sticky adobe all spring. My house was a deserted adobe whose roof was falling in and whose foundations needed bolstering. But the first time I saw it on a walk up into the mountains, something about it claimed me.

The ruined adobe and the land behind it I finally bought from a lifelong resident of the valley, Josephine M. Córdova, whose husband was a rancher and a part-time gambler. With the purchase price she built in El Prado, a settlement on the road to Taos, an adobe building of two or three one-room living units whose rental supplemented her income as a schoolteacher. She became and remained the principal of the small El Prado school for thirteen years. Upon her retirement she wrote a small book, *No Lloro Pero Me Acuerdo*, "I Don't Cry, But I Remember," recounting the old Spanish way of life here, and nearly three hundred Spanish proverbs. A dear friend and a great lady.

Making my small new adobe liveable was a task. I put on a new roof and bolstered the foundations of the walls with the help of Indian and Spanish-American neighbors. There was no heating save the fireplaces in each of the three rooms, which required hours of cutting wood for them and the iron cookstove. Nor was there running water in the house. We dipped water from the stream in front, the Arroyo Seco, and used an outdoor backhouse. Under these conditions, we could live in the house only during the summer.

The land in back was overgrown with chokecherry and wild plum thickets, and wild rose bushes. It had to be cleared and seeded for pasturage and hay for our few horses. The fences had to be repaired. Eventually an electric cooperative ran a line up this way, enabling us to drill a well and install running water and plumbing fixtures.

But I do not wish to emphasize our small effort. When my wife Janey and I first moved into our small adobe, Salomé Duran, a sheepherder in Wyoming, had not yet settled permanently in his small house just above us. But farther above, where the rock-strewn road ended at the base of the mountain wall, Emilio Fernandez was establishing a home for his tiny wife and children. He was a big, wide-shouldered man with an open heart and gentle manner, who spoke little English. Alone and unaided, he built his adobe house, bridging the Arroyo Seco stream, and clearing a road to it. He constructed barns and corral of stout logs, then cleared a mountain slope of huge pines for his pastures and fields. It sounds so romantic when we read of pioneers "clearing the land" for homesites. But the phrase assumes new significance for one watching Mr. Fernandez felling tall pines, burning the stripped branches and undergrowth, and pulling out the huge stumps with a team. Then plowing, planting by hand, and irrigating with water drawn from a mountain stream. Often on a fall night I could glimpse the glow of the tiny campfire beside which he squatted to protect his ripening corn from deer, raccoons, an occasional bear. The corn and squash he dried in the sun for winter use, unable to afford sugar for canning. For the purchase of staples, he sold pine logs for use as *vigas*, or roof beams, and a few head of cattle or sheep.

Only seldom did he have time to go down into the village, riding a pinto horse, although the family walked down each Sunday to attend Mass. As the road was impassable during the deep snows of winter, he moved his family into the village in order to put his children into school. Through all these years of lonely, backbreaking toil, he built up his ranch, reared his children. He still passes by on foot, his muscular frame beginning to shrink, his favorite pinto gone. For him I have great admiration, respect, and affection. He is a true man of the earth.

If I had been unaccountably drawn here, it took me some time to become accustomed to its spirit of place. Not that it seemed as strangely alien and foreign to me as to many friends who called it "Little Mexico." There was some truth in their assertions, for the little village of Arroyo Seco with its mud-brown adobes reminded me of remote pueblos in Mexico. But still the area had a distinctive aura, a rhythm, a flavor of its own. There were so many intangible influences, vibrations, seismic oscillations of feelings between opposite poles! All these invisible forces helped to mold me into their pattern, whatever that is. Gradually they began to speak to me with the voice of the living land, and its chief spokesmen were the two great peaks that rose from the mountains above.

2

El Cuchillo Del Medio

The high mountain wall rises steeply to the east, not far from the house. From it lift two near peaks. To the southeast is Pueblo Peak, the Sacred Mountain of Taos Pueblo which lies at its foot on the opposite side, a horseback ride around it. It is softly rounded in shape, thickly forested with pine and spruce, a benign, motherly mountain. The Indian reverence for it and the exquisitely beautiful blue lake that lies like a turquoise beyond it is quite special. For from this sacred lake, according to tradition, the tribe had made its Emergence to the surface of the earth, and to it the tribe still makes annual pilgrimage to conduct ceremonies no white man ever has witnessed.

Not far north, separated from it by lower ridges cut by two canyons, rises another great peak—this one a malign, masculine mountain. Protruding toward us is a rounded shoulder whose sheer, bare granite side on the south looks as if it had been sliced down the middle with a knife. From this comes its appropriate name of El Cuchillo del Medio.

The peak offers testimony to its negative character. Legend relates that in the long ago two Indian maidens were in love with the same man. Their rivalry came to a tragic climax upon the summit of the sheer cliffside one day when they fought and both fell to their deaths from this falling-off place, El Salto. This name is given more specifically to a narrow rocky cleft on its western side, in which lies a great cave believed to have been used during human sacrifices in prehistoric times. Over the top of the cave cascades a waterfall—*un salto de agua*—which freezes into stalactites and stalagmites covering its opening with a curtain of ice. The phenomenon occurs only in early spring when weather conditions are right. I have seen it but a few times, when from my back pasture the ice sheet reflecting the setting sun looked like a plate glass window.

The cave is fictionally famous. D.H. Lawrence used it and its alleged human sacrifices as a setting for his novelette *The Woman Who Rode Away*, transporting it to the Sierra Madre of Mexico. The rocky back walls of the cave used to be inscribed with prehistoric pictographs and petroglyphs. These have been pried out by tourists and replaced with the usual backhouse inscriptions; but the place now is generally shunned by Indians.

The trail to it is difficult to follow, leading through a dense forest of huge pines flanked by high cliff walls believed to hold the dens of small brown bears and a few large black bears. Every fall the bears come down into my back pasture to eat chokecherries, spooking the horses. Harmless as they seemed to me, all Arroyo Seco viewed them with alarm. One afternoon shortly after I moved here, I heard the bells of church and school wildly ringing, and glimpsed men coming up the road armed with guns, pitchforks, and clubs. What had happened? A small brown bear had strayed down into the village at three-thirty in the afternoon when school had let out, giving rise to the general alarm, I suppose, that the bears of El Salto were attacking the village. Pursued by the mob, the frightened animal fled safely back into the mountains. Since then large black bears occasionally have come down, posing actual problems. Their presence adds another negative aspect to the character of El Cuchillo.

If our immense global rock, the Earth, embodied the principles of cosmic opposites from the beginning, as does perhaps even the power of all Creation, it is not strange that the complementary polarities are manifested in all parts of the whole—even in the malign, masculine Cuchillo and the benign, motherly Sacred Mountain. An interesting parallel

12

to them was called to my attention recently when I was visited here by Professor Robert Gustafson, head of the Department of Philosophy and Religion at Pembroke State University in North Carolina. He referred to Mt. Ebal and Mt. Gerizim mentioned in the Old Testament as the mount of blessing and the mount of cursing, and added that during his recent trip to Jordan he found that the natives of the region still regarded these mountains as good and evil.

That the two bipolar mountains here imprint their forces both on the physical and inorganic world, and on organic life—without the Biblical tradition of Moses' commandments—is borne out in many ways.

The dichotomy is marked by the Arroyo Seco River which flows out of the steep canyon on the south side of El Cuchillo and down through the little Spanish village of Arroyo Seco, a mile below my house. It is paralleled by our rutted dirt road. Along the north side live all the members of the Spanish community. On the south side extends the Indian Reservation of Taos Pueblo, a vast sage plateau whose sparse fields are watered by the Rio Lucero which flows out of the deep canyon on the north side of the Sacred Mountain. Hence our mountain slope is sharply divided into two realms, Indian and Spanish, with different racial backgrounds, culture, and language.

A major dispute has been over the boundary of the land ever since Charles V of Spain in 1551 awarded a large land grant to the pueblo, now comprising its Reservation, followed two centuries later by smaller land grants to Spanish settlers and the founding of the village of Arroyo Seco in 1745. The ramifications of the land dispute are too complicated to detail here, and are still continuing.

Another grievous quarrel has been over water rights. For the Rio Arroyo Seco is no river at all; it is but a small stream without enough water to provide irrigation for the Spanish fields. It has been necessary to divert a proportion of the flow of the Rio Lucero to the Spanish domain. The allocation for a century or more has resulted in violent quarrels. In my early years here when the irrigating water was insufficient for our drying fields and it was obvious that the Indians were stealing our rightful share, my neighbors enlisted me to accompany a group of them to the "division of the waters" on the Reservation. They were all armed with shovels and pickhandles.

Fortunately we encountered no Indians. But at the division, just below the mouth of the Lucero, they had diverted our flow of water into their own irrigation ditch with a dam of stones and mud. Destroying this, we returned home. This crude separation of waters has now been replaced by a cement headwater partition structure, allocating the proper percentage of the flow to both Indian and Spanish domains.

Ostensibly, the centuries-long antipathy between the two segments of our upland community has been based upon differences of racial and cultural backgrounds supported by government-imposed geographical limitations. Fundamentally, I'm inclined to believe it reflects the opposite polarities of the two mountains.

I do not want to intimate in any way that the Indian segment, polarized to the Sacred Mountain, is "good," and that the Spanish segment within the sphere of influence of El Cuchillo is "bad." I am a resident of the Spanish community, yet my belief in Indian values has been rooted in me since childhood.

When I first bought this crumbling adobe and the land behind it, Ralph Meyers, the noted old Indian trader in Taos, was vociferous in his denouncement of it. "The damned location is no good. It lies too close to El Salto. The place has an Indian jinx on it and it's full of Spanish *brujas*. You won't last a month. And how the hell are you going to get up there, eight thousand feet high, in winter anyway?"

I reminded him that I already had bought it. Whereupon he offered his sage advice. "You've got to take the jinx off it. Propitiate the evil spirits. A charm will do it. Piss and a prayer. Just the thing!"

A few days later he came up to execute the powers of the charm. A copious urination was followed by the sprinkling of sacred cornmeal from a small buckskin sack hung around his neck. Apparently that did it. I have never been troubled by evil spirits.

Nevertheless, the aura of El Cuchillo and a bad reputation hovered around Arroyo Seco. In its early days, when its huddle of mud-brown adobes was practically isolated by the tortuous wagon road, the village was believed to be a refuge for horse-thieves and other tough characters nibbling at the fringes of the law. Occasionally Indians rode over for bootleg whiskey. Later, in my own time, the place was regarded as the toughest settlement in the Rio Arriba because of the many knifings that took place among its rowdy youths.

When Bolivar next door got married, I was invited to the house of his mother, Mrs. Quintana, for the great wedding feast given for the host of neighbors. I was then asked to attend the customary wedding dance that evening. But Bolivar drew me aside and suggested that I not come, as there might be a knifing. So just as delicately, I did not accept the invitation. Next morning I learned that the affair had erupted into a knifing, just as Bolivar had predicted. Other incidents of the kind were constantly taking place. I must add that I was never involved in a fracas even though I was an Anglo, and that I was always accorded courtesy and friendship. One could not blame the youths for their sometimes bloody quarrels. Not only were they possessed by a hot-blooded temperament, but they were all poor, without cars to drive into Taos or for pleasure, without amusements of any kind. They sat dejectedly along the road, waiting vainly for something stimulating to turn up. In recent years a succession of enterprising parish priests have had their hands full initiating sports and games.

And of course the area was reputedly full of *brujas*, witches, whose midnight rendezvous was the cave in El Salto. Almost anyone could tell a hair-raising story about them. One verified story comes readily to mind. An aging woman who had been given a pair of new shoes wore them to church one winter evening, and afterwards left to walk home. She was never seen again. When her neighbors tried to track her through the deep snow, they followed her footprints up the steep road toward El Salto, where they ended. There was no other trace of her; she had vanished completely. A couple of years later a woodcutter climbing La Ceja, "the Eyebrow" curve of the mountain slope far to the north, found her decomposed body, which was identified by her shoes. How it got there was inexplicable. An aging woman in new, stiff shoes could not possibly, in bitter cold and deep snow, have walked up the rising road to its end, through several miles of forest, and climbed up the slope of the mountain. The consensus was that *brujas* had transported her there.

Who the *brujas* were, no one knew, of course. But I heard gossip when I was moving into my house that my next door neighbor, Mrs. Alicia Quintana, was one of them. The rumor would have horrified her. She was a descendant of the historic Antonio Martinez who had been awarded this immense land grant. Her husband, José Maria, had been a sheepherder from boyhood, like most Arroyo Seco men, pasturing his flock during the winter in the lower and warmer valleys along the Rio Grande, and driving it up into the mountains for the summer. He and Mrs. Quintana had three sons and five daughters, over whom she ruled with assured authority.

She was a sturdily built woman with an iron constitution. I once saw her watching two of her sons trying to lift a seasoned log. Finally, with a snort of disgust, she walked over, hoisted the log to her shoulder, and strode off with it. The Quintana farm adjoined my own land. While Mr. Quintana was away with his sheep, she assumed its management—supervising the planting and harvesting of the fields, nursing the vegetable garden, tending the stock, and mending the fences. She was up at daybreak— rousing out of bed all the rest of the family. She adhered to the old traditions. Periodically, she made soup, for which I gave her all my bacon grease, in a large cast-iron kettle set on an open fire in front of the house. I observed her once insisting, when her sons were castrating a colt, that the cut be made, not by cold steel but by the teeth. In addition to all this work, she assumed the task of personally caring for the village priest and providing fresh flowers for the church. One of the most remarkable women I have ever known, she was a true matriarch in the old Spanish tradition. It was little wonder that all Arroyo Seco regarded her as a powerful figure.

Soon after I met her, I had a dream about her. I was standing one night in the kitchen of my small adobe. Beside me was standing an Anglo youth with auburn hair. Mrs. Quintana was sitting in a chair in the corner. In the candlelight she looked like an evil old witch. The house too gave off the feeling of eeriness and evil. The Anglo youth beside me was frightened. He cringed against the wall, hands over his face. "You're not used to it," I told him. I too felt the somber, eerie atmosphere, but at the same time I felt cheerful and unafraid. I walked toward her . . . .

In retrospect, I see this dream as constellating the two aspects of my own dual nature. The fearful Anglo youth representing my white, Puritanical component, contrasted with my other shadow self drawn to darkness and evil.

Some time later I had another dream. I was in the house when my sister Naomi, a fey soul with intuitive promptings, came in to tell me of a discovery she'd made. I went out with her to look at it. Along the back fence of the orchard, and hidden under brush, we found an old log carved by Mrs. Quintana into the semblance of a queer animal—short-legged as a dog, but big-bodied, with the protruding snout of a pig. It reminded me of a South Sea or Central America effigy. I knew immediately it was for our protection; and hunting around, I found another close to the house. In its front was carven a symbol which I have forgotten.

I related to Naomi the gossip that Mrs. Quintana might be a *bruja*, a witch, but that lately I had been told she was an *arboleria*. The word derived from *arbol de la vida*, the "tree of life," or *arbol de la ciencia del bien y del mal*, the "tree of the knowledge of good and evil." In other words, she was not only able to cast spells like any run-of-the-mill *bruja*, but to take them off.

What changed my first dream impression of her to a more favorable one was an amusing incident. All Arroyo Seco must have regarded with some suspicion the first incursion of an Anglo into the region. Our boundary fence was broken time after time so that stock could graze at will in our fields and orchard. The dramatic climax came after I had laboriously hauled stones from the river to lay for the floor of our front portál. Upon returning home after a short absence, I found that they had been uprooted by one of the Quintana pigs. That afternoon the pig returned to continue its destruction. Never in my life have I seen such a monstrous animal. It looked exactly like the queer animal effigy in my dream, short-legged as a dog, big-bodied and with the protruding snout of a pig. But monstrous beyond belief, looking like a huge hippopotamus.

At the sight of it, Janey's small and fierce Chow dog, descended from the war-dogs of ancient China, hurled himself against it, tearing out from its flank a chunk of flesh but being stunned by the impact. The monster merely turned around in mild annoyance. At this moment Mrs. Quintana strode through a broken gap in the fence exclaiming, "Madre de Mio! I hope your little dog has not hurt himself!"

Whereupon Janey, with her excitable nature, loosed upon her a violent tirade in French and Italian, not a word of which Mrs. Quintana understood, but whose meaning she comprehended fully. It is quite likely that she had never been so addressed. She immediately had the monstrous pig confined in the corral.

A week or two later, her oldest son Pablo trucked the pig to offer for sale in the public stock auction in Alamosa, Colorado. Pablo reported that he was quite embarrassed by the whole proceeding, shrinking down in the back row. "What am I offered for this gigantic animal?" shouted the auctioneer. "They call it a pig. But it looks like a hippopotamus. Who will make me an offer?"

Thereafter Janey and Mrs. Quintana were the closest of friends. The boundary fences were patched up. And when we had to leave in the winter, I simply turned over the keys of the house to Mrs. Quintana. During the many years I lived alone here after Janey's death, she and her daughter Amada looked after me with boundless solicitude, coming over almost every day and bringing fresh vegetables.

Mr. Quintana was a character himself. He was a short, sturdy man, so small that the teen-age daughters of Ann Merrill called him one of Tolkien's "Hobbits." A peculiar growth of huge warts on his head prevented him from wearing a hat. In due time, the warts were removed at the hospital, only to return. A man of the earth, he had spent his life herding sheep. When at the age of sixty-five he had to give them up, due to both his age and the Forest Service restrictions on grazing in the mountains, he was lost without his sheep. Growing a few head on his own pastures, he helped to shovel snow off my roof in the winter, and while I was away, hayed the horses, and watched the house like a hawk. Until he died at the age of eighty-two, he made a daily inspection tour of my fields and came to visit me every morning.

All the Quintana children and grandchildren familiarly called me "Frank." But Mr. and Mrs. Quintana always addressed me as "Mr. Waters," a formal courtesy I also extended to them. Little wonder that I, with Naomi, Carl, and my niece Susie who came periodically from California, looked upon the Quintanas as members of our own family. Of them all, of course, Mrs. Quintana was the dominating spirit. The beauty in her face grew daily.

Yet in her I sensed a peculiar negative streak that seemed to welcome misfortune. All the Quintanas, persons and animals, were accident-prone. Whenever someone was hurt or became seriously ill, or a horse died of a punctured bowel or broke its leg, Mrs. Quintana came over to report it with an air of positive cheerfulness. She herself developed an unremitting burning pain in one leg for which none of the local doctors could find the cause or the cure. The last doctor she tried gave up the effort, saying, "So it still burns like fire, eh? Well, it'll keep you warm all winter!" Thereafter, every freezing day when she came over to see me, her face pinched with cold, she would slap her ailing leg and exclaim with a joyful chuckle, "Ai. Ai. But this is keeping me warm!"

My turn came one Saturday afternoon when the local dentist extracted all my teeth, slapped in two new plates, and gave me a pill the size of a large marble to stop the pain when I went to bed. In the middle of the night I awakened with blood filling my mouth and nostrils. Sleepily, I stuffed cotton in my mouth and wrapped a towel around my head. Early next morning, Mrs. Quintana walked in the house without knocking, as usual. I could well imagine what she saw from the doorway of my bedroom: a still figure in bed whose face, head, pajamas, pillow cases, and bed sheets were covered with blood. At her first start of shocked surprise, I moved and spoke. Whereupon she let out a small scream of relief that somehow, at least in my imagination, contained that strange element of ironic humor.

"No! I haven't been murdered!" I shouted crossly. "I've just got a bloody toothache!"

She laughed uproariously. "So no one has killed you with an axe, Mr. Waters! But perhaps you will die anyway, losing all your blood, God willing!"

Then, of course, came her deep compassion and helpful hands as she bathed my face, replaced the towel and pajamas with fresh ones, brought more cotton to stuff in my mouth. This went on all day Sunday. For the dentist, a Spanish friend of mine, had forgotten to stitch up my torn gums in his haste to leave town for a weekend vacation, and I could not see him until Monday morning.

What engendered this curious streak in her may have been a healthy ironic humor, or a philosophical acceptance of all misfortunes as the will of God; but it certainly reflected the mood of the locality, the influence of El Cuchillo which lay upon us all its dark shadow.

I never discussed *brujas* with her, knowing her staunch Catholic faith. Still, one incident led me to feel she at least believed in spirits. A young couple in Los Angeles were told of the sacrificial cave at El Salto by my sister and brother-in-law, and resolved to see it during their vacation trip to New Mexico. I was away when their car appeared in my driveway. Mrs. Quintana immediately came over to inquire what they wanted. Upon being told, she offered to guide them to the cave despite the arduous long walk and her fear of bears. Upon their return, and after Mrs. Quintana had gone home to rest, the young couple asked me why she had stopped periodically along the trail to ring a small brass bell before proceeding.

This, I knew, was not to frighten away the bears. It immediately recalled a trip I had made with a Hopi priest, John Lansa, to a sacred shrine in a remote area north of Black Mesa in Arizona. The shrine was known as Kisiwu, the Spring in the Shadows, a mysterious place and the home of several important spirits sacred to the Hopis. The spring itself lay in a cave high on a rocky escarpment rising out of the sandy plain. John preceded me as we climbed up the narrow trail. Four times he stopped, taking off his shirt, pants, and moccasins. Then from a little buckskin medicine-bag suspended from a thong looped around his throat, he sprinkled a pinch of cornmeal on the ground, and gave a loud call. Finally reaching the cave, he offered his prayers and motioned for me to join him. He had of course been notifying the spirits of Kisiwu of our approach, just as had Mrs. Quintana on her approach to the cave of El Salto.

The parallel illustrates how deeply rooted and widespread among Indian and Spanish alike in all this harsh and naked land is the belief in spirits which may be invoked for good or evil. Their innovation for evil is known worldwide as witchcraft. Throughout the Rio Arriba, this region of the upper Rio Grande in northern New Mexico, witchcraft has been perhaps the most prevalent. Documented records for three centuries amply attest that the belief in witchcraft here equalled that in Europe between the thirteenth and seventeenth centuries. The literature on these tragic case histories of trial and torture of accused victims is voluminous, but there is no need to summarize it.

Still, we are told that the word "witch" is derived from the Anglo-Saxon word "wicca," meaning craft of the wise. Hence the craft is not necessarily directed towards evil ends; it may be employed to lift spells cast by lesser *brujas*, and to cure mental and physical illnesses.

If we don't doubt the possibility that demonic powers can be invoked by witchcraft, neither can we doubt that divine powers can be invoked by prayer and religious rites. They seem to be complementary, reflecting the dual forces of all life. The Navajos maintain the tradition of two opposing ritual practices, the religious ceremonial of Blessing Way among others, and the Witchcraft Way. Among the Hopis there emerged in early days a ceremony based on the power of the animal kingdom, *tuvósi*, which became extinct when its members used the power for selfish ends. Nevertheless, its beliefs and practices still exist as witchcraft. *Pósi* (Eye) is the name for a medicine man who uses the eye of the animal kingdom which can see in the dark. The Hopi name for a witch or sorcerer is *powâga* (eye, walking, doing), because he uses the eye of the animal kingdom for evil purposes—destroying crops of his neighbors, bringing winds, driving away snow and rain, shooting ants, insects, and glass into his victims, and causing the deaths of even his own relatives in order to prolong his own life. Who these alleged *powâga* are, no one knows. Yet fear of them is spreading at the same rate as ceremonialism is breaking down.

Evil itself seems to have originated in man with the creation of Adam and Eve in the Garden of Eden, according to Christian doctrine: or, as the Tewas believe, it was brought up by the First People during their Emergence from the underworld. Despite modern psychological belief that evil is a component of man's own nature, it is commonly believed that evil is projected upon us by other persons or forces outside ourselves.

Among the Spanish people here the Church has been the equivalent of Indian ceremonialism as a bulwark against evil. In testimony, perhaps, is the holy power invoked by Mrs. Alicida Duran, my other close neighbor. Salomé Duran, her husband, has been a sheepherder all his life, like Mr. Quintana. When sheep-raising was given up here due to Forest Service grazing restrictions, he began the custom of herding sheep in Wyoming all summer, returning home to live during the winter. A few years ago, he settled here permanently to graze his own small flock of fifty or sixty sheep and goats on his ample pastures. A big, muscular man, he spent all day outside, according to custom: mending fences, irrigating, cutting wood, doing chores, or simply watching his flock. His neighborliness has been of immense benefit to me. For when my own fields, converted into permanent pasture for my remaining horses, became overgrown with wild roses, he turned his flock into them. As goats are browsers, not grazers like sheep, they soon cleared my fields completely. In return, my horses wandered through the open gates to graze on his own pasture. More important, his residence at home lifted from Mrs. Duran the heartbreaking tasks required of a lone woman to keep up the place. It permitted her to spend her time on work in the house and tending to her garden. She is an excellent cook, sometimes working during the winter in a gourmet restaurant, and her flower garden is the best in Arroyo Seco.

An Anglo woman visitor once remarked to me that she couldn't understand why our small homesites in such a comparatively wild area should seem so peaceful and protected. And then, glancing out my window, she pointed to Mrs. Duran's front lawn. "Ah! Of course. I see now. No wonder!"

What she saw was a shrine built of cement blocks upholding a statuette of Our Lady on top, with an array of flowers at her feet, and surmounted by an American flag.

Aside from the conjectural existence of *brujas* evoking evil, I can affirm the presence everywhere of celestial influences imbuing localities, even the small group of aspen trees in my back courtyard. A large grove of much older and higher aspens stands outside, flanking the driveway, but there is something special about this small group. There are seven of them. One of them grew so close to the wall of the house I was afraid the jutting eaves would either stunt its growth or kill it, so I had a hole cut through the protruding roof to allow space for its upward climb. As I lie in bed, their tall, slim, white trunks, ghostly pale in dawnlight or moonlight, are the first things I see in the morning and the last at night.

If aspens long have been my favorite trees, since childhood the Pleiades have been my most intimate constellation. The relationship between them appeared in a curious fantasy. One winter night I seemed to see these seven, white, slim aspens, now stripped of leaves, rising like tall tapers higher and higher toward the seven principal stars in the Pleiades. At the moment of contact their tips were ignited as by a burst of energy, and a glow of soft light was diffused from every bare branch and twig. The fantasy lasted only a moment or two, but it assured me they were intimately related.

The interrelationship of stars, earth, and man posits, of course, an exchange of influences. Yet this area—despite its natural beauty, its often joyful moods, my good neighbors, and the connection between my seven aspens and the Pleiades—is nevertheless curiously impacted with the negative spirit of bare-faced El Cuchillo.

I still ask myself what drew me here to spend such a considerable span of my earthly existence. Undoubtedly, our karmic propensities were much the same, and El Cuchillo and I are kindred spirits in some way. It has affected me profoundly, of course. But has my presence here affected it? Am I exerting in some small manner an influence upon that stark bare peak, or am I projecting upon it the negative aspects of my own being, or do I merely maintain with it a polite and guarded speaking acquaintance, as it were? At least we jibe without conflict, even at night when the October wind shrieks at the eaves and I feel pressing down upon me the heaviness of its dark power.

3

The Sacred Mountain

How different seems the benevolent, maternal Sacred Mountain! You feel its full force when you cross the road, lead a horse through a gate, and ride south around the base of the peak.

This is Indian land, the Taos Pueblo reservation. A great upland expanse of waist-high sagebrush sloping west from the foot of the mountains. The sage glints silver-green in early sunlight, interspersed with yellow-flowered chamisa, tall sunflowers, and clumps of juniper and piñon trees. It is an unspoiled land overlooking the desert below cut by the narrow slit of the Rio Grande, and the upturned blue horizon far to the west. To the left, the Sacred Mountain looms bigger, softer, and greener. And from the mouth of Lucero Canyon there extends a road and the narrow, government-built cement irrigation ditch.

My mare, Cry Baby, knows the overgrown wagon road well. It leads through a thick growth of piñon trees. In the fall, one can dismount here and gather up from the ground a sack of piñones, the small sweet nuts which are roasted and sold throughout the Southwest. The road peters out into a trail that dips down into a *glorietta*, a marvellous glade hidden in great cottonwoods and pines, and cut by a clear stream that widens into a deep pool. The grassy, isolate meadow is a favorite camping place for Indians, especially for newlywed couples. Janey and I often used to strip and bathe in the pool and then dry out on its grassy banks.

From here there are trails in several directions through groves of cottonwoods and pines. Cry Baby drinks from the pool, gingerly fords its rocky bottom, and waits for further direction by a pressure of the reins.

One of them, after climbing out of the sequestered *glorietta*, leads across an open meadow toward the dark lower slope of the Sacred Mountain. She takes it in an unreined, furious gallop, heading straight for a lone cottonwood. Here, I slow her winded pace. For we now climb a trail beside an irrigation ditch, past flanking pines, spruces, and the first aspens, through carpets of bluebells, lupine, crimson paintbrush, white onion, and purple asters, to the cliff-walled mouth of the Lucero—to the division of its waters.

It is one of the wild spots we seldom see. The water pours down, white and foaming, from the snowcaps above. Many are the picnics we have had here with Indian neighbors. One of them included "Grandma" Concha, nearly eighty years old and blind. She wanted only to be set at the foot of the falls where she could listen to the voice of the water.

The Lucero in the past has been a good trout-fishing stream. It is a tortuous stream to follow, swift, narrow, obstructed with fallen trees and boulders, necessitating one to cross it from side to side. Up above, the canyon seems filled with one solid forest of towering aspens through which the light is filtered in a greenish haze in summer, or a deep yellow glow when the leaves turn in the fall. There sounds the chattering of squirrels, then the explosive burst of a mountain grouse from darkness into silence.

From the mouth of the Lucero Cry Baby knows the way home. The short way is impassable by horseback, leading through a tangled jungle of scrub oak directly to the road past my house. So we must ride the longer way: down the road and back across the sagebrush.

Beautiful as it is, the mouth of the Lucero has about it an aura of mysterious, eerie wilderness in which a strange thing happened that my sister Naomi and I once experienced. I say "aura" advisedly, because the strange occurrence apparently was not caused by a material incident.

It was late afternoon. My brother-in-law Carl had gone fishing and had not yet returned. While waiting for him, Naomi and I went for a walk up the road toward the base of the mountains. When the road ended, we cut south toward the mouth of the Lucero across an open, high meadow. It was a lovely spot whose peace and silence were enhanced by the wild flowers underfoot, the mellow glow of the sinking sun. Ahead of us lay the thick growth of scrub oak I have mentioned.

Suddenly Naomi, with her acute perceptions and fey intuition, stopped short, and I noticed on her face a look of trepidation. At almost the same time, I was halted by what seemed an invisible and intangible barrier. For a moment, I believed that she had instinctively sensed the presence of a bear, which had come down to feed on the acorns. Previously, I had been warned not to ride in this vicinity, as Cry Baby would be spooked by the smell of bear. Yet as I tried to step forward anyway, I was held in check by that mounting, intangible wave that had no sound nor smell, but was more impassable than any physical barrier.

At this instant, the cloying silence was broken by a shrill cry that seemed to come from the cliff walls at the mouth of the Lucero. It was so loud and clear that it filled the meadow. Wild and frightening, it came from a human voice imploring help, but in words I could not understand. Surely someone over there, perhaps an Indian, had been attacked, fallen from a cliff, or met with another serious accident. Unable to ignore its wild plea, I gave a loud shout, although that intangible barrier prevented me from moving forward.

As we stood there rooted to the spot, another shrill cry sounded. Now years later, I cannot describe it though it is etched indelibly in my memory. It was as if it were uttered by someone who had been pushed or jumped to his death from the cliffs; and now, too late, gave one last despairing, agonizing death-cry. An earthly cry, but unearthly, too, as if it had been filtered through an abnormal or supernormal medium. It filled our small world with a horror that destroyed completely all serenity, and broke against the benevolent Sacred Mountain its soul-torturing anguish.

Naomi, her face pale and drawn, and I turned about and trudged home without a word. In the house, we still sat wordless and shaken. We could not ignore those two heartrending cries. I proposed saddling Cry Baby and riding the long way around to the mouth of the Lucero. But by the time I caught, saddled, and rode her there, it would be too dark to see anything. Still we had to do something. So leaving a note for Carl who had not yet returned from fishing, we got in the car and drove down to the pueblo.

Albert and Clara and one of their sons were eating supper by the light of a lamp. I explained what we had heard, suggesting that I drive Albert and some other Indians up there to find out if someone from the pueblo had met with an accident. Albert's son quietly rose from the table and went out. In a little while, he came back. Apparently, he had reported the incident either to the Governor or to the War Chief, the "Outside Chief" who is responsible for all happenings outside the pueblo itself. No Indians had gone up the Lucero that day, no trouble had been reported, nor were any Indians reported missing. Albert seemed disturbed, but said to us simply, "Come back tomorrow."

Early next morning, we drove back to see him, still disturbed ourselves. Albert gave us coffee at his kitchen table. He affirmed that further inquiry had revealed no accidents at the mouth of the Lucero, no Indians missing from the pueblo. The door was open. The morning sun shone in, bright and clear. Out in the plaza, people were serenely going about their daily chores. Yet all this only accentuated the frightening cries we had heard the previous evening, the intangible barrier we had encountered.

Albert was a man of few words. He finally said simply, "Long time ago that happen. You just hear it now."

Nothing puts into such few words the belief—not only Indian—that time is not a linear flow, as we think it is, into past, present, and future. Time is an indivisible whole, a great pool in which all events are eternally embodied and still have their meaningful being. Into it we may dip by chance, or by a meaningful flash of supernormal or extrasensory perception, and glimpse something that happened long ago in our linear time.

And this, I believe, is what happened that late afternoon. We did not break completely through the time barrier—that intangible, mysterious wall—to glimpse what had happened. But the cries had penetrated it, and we were momentarily, psychically attuned enough to hear their audible vibrations.

To return to the *glorietta* . . . .

The alternate route of Cry Baby and myself from here is a wagon road curving around the base of the Sacred Mountain to the pueblo at its foot, directly opposite the northern side of the peak from my house. The road opens up a new perspective of the Sangre de Cristo range. One sees between and behind the Sacred Mountain and El Cuchillo the majestic snow-covered Vallecito, hidden from sight at Arroyo Seco because we are too close to see it. It in turn obscures, at our still relatively close range, the mighty mass of Wheeler Peak, more than thirteen thousand feet high and the highest mountain in New Mexico. This is the peak below which lies the sacred Blue Lake of the pueblo, from whose drainage of snow waters come Pueblo Creek and the Rio Lucero. The summit of Vallecito contains a depression which appears to have been scooped out by a spoon, and from this it is locally called La Cuchara, the Spoon. One asks a neighbor if he thinks there has been enough snow in the winter to provide irrigation water all summer. He points with his chin to Vallecito and answers simply, "The Spoon is full."

This view of the snowy Vallecito between and behind the Sacred Mountain and El Cuchillo throws into larger perspective not only their geographic but their psychical relationship. It is as if they are cupped within the enclosing Sangre de Cristos as the Yin-Yang symbols are circumscribed by the circle of cosmic unity. For if most local storms seem to originate from the dialogue between them, their result is a unifying snowpack which provides life-giving water for all of us, Spanish and Indian alike.

The road now winds through outlying fields and solitary adobes. For while all Indians are required to occupy their pueblo apartments during a portion of the winter—"The Time of Staying Still"—they are permitted to live out on the Reservation in their "summer homes" in order to farm their individually owned land. Their small fields of corn, squash, beans, and wheat delight the eye. They are not mathematically laid out as if by a ruler in rectangles and squares, as are those of the Anglo and Spanish. They conform to the flowing, natural boundaries of the land, its hillsides, streams and arroyos.

Through them, the road curves on its way past thickets of wild plum. In the spring, these beaches of white blossoms perfuming the air give the landscape a decidedly Chinese look that only Lao Tsu and Chuang Tsu could describe. And then—in high time, for Cry Baby is sweating—we ride into one of the most perfect architectural forms in America. The two halves of the five-storied, adobe pueblo are separated by a large open plaza through which flows Pueblo Creek. The whole was originally surrounded by a wall, battered down last century by American howitzers. It still preserves the feeling of a self-enclosed unity isolated from the encroaching influences of Spanish and Anglo invaders. It owes its allegiance only to the maternal mountain mass that rises above it, whose outline it architecturally reflects in its tiered, pyramidal form.

I loved to come here simply to enjoy its peace and the slow tenor of life. Women walking down to the creek to fill their pottery jars or tin pails with water. Men herding their horses in the corrals. Children running up with pleas for a "nickle-penny." The fragrant smell of piñon from cooking fires. There were always friends who had a pot of chile warming on the stove, an armful of hay for Cry Baby. And then, after a rest, we would ride back home.

This was the long horseback ride which Albert took each day to Arroyo Seco and back when he helped with the work on my small adobe. Often, he brought his small son Red Bird for company. Becoming bored with watching us work, the boy would beat a small drum, sing in his childish voice, and dance. Later, I depended upon Frank to help break our colt Star, to shoe our horses, and to build another room. He, too, rode horseback from the pueblo and back again after his hard day's work. The work was backbreaking labor indeed. Every adobe was of mud dug from the back pasture, mixed with water and straw, molded in wooden forms, dried in the sun, and then laid in the walls. Each huge viga or roof beam was a lofty pine felled in the mountains above, stripped of branches, and snaked down by a team of horses. Preparation of it followed Indian tradition. The tree had to be cut in the phase of the waning moon, when the sap was low. Once brought down, the trunk was carefully covered by chips of the bark stripped from it, and, thus protected from the sun, allowed to dry out gradually. Only then was it hoisted into place to support the heavy roof. Otherwise, the viga developed the long cracks often seen in those supplied by less careful Anglo building contractors.

My nearest Indian neighbor, old Juan Concha who had been a Pueblo governor for several terms, lived in a summer home scarcely a mile away. He visited me often—always at mealtimes. When entering the house, he always exclaimed, "This Indian house!" And upon this theme he launched into its history. Evidently, in previous times, the Rio Arroyo Seco had followed a course in back of my house, still marked by a shallow arroyo between the house and the barn. The stream then, as now, had been established as the boundary between Indian and Spanish land, but the Spanish had diverted the stream to flow in its present channel a hundred yards south. Hence, Old Juan called my house "La Isla," for it stood on an island, as it were, between the former and present channels of the stream. It was his contention, of course, that the land between them still rightfully belonged to the pueblo, and he prophesied that the Indians would eventually get it back.

The prospect is improbable but not impossible. At this late stage, after having enjoyed it for many years, I would be discomfitted at losing it, but would make no rumpus about it; for I have always upheld the efforts of all Indian tribes to regain the land unjustly taken from them by the federal government. And from recent developments, it seems that the Indian cause is gaining ground, literally and ideologically.

The long and obdurate fight of Taos Pueblo for restoration of the mountain wilderness around its sacred Blue Lake is a heartwarming example. I have detailed it in books, articles, and essays, but a few pertinent facts may highlight it.

In 1551, when King Charles V of Spain established claim to New Mexico as a Spanish province, he gave to Taos Pueblo a land grant of 130,000 acres. The grant was confirmed by Mexico in 1821 when she gained independence from Spain, and by the

United States in 1848 when it acquired sovereignty over New Mexico. Meanwhile, much of the land had been preempted by Spanish and Anglo settlers who founded upon it the modern town of Taos, a few miles from the pueblo. Then in 1906, President Theodore Roosevelt established the Taos National Forest (now Carson National Forest), taking for it 50,000 acres of pueblo land, without compensation to the Indians. Then began the fight for restoration of their land.

In 1926, a Pueblo Lands Board found that the United States had unlawfully extinguished Indian title to the very land on which stood the modern town of Taos, and offered to pay the pueblo the 1906 valuation of the land, $297,684.67. The pueblo waived payment in consideration that it be given clear title to its sacred Blue Lake area of 50,000 acres. Instead, after a delay of seven years, a Congressional act was passed, authorizing only a fifty-year use permit to Taos Pueblo for only 32,450 acres.

Hampered by lack of funds to pay lawyers' fees, the pueblo continued its agonizing legal fight to gain complete restoration of its land. It was a stormy period during which I wrote innumerable letters for the Pueblo Council and attended meetings with its members and its friends, including Oliver La Farge and John Collier. Adverse publicity was generated on all levels. By the senior United States Senator from New Mexico, who introduced his own bill proposing that the pueblo be given only 3,150 acres. By the Forest Service, eager to appropriate and cash in on the sale of the area's virgin timber, and to open it to recreational development. And even by the Town Council of Taos itself, which supported the unfounded allegation of the editor of the town's weekly newspaper that the Indians were attempting to steal land in the public domain, thus obtaining title to the watershed, blocking off the rivers and streams and depriving the Spanish communities of water for their fields. A petition condemning this outrageous Indian theft was signed by members of all Spanish communities, including my own Arroyo Seco neighbors. My own refusal to sign was an unfavorable exception.

The mounting national controversy was highlighted by the appearance at a Congressional hearing of ninety-year-old Juan de Jesus Romero, the *cacique*, or religious leader, of the pueblo, who testified to the religious significance of the Blue Lake area with its many sacred shrines and sanctuaries. He was supported by other Indian tribes throughout the country, by church groups, civic organizations, and thousands of individuals, all acclaiming the constitutional right of Taos Pueblo to religious freedom and preservation of their wilderness "church." Finally, on December 15, 1970, Congress passed a bill providing that the area would be kept in wilderness status under Pueblo ownership, with the federal government acting as trustee.

We may view this Congressional action in perhaps not too exaggerated perspective as a significant victory of the Sacred Mountain and the wilderness area it imbues with its benign blue spirit. I say "blue" advisedly. For not only the sacred Blue Lake reflects its ineffable clear color. The whole region vibrates to this one section of the spectrum—the entire landscape of mountains, sagebrush, and desert; and in times past both Indian and Spanish villagers painted their doors with that shade which came to be called "Taos Blue." One notices it immediately upon climbing out of the brown rocky gorge of the Rio Grande, when all the visible world seems permeated by an invisible, mystic blue spirit. It is little wonder that Indians, Anglos, and Spanish alike have developed a mystique about the Sacred Mountain with its living blue spirit. I don't doubt its existence after experiencing it myself in this curious dream:

I was alone in my living room in the dead of winter. It was dark and bitterly cold. The electric power was off again, and my only dim light was an old coal-light lamp with a dusty, fly-specked chimney. The butane tank had not been refilled, so there was no heat from the gas stove; and there was no wood in the fireplace. I sat shivering in darkness, rubbing my cold hands together.

Then, I noticed through the front window a peculiar blue glow on the Sacred Mountain, which I first thought might be a forest fire. Getting up and walking to the window, I saw then that it was deep inside the peak, diffusing its light through the rocky cliffs and forested canyons. The glow was round in shape, vivid blue in color, and radiant with warmth. I felt immediately that it was the energy-giving blue spirit of the mountain. So I spread my cold hands, knowing that it would keep me warm. . . .

4

Mountain and Plain

I suppose that at heart I'm a Mountain Man. The term, capitalized, has come to designate specifically that strange breed of men who in the first half of the last century trailed into the Rocky Mountains to trap beaver. Solitary men for the most part, undergoing unbelievable hardships in an unexplored wilderness, they found plenty of beaver. Bales of pelts, or plews, which they packed into their yearly rendezvous at Taos, Green River, or elsewhere, and sold for a tidy profit. The money was worthless to them. They squandered it in a brief orgy of whiskey and women. Then again they set forth for another lonely year in the vast unknown with little more than their traps, lead and powder, knives, and salt. What they were really seeking, they did not know. But as the great bulks of the mountains heaved up inside them as around them, the rivers ran wild in their blood, and the mighty canyons and abysmal gorges shaped the dark depths within them, they knew unconsciously they had found it, whatever it was. Self-isolated from their little villages back across the wide buffalo plains, from comfortable homes, families, the fellowship of their kind, they never went back. The immense wilderness had claimed them forever, the first of us newcomers on whom the great spirit-of-place of the inimical and unknown heartland of America had set its invisible seal. This was what made them Mountain Men.

Yet people of the wild mountain uplands have always, everywhere, differed from those on the gentle lowlands. Most major civilizations have been nurtured in great fertile river valleys. Crops were easy to cultivate. Agriculture gave way to industry and trade; great cities arose; and with them a civilization spreading its culture and religion.

The mountain highlands, on the contrary, have not been favorable for extensive settlement and the refinements of civilization. In them gathered the effluvia of society—bands of outlaws and brigands, political outcasts, spearheads of colonists attempting to extend the perimeters of their motherland, strange religious sects fleeing persecution. All non-conformists and discontents isolated from the mainstream of life. The wilderness insured their isolation and ingrownness, a certain wildness, and a peculiar psychic response to the tremendous forces of nature which enclosed them. They became mountain people.

This was as true of northern New Mexico as anywhere else. The great Rio Grande River valley was popularly separated into two sections. The Rio Abajo, south of La Bajada Hill which marked the drop from the mountains to the plains, comprised the lower region in whose fertile bottomlands the Spanish colonists had established their large haciendas and founded Albuquerque, now the largest city in the state. The Rio Arriba designated the upper reaches of the Rio Grande. It extended northward along the river's deep, tortuous gorge, through Taos to the tiny settlements in southern Colorado which marked the limit of Spanish colonization. It was all mountain country, long unmarked by the wheels of progress.

Sante Fe, midway between the Rio Abajo and Rio Arriba, never quite gave full allegiance to either. When I first saw it, some forty years ago, woodcutters with burro packs of piñon were still parading around the cobblestoned plaza. Even today, this oldest capital in the United States and the capital of New Mexico has no open airport. Here in Taos, one must drive 150 miles to Albuquerque to board a plane.

Taos, seventy miles upriver, was of course a major rendezvous of the early Mountain Men. It was noted for its rotgut whiskey called "Taos Lightning," and as the birthplace of constant rebellions against established order, whether Spanish, Mexican, or American. I remember, a little too fondly perhaps, its many saloons and open gambling halls around the central plaza, the hitching rails at which stood Indian horses and Spanish wagons in defiance of the occasional Tin Lizzies from the City. Even today it is still regarded as the Last Outpost of Individualism, with its hordes of artists, those cultural nonconformists to our mechanistic society, pseudo-artists and hangers-on, its varied array of delightful crackpots, and later hippies. It is still a mountain town at heart, as it always has been.

There are many such towns, smaller and less known, throughout the Sangre de Cristo Mountains of northern New Mexico. All reflect the same forbidding qualities of remoteness, isolation, and wildness. All of them are dear to me, especially Mora.

It lay in a narrow, high mountain valley to the east of Taos. The village had been founded by a group of seventy-six Spanish colonists from Mexico along a stream discovered by French trappers; their Act of Possession of the Mora Land Grant is dated October 20, 1835. When I arrived there a century later, it was still remote and isolated. The rocky dirt road to Las Vegas, about thirty miles to the south, required an hour and a half of careful driving. The mountain road to Taos was worse, corkscrewing up a high pass to the north, modestly called Holman Hill, and crossing the mountain ridges to the west. I have been stuck on it by spring washouts, summer cloudbursts, fall freezes, winter snows. The tiny primitive hamlets up the surrounding canyons—Chacon, Guadalupita and the like—were locked in for most of the year. Only for Christmas Mass did a few of their inhabitants drive into town, huddled in straw-filled wagons.

When I moved there in 1936, Mora, with its straggle of old adobes, looked like an ancient Indian village in the remote mountains of Mexico. Its focal point was a tiny plaza between the parish church and the mercantile store or trading post of Peter Balland, a Frenchman with a wooden leg and the brother of a former priest. Across the dirt road stood the Butler Hotel, an historic building erected when the American cavalry troops at Fort Union relied upon Mora farmers for hay and grain.

The Butler Hotel—or Mora Inn, as it is often referred to—was a rambling eighteen-room adobe, Spanish-Colonial in style. Fronting the street was a long, wide portál of great flagstones.

Walking inside, you entered the lobby, on whose right extended a long mahogany bar said to have been brought from the Barbary Coast in San Francisco, and which was now used as the desk. Behind it hung the reputed personal effects of the noted Mountain Man, Kit Carson—frying pan, cooking pot, sheath knife, and metal plate. To the left stood an immense grand piano which had been brought over the Great Plains by oxcart to the officers' quarters at Fort Union. On it were several old sheets of music and a book published early in the 1800s, containing model letters, one of them to be written by a young lady to her escort after an enjoyable sleigh ride. On the wall above hung two especially fine prints brought from France by Father Balland. Beyond lay a bare dining room and Mrs. Butler's own room, flanked by the kitchen.

Walking outside from the lobby through a small *placita* enclosed by several rooms, and then through a *zaguan*, one came into a large, weedy garden walled on one side by a wing of small dark rooms. Each contained a small wood-stove, and an immense walnut spool bed with a feather mattress also brought from Fort Union when it was abandoned. At the back of the garden teetered the decrepit wooden toilet.

Here in this historic old adobe, I lived off and on for two years, feeling the weight of the enclosing mountains, the isolate remoteness, and the wilderness pressing in upon me and everyone in town.

Of the few Anglos in town, four lived in the hotel—its only permanent inmates—and three of them were part Indian. Monte Butler, who had established the old inn, had fled here some years before to escape a criminal charge against him in Indian Territory. A gambler by profession, he made the hotel pay by running games in it. He had met his wife, Sybil, in Las Vegas soon after she had come West to work as a government stenographer or clerk of some sort. Eventually, he began to go blind. Then, fortunately, there arrived from Oklahoma a younger man, half Cherokee, who also sought refuge here with a price on his head.

It was old Monte's belief that "You can't make a race-horse out of a mule, a lady out of a whore, or put gambling blood in a shit-heel." The young refugee—Ralph, as I shall call him—

evidently possessed the gambling instinct. So patiently, for months on end, Monte taught him how to deal cards: black jack, stud and draw poker. Ralph became miraculously adept. He could deal any card from top, bottom, or middle of the deck with uncanny precision. I've seen him, one hand outstretched on the table before me, deal me any hand I called for. If the decks he used were marked by the manufacturer from whom he ordered them, I could never detect their markings on close examination.

When Butler died, old and blind, Ralph stayed on in the hotel, doing all the chores. His only earnings were the winnings from the games he conducted at night for the benefit of a few surveyors, cattle and sheep buyers, road construction workers, or visiting government officials. Mrs. Butler complied with his necessity. She would retire to her own room early in the evening, bolting her door with a huge cast-iron Spanish lock, so Ralph could open his game in an empty room.

Mrs. Butler was an odd, middle-aged woman with bright blue eyes. I was fond of her. During all the years she had lived in this completely Spanish community, she had not learned one word of Spanish. Her reason was simple. The human brain has a lot of cells, like a honeycomb, and when these cells were filled with information—in her case, English words— they had no capacity to absorb more, especially Spanish. I will have more to say about her later.

The only permanent guests in the hotel besides myself were my treasured friends, Ed and Fran Tinker. Ed was a black sheep member of a prominent Osage family in Oklahoma. His brother was the now-famous Major General shot down at Midway, and for whom the Tinker airport in Oklahoma City is named. Ed was a handsome six-footer. A true Osage, he took life as it came, ineffectually dabbling in local politics, building a couple of bridges on the road up through Guadalupita to Black Lake, and generally relying on Fran's earnings.

Fran, his wife, was a tiny, resolute woman. When Ed's Osage father finally met her in Mora, he exclaimed forthrightly, "Well, I can see you sucked the small tit!" Fran, however, was one of the most remarkable women I've ever met. Her father had been a judge in Sante Fe, and she spoke Spanish as fluently as English.

In Mora, she was employed in a W.P.A. program to teach families in the remote canyons the use of pressure cookers. These enabled the people to preserve meat, vegetables, and fruits for winter use instead of drying them in the sun. Her other duties varied widely. I've seen her deliver a baby, set a bone, break a fever, and teach children how to embroider discarded flour sacks; and she knew the uses of native herbs and plants. She and Ed lived in two rooms in the hotel, where Fran cooked their own meals. I took suppers with them; and being an early riser, made my own breakfast in the hotel kitchen.

A part-Picuris Indian girl helped out with the work in the hotel. Maggie had a clear, rose-brown complexion, and was a hard worker. Born in El Alto, a tiny settlement of Picuris only a spitting distance away, she had never ventured farther than Mora and did not know what a train looked like. Her curiosity was appeased one day when Fran and Ed drove her to Las Vegas and put her on the train for Raton. Ralph met her there and drove her back home. Maggie was a different person after that, one whose outlook had been extended far beyond her geographic boundaries.

Court Day—which sometimes was extended to two or three days—was an important occasion for the Butler Hotel, for all Mora. Here in the county courthouse gathered judges, lawyers, litigants, and spectators to hear impending cases. As the hotel offered the only accommodations, its dining room and sleeping rooms were filled to capacity. All of us worked. Mrs. Butler cooking meals that at best were simple and filling. Ralph waiting table, plucking chickens and butchering a pig, cutting wood for the stoves in all rooms. Maggie helping with the cooking, washing dishes, and she and myself making beds after the guests had left for the courthouse.

In the evening, of course, Ralph opened his game in Fran and Ed's bedroom, the only room available. It was his one big harvest time after weeks of drought, and he ruthlessly ran a tight game for high stakes until dawn. Ed, with the Osage love of gambling, insisted on changing in although he was some months behind in his hotel rent. He was not a good hand at cards and lost continually, Ralph showing him no mercy. I felt sorry for Fran, trying to sleep fully dressed in the smoke-filled room, then patiently getting up to make coffee in the morning. When all the players had left, Ralph cut loose on Ed, high, wide, and handsome.

"Goddamn your miserable soul! I told you not to sit in on this game. You're a chicken-shit gambler who doesn't know his ass from a hole in the ground. What do you mean, drawing down to shorts like a millionaire when you owe Mrs. Butler three months' rent? And how much do you owe me now?"

He peeled off a hundred dollars from a roll of bills, slapped them on the table in front of Fran, and stalked out.

Someone in Mora, perhaps it was Peter Balland, always referred to the enclosing mountain walls as "Wall Street" because they were high and hard, sometimes blowing hot and sometimes cold. And in October, when the snows began, Wall Street pressed in upon us, accentuating our enforced intimacy. Family squabbles, long-dormant feuds, and repressed impulses to violence began to erupt. National elections were approaching, and political differences added to the dissension. Horsemen rode up on the hotel portál one midnight, battering with pistol butts the window shutters and bolted doors. A man completely disembowled was found next morning in the churchyard.

One night, while I was propped up in bed reading the current best seller, the phenomenal *Gone With The Wind*, a rifle shot tore through my one small window fronting the lane which opened to the road to Guadalupita. The bullet imbedded itself in the adobe wall just above my bed, sending down on my head and book a shower of dirt. Hardly had I jumped up to put out the light, than Ralph burst into the room. Wearing a long nightgown and pointed cap, with his revolver strapped around his waist, he shouted with his usual profanity, "Who in the goddamn hell is taking a pot-shot at you? I'll bet you've been sleeping with some girl on the sly, and her lover's jealous. I'll fix the son-of-a-bitch right now!" He dashed out the door, stalked up and down the street, and finally went back to bed.

Next morning, we all reviewed the incident in a calmer mood. My writing table was placed in front of the small window, and fortunately I had stopped work about midnight and gone to bed to read; otherwise I would have been shot. Mrs. Butler mildly observed that the presence of an Anglo in town presented temptations, and suggested I move into another dark, window-less room. Ralph, high-strung and irritable, insisted I leave Mora before I was assassinated. Fran, resolute and calm as always, was sure I had made no enemies. She pointed out that the shot had been fired shortly after the saloons had closed at 1:00 a.m., when their inmates gathered along the lane outside my window to continue drinking. Whoever fired the shot, she believed, was no more than a drunken brawler. I was inclined to agree with her. So, I slowly walked up the road to the house that served as a post office, stopped in the saloon for a beer with all its regular customers and then for a chat with Peter Balland in the trading post, and slowly walked home. There was no expression of enmity, and no more shots through my window.

Winter locked us in. Only a few stragglers came to the hotel to stay overnight, contributing a pittance to Ralph's poker games. All Mora suffered cabin fever, as if we were confined in a teakettle under great pressure.

Community release came in Holy Week. It was spring, when the snow on the peaks began to melt, releasing rivulets and torrents to plunge down the mountainsides with avalanches of earth and uprooted boulders; when the ice on the streams began to break, the pussywillows began to bud, the stallions showed new vigor, and the crows circled over the stubble fields. The people conformed to resurgence of life in nature with the literal observation of the meaning of Easter.

It was not unusual that Mora was a stronghold of the Penitentes. The Order of the Hermanos Penitentes—Penitent Brothers, or Los Hermanos de la Luz—Brothers of Light, was brought to New Mexico in 1598 by the Spanish colonists under Don Juan de Oñate. Outlawed later by the Catholic Church, its rites were still secretly carried on in these isolate mountain settlements. Most of the people of Mora were Penitentes, under the threat of excommunication if found out. Their thick-walled, windowless, adobe *moradas* were hidden in lonely dark canyons, and during their rites armed guards protected their secrecy.

It was a compliment to me that, as I was walking down the street, a man came up and suggested that I stand, next afternoon, under a certain great cottonwood at the mouth of a nearby canyon. The next day was Good Friday, and I understood I was invited to witness the great Passion of the Penitentes.

I have described it in detail elsewhere, and will not repeat it here. A long line of men, voices raised in a Gregorian chant, coming down the canyon to surround me and march me back up the canyon to the massive *morada*. Inside the candlelit darkness, the singing and praying. Then the *Procesion de la Sangre*—the long file of men marching farther up the canyon between snowbanks to the *Calvario*. The self-chosen Cristo staggering under a heavy cross. The Pitero eerily sounding his flute. The Rezador leading the ancient chant. And behind the Hermano Mayor, the Penitent Brothers rhythmically whipping themselves with cactus scourges. In the *morada*, the Sangrador had gashed their backs—four cuts down and across in the shape of a cross—to allow the blood to flow freely without raising welts. The sound of soggy blows, the snowbanks crimsoning with spattered blood. And then at the *Calvario*, the binding of the Cristo on the mounted cross in emulation of the crucified Savior.

Although the rite was Christian in origin, it derived the stark drama of its enactment and its overwhelming emotional force from that yearly resurrection of nature and the people's release from the tensions of their long confinement. By it, they expiated all their guilts, released their repressed passions and proclivities to violence. And in its bloody and sometimes fatal rites, they expressed as a mountain people their wildness and remoteness from a more gently ordered society.

I left Mora for a few months to do some work on a new book in Colorado Springs, Colorado. It was necessary, but it was also an escape from the constrictions and tensions in Mora. While I was there, a telephone call came about midnight. The caller, who did not identify himself, asked me to pick him up under an arc light on the edge of the railroad yards. The man turned out to be Ralph, dirty and begrimed with soot, and with the seat of his trousers torn out. On the way home he related what had happened.

The day before had been Court Day in Mora, and all the visiting judges, lawyers, and politicians had come to the Butler

Hotel for lunch. Ralph was waiting table when he overheard one of the men remark humorously to his companions, "Now boys, be careful when you break open Mrs. Butler's biscuits or you'll get a spurt of flour in your eyes!"

Ralph, in the act of pouring water in their glasses, promptly crashed the water pitcher on the speaker's head. Confronted with the sight of him stretched out on the floor with blood spurting from his cracked skull, and all the other diners crowding around him, Ralph fled from the hotel. Out on the street he thrust a bill into the hand of a man in an empty car who was willing to drive him to Las Vegas. But first, the driver ducked into a saloon to buy a bottle of whiskey. This did not expedite the trip. On the way, the car ran off the road, sideswiped a telephone pole, and threw Ralph through a barbed wire fence, tearing out the seat of his pants. On foot, Ralph made it to the railroad tracks where he hopped a freight train to Colorado Springs.

I was living at the time in a two-room tourist cottage on the outskirts of town. Here, I kept Ralph for a week. Radio reports and letters from Mora were not encouraging. The man whom he had conked on the head was the district attorney in Las Vegas. He was still in the hospital and it was not known whether he would die or not. A warrant had been issued for Ralph's arrest, and a $10,000 reward was offered for his capture and conviction, with talk that a previous charge against him would be investigated.

While Ralph sat listening to the radio all day long, he groomed his hands for more serious work: cracking his knuckles, rubbing glycerine into the tips of his fingers, dealing cards continuously. There was only one table in the cottage, and on it I was trying to correct galley proofs. With Ralph sitting opposite me, cracking his knuckles, it was a test of endurance.

There came answers to the letters he had written. He was offered a job as a dealer in the Colorado mining towns of Durango and Silverton. So, we packed up the car and headed south. I left him at Fort Garland, where he could hop a train to Durango, and continued on to New Mexico.

When I crossed the state line a few miles south, the immigration officer, who had been a former local judge in Mora, questioned me closely about him, saying that he had received orders to stop Ralph if he tried to leave New Mexico. It seemed prudent to me, as I was known to be his close friend, not to return to Mora. So, I settled in a small house in Taos, rented sight-unseen from Spud Johnson.

During the following months Ralph wrote me often from Durango, Silverton, Ouray. Always under the alias of J.R. Smith, and addressing me as "Frankie" or "Frinkie" in his scrawled, illiterate handwriting. And always asking for money. The ten or fifteen dollars I sent him were not enough. Not having the sums he urgently requested, I went to the gambling fraternity—Long John Dunn, Curly Murray, or Mike Cunico, who later killed a man in front of his dance-hall and gambling rooms, was exonerated but had to leave Taos. I would stand behind Curly, for example, when he was dealing blackjack and say simply, "A friend of ours in Silverton needs two hundred dollars immediately." Curly, without looking up at me, and without a pause in his dealing, would hand up over his shoulder a roll of bills. No questions asked, no receipt requested. What wonderful, mutual trust these gamblers had in one another! Try and borrow a hundred dollars from the bank!

A couple of months later, Ralph arrived, slipped across the state line by an obliging friend. He wanted to pick up his clothes and some money concealed in his room at Mora. Also, he was red-hot to collect the money owed him by Ed. Hence, at night I drove him to Mora and back again. Here in Taos, I kept him for several days.

A month later, he showed up again with Mrs. B., a middle-aged woman dressed in fringed buckskin, and loaded with Navajo silver-and-turquoise beads, pendants, rings, bracelets, and a great concho belt. The widow of a well-known Navajo trader, she had taken a liking to Ralph, who was now working at the Buckhorn bar and dance hall in Farmington. They stayed at a motel in town, but took their meals at my house for fear Ralph might be recognized, bringing steaks, eggs, whiskey, wine, and beer. At night, they visited Mike Cunico, Curly Murray, Shorty, and the other gamblers to repay them the money I had obtained for him. Mrs. B. declared her intention to buy the Buckhorn for Ralph, and insisted I join them there. Fortunately

I did not, for their affair soon ran its course and Ralph vanished to parts unknown. I never heard from him thereafter.

The following summer, I returned to the Butler Hotel. The district attorney in Las Vegas had recovered from his cracked skull and the excitement had died down, although his charges against Ralph had not been removed from the books. Mrs. Butler finally had given Ed and Fran notice to move out due to their months of unpaid rent, and they had rented a small house on the outskirts of Mora. Maggie had given birth to a baby girl, Margie, and was practically running the hotel. Sybil wanted to sell it for enough money to live on with relatives in San Francisco. She considered me the most likely buyer, offering it for $5,500 with all the furnishings. I had great plans for it, but lacked the money.

Hence, I petitioned the State of New Mexico, the University of New Mexico, and the Museum of New Mexico to buy and preserve this historic site. None of them was interested. Nor did Peter Balland receive any replies to his offers to sell his superb collection of old *Santos*. These pictorial representations of Christian saints when painted on slabs of cottonwood were called *retablos*. Those carved in the round from wood, and often attired in appropriate dress, were known as *bultos*. In either form, these *Santos* were images of the saints envisioned by the simple, devout people of the remote mountain villages.

Peter Balland had collected them for many years in payment of debts for purchases from his trading post. They were so numerous he hung them on the walls of his back butcher shop. It seemed clear that New Mexico was not interested in such superfluous reminders of her outmoded past. Eventually a huge truck hauled Peter Balland's entire collection to the Fine Arts Center in Colorado Springs, whence it was taken around the world for display.

The shoe was beginning to pinch Sybil. Ralph had been slipped out of New Mexico by a friend; we never saw him again. There was no one to manage the hotel save herself and Maggie, and they were not able to do all the work. In despair, she recalled Fran and Ed, renting them the hotel. Even so, it

46

was not a paying venture without Ralph's games at night. Getting desperate for money, Sybil began selling treasured articles to people in town for a pittance of what they were worth. She again offered to sell me the hotel, this time for $4,500, so she could leave Mora. It hurt me to have to refuse her, but in an attempt to help her in some way, I gave a huge party at the hotel. Inviting all our friends in Mora and everyone in Taos who wished to come, I hoped that some wealthy person in the latter group would be impressed by the historical importance and undeniable charm of the old hotel and finance it.

The occasion is one of my warmest memories. Crowds of people came, squeezing into Fran and Ed's rooms which had been converted into a bar. They filed into the dining room for buffet plates of roast beef, fried chicken, Sybil's now-famous biscuits, enchiladas, refried beans, and fresh green chiles. They admired the Italian tapestries loaned by Mable Luhan for the occasion and hung on the wall of the parlor. They swarmed in all the rooms, the placita, and the garden bringing the old inn to life as it must have been, and could have been again. But of course no one offered financial support. That evening after they all had left, I realized that I had seen the last bright effulgence of the Butler Hotel's sinking sun.

Sybil sold the hotel to an Armenian merchant who promptly tore it down and erected a barny mercantile store. The huge walnut spool beds were sold to takers at their own price, as were the historic fixtures and artifacts; the two exquisite French prints finally wound up in the Museum of New Mexico. Sybil, with the little cash she received, went to live with her relatives in San Francisco. I moved back across Wall Street and finally settled in another mountain town, here in Arroyo Seco.

There were many to choose from—Las Trampas, Las Truchas, Penasco, a dozen others. All were remote and isolated, with an air of independence and individuality compared to the conformity and mediocrity of the sprawling cities on the plains below. Small and tawdry as they were, they reflected the influence of mountains everywhere. For even as mountains slowly build up the fertile plains below with their eroded detritus, it is from their high places that saints, prophets, and lawgivers throughout the world have brought down the spiritual teachings which have enriched civilizations.

But, for some reason, Arroyo Seco became my *tierra*. I gradually became aware not only of the influence of its two signal peaks, but of those eternal forces of water, silence, and spirits which I, like most of us, had taken for granted.

5

Silence

It is my habit, weather permitting, to observe a moment of meditative stillness each morning when the sun first tips the rimrock of the mountain range behind my adobe. The place for it is always the same. An unprepossessing spot on a slight rise in the waist-high sagebrush, flanked by a clump of huge gnarled junipers—cedars, as we call them. There are many more beautiful, if not more striking "scenic" spots within the half-moon curve of mountains, and I did not choose this one. It simply drew me years ago by some curious magnetism, until I have now worn a barely discernible trail to it through sage and chamisa, around clumps of piñon and cedar, and across dry arroyos.

Here I stand, sniffing the early morning breeze and spying out the vast landscape like an old coyote, as if to assure myself I am in the center flow of its invisible, magnetic currents. To the sun, and to the two oppositely polarized peaks, El Cuchillo and the Sacred Mountain, I offer my morning prayers. Then, letting the bright warming rays of the sun engulf me, I give myself up to a thoughtless silence.

One, I suppose, could call it meditation. I don't, for I'm not sure how one is supposed to meditate. Once, I attended an hour's talk on meditation given by a noted esotericist from England. He carefully explained the best hours of the day to observe it; how to choose a corner of the room; what kind of a religious painting or photograph to hang on the wall with a burning candle beneath it; the choice of the proper incense to burn; the posture to assume. By then his hour was up. I left the hall, thinking of a question that Dr. Evans-Wentz once had asked Sri Ramana Maharshi, the famous sage of India.

"Is it helpful to sit on a tiger's skin?" he asked. "Should one sit in the lotus position, or may the legs be kept straight? What posture is best?"

"All of this is unnecessary," the Maharshi answered. "Let the mind assume the right posture. That is all."

Meditation may mean prayerful contemplation to some; to others, concentration on one form or object; or to still others, the fixation of the mind on one thought in order to empty the mind of all other thoughts, often aided by controlled breathing. None of these techniques or yoga disciplines have I followed. Nor have I had a specific goal to achieve. It is enough for me, as a prelude to a busy day, to attain for a moment at sunrise a measure of unbroken silence, of profound stillness within.

It doesn't come immediately, the crisp morning is so invigorating. There isn't a cloud in the sky. The earth emerges pristinely pure, virginly naked in its beauty. The snow-tipped peaks of Jicarita and the Truchas to the south, down toward Santa Fe, rise sharply into the blue. Beyond the slit of the Rio Grande to the west, the upland desert rises to the southern thrust of the Colorado Rockies. And to the east and north, directly behind me, the Sangre de Cristos curve in their great semi-circle. From down in Arroyo Seco, a mile below, sounds the clear pealing of the church bell. Reluctant wisps of smoke rise from the adobe village. Around me, the magpies are stirring awake. How cleanly beautiful these Rocky Mountain peacocks are, with their snowy wing patches and long, blue-black tails. A chipmunk scurries out from a rock. So much to see and hear and smell, as if one had never noticed it all before! And with all these appeals to the senses, the mind like an alarm clock jangles out a discordant medley of thoughts. "Are there any eggs left for breakfast, or must I have another bowl of atole? . . ." "What became of that coyote I heard last night? . . ." "Don't forget to put air in that tire when you drive to town. . . ." The tyranny of thought. When will it ever end?

But end it does. Abruptly, without warning, just as sleep overtakes you. As if one had suddenly broken through an invisible barrier, to be becalmed in an immeasurable, profound quietude, broken only by the voice of silence itself.

Silence. One would think, as I do now, that it is incongruous to break it with these random remarks. Still, there is much to be said for it. For silence has many gradations of its own, and comparative degrees depending upon where and how we experience it. Occasionally, out-of-town guests spend a night or two in my spare bedroom, like a recent couple from New York. In the morning I casually asked the lady how she had slept.

"I couldn't sleep at all!" she replied, rushing to the coffee pot. "Not a single wink, it was so ominously quiet!"

Her remark momentarily amazed me; I thought she might be deaf. For all night long could be heard the ripple of the stream, the thin clatter of leaves in the aspen grove, the deeper rustle of the cottonwoods in every breeze. At dawn one could hear the clip-clop of a horse's hooves as the Major-Domo, the Master of the Ditch, rode by to make his daily round of inspection. The constant tinkle of a bell from Salomé Duran's flock of goats and sheep was musical and reassuring. And at sunrise bird calls and the bell of the village church ushered in the new day. Still I could understand why a woman from New York, accustomed to all the noises of city streets and the ever-present roar of the city, had not heard these sounds. She was not attuned to their spectrum in the wide range of sound.

Living here alone for so long, I still do not have a phonograph, a recording machine, a TV set. My little portable radio I turn on only for a newscast at breakfast, interrupted by wordy and singing commercials. Not until a few years ago did I have a telephone. The comparative silence, I have grown used to.

But this is only an upper layer of silence; its lower layers I experienced when I was snowed in for several days. I began to feel it in the still, warm hush that always precedes a heavy snow. It was like a blanket muffling all sound. Then as the big, soft flakes fell steadily through the late afternoon, all night, and next day, covering fields and mountains, this whole little world seemed smothered in snow and silence.

Salomé I could see occasionally clearing a path to his immense woodpile or throwing hay to his flock, but they seemed like moving figures on a movie screen not wired for sound. Occasionally, to get out, I plodded through the drifts up to the mouth of the canyon. The absence of all movement seemed to contribute to the quality of stillness, for it is movement that creates sound. The branches of pine and spruce hung motionless and heavy with snow. No birds stirred among them. No animals moved through the weighted sage, although I could see the hieroglyphic marks of their tracks—rabbit, deer, a fox or coyote. What I noticed most was the stillness of the stream that usually rippled noisily in its swift flow, booming at the waterfalls, gurgling in the trout pools, singing through the small glades. It, too, was iced over and covered with a heavy blanket of snow, moving in its subterranean course without betraying a sound of its serpentine passage.

But gradually at night, my hearing opened up to a new spectrum of sound. It was curious how faint yet how distinct these sounds were. The house had something to say. Every room spoke with its infinitesimal creaks and groans. I could tell when the cold was increasing by the faint changes in whine of the water pump. One midnight, I was awakened by a loud, sharp explosion outside. Next morning, I saw the smooth white trunk of one of the aspen trees split open in a long vertical crack. Many other aspens in the grove bore such cracks. No one knew what caused them. The most prevalent conjecture was that they had been struck by lightning—which seemed improbable, considering that there were so many. Now I thought I knew the cause; the bark had been split by the expansion of its sap frozen by extreme cold. For sap rises in trees, not in the heart of their trunks but in their bark—which is the reason one can kill a tree simply by ringing its bark.

How still it was! I could even hear a rabbit munching at the alfalfa I had spread out in the snow. A small plop of snow, whenever a half-frozen, puffed-up bird moved on a twig outside my window, was just as distinct. One dawn, I heard a faint twinkle of ice in the stream out front, so unusual I wondered what caused it. In the morning, I found tracks there at an air-hole. A deer smelling water had come to drink, breaking through the rim of ice. Long before sunup I could hear the muffled sound of my two horses' feet, padded with snow, as they came up to the rail of the corral to stand waiting for their morning feeding. And when I didn't rouse out of bed promptly, their low, throaty neighing would have awakened a saint out of his contemplation. At the same time, there came a bombardment of wings and feathers on the portál, as dozens of large, crested bluejays launched themselves to the table on which I spread their breakfast of birdseed. What a racket they made! With them came, of course, the Duran's cat, crouching under the table for the opportunity of springing upon one of them. The large magpies were more wary. They waited for the suet I hung in the trees. And then came the multitudinous common people of the bird tribe, the little birds, to feed on the table leavings of the rich.

Eventually, little Robert Quintana came over to help me shovel snow off the roof, and Celestino to clear my driveway with his tractor and blade. Next day, the road was cleared and I drove into town. Seeing people and hearing sounds and voices suddenly made me realize the quality of silence I had experienced, a quality not measured by the few days of its duration.

Could it be that silence expresses itself visually as well as audibly, having the same gradations as the color spectrum? The silence of a forested mountain often seems dark blue or violet, while that of the desert at high noon takes on the quality of yellow. These colors may be imaginatively evoked, of course, by the predominant colors of their landscapes. White silence is the most profound; but curiously enough, its evocation is not restricted to a snowy mountain valley, for example. It may be felt among brilliantly colored surroundings and in the darkness of the night. Its complete absence of sound, its deep profundity, seems confirmed by the fact that white is the composite of all colors in the spectrum.

Many years ago, a Buddhist friend of mine from Bombay, India, Dr. Sakhârâm Ganesh Pandit, gave me a bit of advice just before I was inducted into the army at the outbreak of the Second World War. He recommended that whenever I was emotionally upset I remain absolutely quiet until I could hear the constant ringing in my ears. This advice I have tried to follow. Whenever I was called to speak to a large audience—a chore for which I am temperamentally unfit, which I have always dreaded, and which made me extremely nervous—I stood silent at the podium until I could hear the deep sound in my ears. This practice I have passed on to other speakers, to singers and the like, who have found it helpful.

And so it is this deep silence, this white silence, that I experience during my moment of meditative stillness in the sagebrush at sunrise. All the sensual morning sounds seem to merge into one sound, the steady ringing in my own ears which merges into the steady hum of silence itself, the voice of the living land, or perhaps the sound of the moving universe itself. *Quien sabe?* I myself have never questioned it.

It seems odd that Western science, in breaking the so-called sound barrier with fast jet planes and exploring the perimeters of outer space with manned capsules propelled by rockets, has never investigated the unknown element of silence. Perhaps because it has never remained still enough to listen to the ringing in its own ears. Eastern religious-philosophy on the contrary, which we envisage in the image of a "naked fakir" perpetually sitting still, has reported many properties it possesses.

The Hindu sage Sri Ramana Maharshi asserts that *mouna*, silence, is eternal speech. It is achieved by meditation without mental activity, and practiced by most sages. "How does speech arise?" he asks us. There is unmanifest abstract knowledge. From it rises the ego, which gives rise to thoughts and then to words. Words are therefore the great-grandson of the original source. If they can produce an effect, how much more powerful can the effect be through silence? Take preaching for an example. Compare a man haranguing a crowd for an hour without effect with one who sits silently sending forth intuitive forces to play upon the world to its great benefit.

If this is true, we must question the word-conscious premise of Western civilization with its ever-mounting flood of books, magazines, and newspapers, its unremitting barrage of wordy radio and TV commercials. To a bar of soap they impute emotional properties, and project on it our physical desires, sexual imagery. And our diplomatic gobbledygook seems dedicated to expanding our foreign markets for it. Benjamin Lee Whorf, formerly regarded as a great linguist but who is now out of fashion, pointed out that our manner of thinking depends on the language we use, the shaper of our ideas. We are not only saying what we are; we are what we are saying.

If I have not been wholly receptive to these wordy harangues, I have been more susceptible to the silent exhortations of the spirits of the living land. Our communion with these nonverbal spirits is achieved in that strange element of silence in which our inner selves are as much at home as our outer selves in the world of multitudinous sound. For in it, the human spirit discovers its own identity and its kinship with the spirits of distant stars.

6

Water

Water in this great arid Southwest always has been man's primary concern. With poetic prayer and dramatic ritual, the prehistoric pueblo-dwellers called into their sparse desert cornfields the tall walking rain from out of the house of massed clouds. Still enacted is the great Hopi ceremonial culminating in the Snake Dance, the magnificent Corn Dance at Santo Domingo, and the impressive dances for rain observed at Zuni and other pueblos—dances which may embody, as many observers believe, the finest and purest art forms yet achieved in America. Among the later Spanish-Colonial settlers, water rights provoked knife thrusts, family feuds, and legal battles for a century or more. And still today, we Anglos are quarreling over rights to water still precious as ever.

Just off the road above my house is the junction of two water courses. One is the little Rio Arroyo Seco, which flows down from the mountains above and marks our boundary of Spanish land. The other, as I have already recounted, is our allocated portion of the Rio Lucero which originates in the mountains within the pueblo reservation. The junction, small as it is, formerly was a deep, gurgling pool hemmed by a thicket of squaw berries. Here, the water was again divided by rude earth embankments. One portion was still allowed to continue down the bed of the Rio Arroyo Seco, from which my neighbors below dipped out pails for their household use. The other portion was diverted above into an irrigation ditch that supplied their fields.

This Acequia Madre, or Mother Ditch, wound its leisurely way in a great curve north and west, being channeled off to flow into the fields. It meandered by loops through open fields, thick brush, and my own back wilderness of lofty cottonwoods and slim aspens. Here, it formed deep pools where in summer we could bathe and dry out before picnic fires on its banks.

Just the same, it posed difficulties. The Mayor-Domo, the Ditch Boss, granted permission to irrigate only on certain days and during certain hours. If one's turn came at midnight, one had to rouse out of bed and with lantern, shovel, and axe to dam up the Acequia to divert the water through his ditch to his field. A small wooden headgate would have served the purpose. But no. It was the custom to cut brush for yards around, and shovel in rocks and dirt for a dam that would be torn down when one's time was up. This decidedly inefficient and primitive custom was replaced a few years ago by the advent of Progress.

A large concrete headgate was constructed at the junction up the road. Over it was erected a sign bearing an astounding array of letters:

U	A C P	A
S		S
D		C
A		S

What they all stood for, I first didn't know, but assumed they represented, as do so many such alphabetical crossword puzzles, the federal, state, and county commissions, departments, and agencies empowered by the incontestable forces of law and financial appropriations to raise the technological level of our welfare. These hieroglyphs, duly translated, announced the beginning of a Special Project of the Agricultural Conservation Program for Community Ditch Improvement by the Taos County A.S.C. Committee.

Work started at once when a huge Juggernaut began replacing the meandering Acequia Madre with a new cement ditch. It ran straight as an arrow, tearing down fences, uprooting trees, and clearing brush. Obviously, it was headed my way. In my small wilderness, I discovered a line of sharpened stakes to mark its route directly through a virgin glade surrounded by towering cottonwoods. There always seemed something holy about this power place. In it, a fox had its den. There were always rabbits nibbling on the grass, and on moonlit nights one could see deer. The trees were a sanctuary for the birds. The line of stakes disturbed me, for their pointed ends were dangerous for my horses, and I had not given permission to plant them there, or to cross my property with the new cement ditch.

It would have been sensible to obtain a court injunction against trespass. But rather naively, I complained to local officials of the A.S.C. Committee, a state engineer from Santa Fe, and the boss of the approaching Juggernaut. All devoutly assured me that no damage would be done to the land. They even selected a new route for the ditch, a narrow little ditch, that would not necessitate cutting down any trees for its passage.

Not until the fence was torn down to admit the Juggernaut did I realize that it dug the ditch and cemented it in one operation. What an immense technological monster it was, a triumph of engineering! There was barely room for its passage between the trees, but in forcing its way it barked and scored the trunks so deeply, and cut so many roots, that the trees were killed. Within a few months, the glade was an impassable tangle of fallen cottonwoods and chokecherries. The great pools of the former Acequia Madre were drained by cutting a wide, four-foot-deep arroyo through the whole area, impassable for the horses. Nor could they cross the new ditch to the back pasture beyond; it was necessary for me to build a bridge later. Moreover, the boundary fences on each side were not rebuilt until I employed a man to replace them. In short, the havoc completely destroyed what should have been preserved as a small wilderness oasis.

The field in its course fared little better. There were few outlets along the new ditch, so that the water could not be spread easily. And there was no seepage to sustain the growth of grass, trees, and brush along it, and to build up the underground water level. The water simply raced along in its cement walls through bare fields.

If I take umbrage at what has happened here to our little Acequia Madre and a few acres of sentimental value only to me, it is not wholly because of a personal pique. A similar, larger Bureau of Reclamation project was laid out a few miles downriver for building a huge dam across the Rio Grande just above the historic Spanish village of Velarde. The village and its little valley had become part of the Sebastian Martin land grant in 1712, guaranteed to its residents by the United States under the Treaty of Guadalupe Hidalgo in 1848. Fifty years later, the land grant was sold to the federal government. It then came under the control of the Bureau of Land Management which now sought to exercise its authority. From the projected dam upriver, it proposed to divert the water through a nineteen-mile concrete canal running throughout the valley. This would have destroyed the existing acequia system, one of the nation's oldest irrigation networks, and the valley's orchards famous for their apples, peaches, apricots, and plums which helped to support Velarde's residents. As happened in my own back land, the villagers were not aware of the proposed canal until they happened to see the stakes marking the surveyed route. But wiser than I, they took prompt action, forming an association to protest the canal through publicity and legal measures. They were finally successful in forcing the Bureau of Land Management to abandon the project for the time.

These two neighborhood examples reflect in miniature what has been happening to large river systems throughout the nation, like that of Colorado. Assuredly, the Colorado is one of the great rivers of the world. Its immense drainage area covers nearly one-twelfth of the continental United States, including portions of seven western states, and two portions of Mexico. It contains the highest peaks, the largest mountain ranges, the widest plateaus, the deepest canyons, and the lowest deserts in America—until fairly recently all comprising the greatest and last wilderness of the nation. How different today is the wild, turbulent river that once threaded it from 14,000-foot-high peaks to a desert 248 feet below sea level. It is now virtually a cement-lined canal from source to mouth. My old friend Cliff Tabor, president of the Colorado River Water Users Association, assures me that not one drop of surface water now reaches the mouth of the Colorado at the Gulf of California.

Nine colossal dams with backed-up lakes to serve as storage reservoirs, hydroturbine power plants, pumping works, and aqueduct systems have blocked its free flow through the living land. The immense cost of the first of these great projects was borne largely by the sale of electric energy generated by their power plants, primarily to the ballooning population centers of Las Vegas, Nevada, Phoenix-Tucson in Arizona, and the mega-lopolises of Southern California. The ready assumption must have been that still more dams and power plants would provide still more power for which a lucrative sale could be created by developing demands for new gadgets like electric toothbrushes and backscrubbers. Hence another huge federal dam was erected, resulting in the needless flooding of exquisite Glen Canyon. Still another was planned for Marble Canyon, which would have flooded one of the greatest natural wonders in the world—the incomparable Grand Canyon itself. At least for the time, a wave of indignant public opinion fortunately stopped this catastrophic sellout.

Since 1970, the National Environmental Policy Act has re-quired the federal government to prepare a full analysis of all current and future projects in the Colorado River Basin to study their environmental impacts. In 1978, a lawsuit by the Environ-mental Defense Fund against the U.S. Bureau of Reclamation and the Department of the Interior was filed to compel a com-prehensive Environmental Impact Statement on all dams and other water projects in the Basin. These projects include more than sixty-five dams, hundreds of miles of aqueducts, canals, tunnels, and other public works already built; seven major water projects now under way; thirteen new projects set for construc-tion by 1980; and some thirty more in the planning stage. The government reaction was a Senate amendment to the NEPA permitting construction of these new projects before completion of an impact statement, and denying funds to prepare one. Despite crocodile tears over this situation, the prognosis for the future of the entire Basin, the heartland of the West, is not encouraging.

Straightening a river not only changes the land; it also affects the ground-water reserves and its subterranean capillary system. Theodor Schwenk illustrates how completely the fine network of veins is changed as the deepened and straightened river sucks away the surrounding water from a wider and wider area, which then is in danger of becoming arid.

This danger is drastically enhanced by the pumping of ground water for industrial use, as is now occurring on the 3,300-square-mile Black Mesa in the Hopi and Navajo Indian Reservations being strip-mined for coal. In the mining operations, to be detailed elsewhere, the required water is drawn from mile-deep wells at the rate of 3,000 gallons a minute or 40,000 acre-feet a year. The entire area, as the Hopis say, is being drained as if by an enormous sponge. In a desert where the annual rainfall is less than ten inches, this depletion devastates the land, and changes the circulatory system and metabolism of the earth itself.

Water plays a key role in Indian myth and ceremonialism. Among the Pueblos, certain lakes are said to be places of emergence from the underworld and the abode of spirits, such as Taos' Blue Lake and the Lake of Whispering Waters under which lies the town of Zuni kachinas. The Tewas along the upper Rio Grande River associate a lake with each of their four directional sacred mountains.

The belief that water was the primordial home of man is detailed more specifically in the symbolism of the great Mayan and Aztec pyramids. In the Indian number system, which will be explained later, 0, or zero, represented the ocean, endless space and time. Significantly, the Mayas developed for the first time the concept of zero. Hence the "foundation" of the pyramids was water, the first "lifting up," or step, in the massive stepped pyramids symbolizing the first world of water. The second step symbolized the second world of fire, the third of earth, the fourth of air, the fifth of human beings, and the sixth was personalized by Tlaloc whose huge carven heads alternating with those of Quetzalcoatl decorate the Pyramid of Quetzalcoatl in Teotihuacan. Conch shells signify water, hence they decorate the walls of Teotihuacan temples. In Tula and Mitla, walls are garnished with a frieze of "Greek" frets. These mosaic frets and meander designs also designate water. The seventh step of the pyramid, as number 7 in the number system, symbolized spirits. Here on top, was the place of ceremonies and of kachinas. The pyramid, with a new step or level built at each cycle, thus architecturally portrayed the progression of life forms symbolized by the number system.

Today we are also beginning to realize the importance of water. Of the interrelated elements of our one vast global entity—earth, air, water, and sunlight—water comprises nearly three-fourths of the surface body of the planet and of the body of man. It is a living element with a spiritual nature which relates us to all the others. It is sensitive to planetary influences, reacts to an eclipse, and is in tune with phases of the moon. The ground water within the earth, the tides of the sea, and the female menstrual periods all reflect the course of the moon. Rivers spread out at the full moon and narrow at the new moon; hence lumbermen float their logs downstream during the new moon lest they be beached on the banks during the full moon. Sap in trees follows the same rhythm, as my Indian neighbors know; they fell pines for our vigas at the new moon, when the sap is low.

Theodor Schwenk's revealing study of water, *Sensitive Chaos*, shows that running water always tends to take a spherical form, a totality, in its meandering loops and spirals. We observe them in the Southwest in the famous "goosenecks" of the upper Rio Grande and the San Juan farther west, and even here in the S-curve windings of little Pot Creek outside of town. This tendency to take a spiralling course is reflected in the archetypal forms of all living creatures: in seashells, antelope horns, the bones and muscles of our own bodies.

The forester Roy A. Rappaport confirms Schwenk's findings in a statement made in *Manas* magazine: "The problem of how we may live in harmony with our forests is the problem of controlling man's linear purposes so they will not destroy the circular ecosystems to which contemporary humans remain as indissolubly bound as were their ancestors of a million years ago. If we are to live in harmony with our forests and other ecosystems, we must restore and maintain their circular ecological structure. The problem of how to live harmoniously with our forests is not a problem in forestry. It is, rather, a set of social, economic, political, conceptual, and even ideological problems. Their solutions are not to be found through simple changes in forestry practices. They are to be found in changes in the organization of our thought and of our society."

If we are aware of these relationships, it seems obvious that by damming, straightening, and contaminating rivers, as well as by despoiling the land and polluting the air, we are destroying the vital coherence of the whole circular ecosystem of nature both outside and within us.

7

Air

The proverbial clarity of the air throughout the Southwest was first brought to my attention during my boyhood in Colorado Springs, when I was selling newspapers at the Santa Fe railroad station. Number 5, a breakfast train, had just pulled in on time at seven o'clock. The big brass gong at the Fred Harvey lunch and dining rooms was booming welcome to the passengers disgorging from coaches and Pullmans. Among them were two women who stopped near me on the platform.

"Look at those beautiful high mountains!" said one. "What are they called, boy?"

"The big one's Pike's Peak," I answered, and pointing down the brick platform, "that's Cheyenne Mountain."

The woman turned to her companion. "Honey, I think I'll walk down to that mountain before breakfast. We've got thirty minutes here, you know."

"But lady," I told her, "the foot of that mountain is seven miles from here."

"Of course, dear," said the other woman. "It's the clarity of the air that makes it seem so close. The fresh, pure air. That's why this town's a health spa for hundreds of people coming to cure their lung trouble."

Her remark threw into focus a small brown paper container I once had picked up thinking it was a pocketbook, and others I had noticed discarded on the platform and on the streets. Sputum cups! I realized then why there were so many sanitariums, health resorts, and rest homes. All filled with "lungers" seeking relief from tuberculosis, asthma, and emphysema in the clear mountain air.

Well, the air has changed considerably since then. Most mountain ranges don't stand out close and clear-cut any more. They're covered by a thin, tenuous, gray veil compounded of dust, smoke, particulate matter, smog, and an assortment of noxious fumes. In fact, you can hardly see across the street when the alert sounds in our large cities. Nor can we see the radioactive fallout from the mushroom clouds of nuclear explosions which encircle the entire planet.

Still, on the slope of the Sangre de Cristos the nearby peaks of El Cuchillo and the Sacred Mountain loom up distinct to every detail: and one can see from the Colorado line south to the gorge of the Rio Grande, a wide expanse of nearly seventy-five miles. To the air which enables us to see with such perspectives we here give little thought. Mere air. Yet as the uneasy feeling grows that it may run short like everything else, our more distant neighbors are beginning to peer at it more closely before they have to don gas masks as part of their usual dress.

In ancient times it was believed that man and the universe were composed of four primary elements—earth, air, water, and fire. All were living elements with physical and psychical properties. Each moved in rhythmic cycles attuned to the movements of the heavenly bodies.

The Zodiac astrologically represented these four elements:

Fire: Aries, Leo, Sagittarius
Earth: Taurus, Virgo, Capricorn
Air: Gemini, Libra, Aquarius
Water: Cancer, Scorpio, Pisces

Hence mankind was particularly influenced in turn by each of these elements during the complete zodiacal cycle of 2,160 years, the period we term an "Age."

Of late years, this ancient belief in our intimate relationship to the entire universe is becoming more acceptable. We acknowledge scientifically, as our Indian friends do simply, the patrimony of our Father Sun which impregnates our Mother Earth with the life-giving powers of fire, heat, and light. From the living earth are born all forms of life: plant, animal, and human. The importance of water has never been questioned. Water comprises nearly three-fourths of the body of man and the surface of our planet. It, too, is a living element, sensitive to planetary influences. The functions of air and its effects upon man and the world seem less obvious, yet a great deal has been discovered about it.

Air, or the atmosphere, has been found to be a thick envelope or shell surrounding the earth. The bulk of it lies within forty miles of the surface. About fifteen miles up, it contains a thin layer of ozone, a rare form of oxygen, which absorbs invisible ultraviolet light from the sun. If this reached us, it would blister our skin and injure our eyes. So within this protective shell, like chicks within an eggshell, we breathe and live.

The analogy is not totally apt. The atmospheric shell is neither visible nor rigid; and, like the other three elements, the air is in constant motion. It circulates throughout the world in the orderly movements of the prevailing easterlies and westerlies, like the great currents of the sea. It ascends over warm areas of land and descends upon cool areas, following the change of temperature day and night, the "breathing of the continents." Within these great movements are innumerable lesser movements with which one becomes locally familiar.

Little invisible currents and drafts are felt in curious locations everywhere. One of them is between my house and barn, a spot much colder than those on either side. My horses avoid it in winter, preferring the open pasture. The reason, I think, is that this spot lies in what used to be an arroyo, gashed out by water from the mountains above. The arroyo is now filled in and dry, but the old course still serves as a channel for an imperceptible flow of air. There are other such spots, curiously warm or cold, which the horses frequent at certain hours of the day, like trout visiting their favorite pools.

More and more, air takes on a tangible reality, as if we are immersed in a sea of changing currents and tides. On a still, hot morning when I'm sitting in my back courtyard, the aspens reveal the first slight ripple on the surface. A tremor runs through their topmost limp green leaves. They turn slowly on their narrow stems, showing the pale silver of their undersides. Then, the current gradually descends until every leaf is beset with that nervous quiver and its curious brittle sound. No other trees are as susceptible to the slightest breeze as quaking aspens. The tall, sturdy cottonwoods out in front have a sterner character than these slim, white-trunked ascetics. Not for an hour do their leaves begin to murmur.

Then in the afternoon, the big tide rushes in from across the mesa and the desert to the west. Our prevailing winds are westerly, and sometimes they kick up a lot of dust. Billowing yellow clouds of it, piling swaths of tumbleweeds against the fences. Occasionally, a tall, slim, snake-like form rises from the flat plain and glides across the sand. These gyrating, sinuous dust serpents, formed by whirlpool currents of air, are known as dust devils and superstitiously are believed to be lost souls or evil spirits. And indeed, for the moment, they suggest that their element is imbued with life.

Air actually does support myriad forms of life in swarms of gnats and insects too small to see. You know their presence at twilight when you hear the sound of buzz-bats overhead. Buzz-bats, as cowboys call them, are a species of swallows which buzz down upon them for their evening meal. Still higher wheels the Lord of the Air, the eagle; no other bird has soared alone so high and is more revered throughout Indian America. Yet thousands of feet above the earth, the air has been found to contain swarms of living creatures—a sea of aerial plankton.

Placid as the aerial sea usually is, with its many changing currents, it is sometimes aroused to fury. Then indeed it seems a living element. The clouds blacken and lower. The air grows electric. Curtains of heat lightning illuminate the earth. Then come the jagged, blue whiplashes followed by bursts of thunder. Now it's high time, if you're riding horseback, to dismount and head for a clump of trees. Too often iron-shod horses have been struck and killed. I remember seeing a white gelding, Tony, bowled over. Curiously, he wasn't killed, but blinded in one eye.

The windstorms are something else. On an October night, they whistle around the rock-bare summit of El Cuchillo, moan through the pines and shriek at the eaves. During a winter blizzard in the mountains, the air attacks with all its claws and fangs. The great pines bend and groan, dead trees and branches snap and fall. The ice-laden wind cuts like a knife. Finally, the storm is spent; the falling snow heals over all wounds and piles up in drifts. And in the eerie silence, the motionless forest appears like a subterranean growth of pale seaweed.

How alive air is, with all its movements and changing moods! One wonders just what it is and how it contributes to the life of man and earth.

Its chief constituents are nitrogen and oxygen. Nitrogen comprises 78 percent of the atmosphere, and is found in all living tissues. The so-called nitrogen balance between the intake and loss of nitrogen in the human body and in the soil must be maintained to insure life. Hence the widespread use of nitrogen fertilizers. Oxygen comprises 21 percent of the atmosphere, and is found in rocks and minerals as well as in all organic compounds. Without oxygen, man would suffocate to death.

Another relationship must be maintained to insure the ecological balance between plant and animal life. Carbon dioxide is exuded by animal life and the decomposition of organic substances. It is absorbed from the air by plant life in photosynthesis, which in turn gives off the oxygen necessary for animal life. By destroying areas of vegetation like the fields, prairie grasslands, forests, and great primeval Amazonian jungles, while increasing the air content of carbon dioxide created by combustion during industrial processes, we are changing the composition of the air, upsetting the balance of nature, and endangering life on the planet.

Dolores La Chapelle, in *Earth Wisdom*, explains why the air of high mountains is so beneficial. Atmospheric electricity depends upon gaseous ions in the air. An ion is an atom electrically charged. An atom is electrically neutral when the number of electrons surrounding the nucleus is equal to the atomic number. It becomes a positive ion if it loses one or more electrons; a negative ion if it gains additional electrons. Ionization takes place when an atom receives enough energy from cosmic rays, solar energy, or radioactivity to break loose the outer electrons. High mountains receive more of these energies than the surrounding lowlands, and their atmosphere is more easily ionized. The positive ions are pulled down the mountain by the earth's force fields, while the negative ions tend to rise, leaving a greater concentration on mountain tops. "Negative" and "positive," as used here, refer to the ions' electrical charge. Applied to human beings, negative charges have good effects while positive have bad effects.

Ionization of the atmosphere, we are told, is also affected by approaching storm fronts. The negatively charged cloud base induces a preponderance of positive ions below it. The restlessness this causes among animals, I observe in my horses. How uneasy, how nervous and spooky they are, sensing the approaching storm long before I do. People also are affected by headaches, depression, and bad temper. Once the storm is under way, the ion balance is restored and people feel better. The windstorms variously known throughout the world as the Mistral, Sirocco, Foehn, and our local Chinook, all cause these effects.

Aside from these effects upon man and environment, air performs a significant function within the ecological system of man himself. It inter-meshes with the other three primary elements within him, and links him with the outer universe. Theodor Schwenk, already quoted, explains that man breathes 18 times a minute, 25,920 times a day. Hence he is connected with the sun, for it takes 25,920 years for the vernal equinox to move through the great Precession of the Equinoxes. Air also relates man to the element of water. For every 18 breaths there are 72 beats of the pulse, a ratio of 1:4 for the circulation of blood. This confirms the fact that propagation of sound is four times faster in water than in air, blood being the archetypal organ of liquid flow in man as water is throughout the earth.

Breathing and the heart beat, as Alan McGlasham further asserts, are the two basic rhythms in man. The heart beat relates him to organic life, and breathing to the life of the spirit. That they are closely connected is shown by the fact that the pulse rate can be changed by ordered breathing. The relation of breathing to the life of the spirit has been, for centuries, a major concern of the traditional religions of the East. The meditation disciplines followed by Hindu and Tibetan yogins and adepts feature the control of breathing. For with every breath, there is a change of thought; and in order to eliminate the constant stream of trivial distracting thoughts, and to achieve "one-pointedness" of mind toward the goal of realizing supreme universal consciousness, the observation and control of breathing is prescribed.

The breathing of air poisoned by noxious fumes from industrial plants and automobiles, the smoke and smog of large cities, is not conducive to the practice of these disciplines. Purer air is necessary. For ages, the saints and sages of India and Tibet have followed the custom of retreating from towns and villages to carry on their meditations in the undefiled air of the high Himalayas. Tibet especially has been long recognized as a focal area for their spiritual strivings.

The air they breathe, being a living element with both physical and psychical properties, carries a subtle vital energy. This in India is named by the Sanskrit word *prāna*; in Tibet it is called *sugs*, in Aikido, Japan, *ki*, and in China, *chi*. By controlling its circulation throughout the body, man is able to attain spiritual enlightenment or illumination.

In the full meaning of *prāna* we learn the basis of Hindu and Buddhist Tantric yoga, so clearly explained in the comprehensive series of volumes by Sir John Woodroffe. The word *prāna* derives from the Sanskrit root *An*, to breathe. Breathing is the manifestation of the life-principle *prāna* which pervades plant, animal, man, sun, and the planets. When breathing ceases, life ceases. But physical breath cannot be equated with *prāna*. For breath is simply air which is inhaled and expelled, and the action of breathing may be seen and known. *Prāna*, manifested as breathing, is itself invisible. It is the breath of life, the principle of movement, the rhythm of the universe, the one source of all individual and collective life. Breathing, then, is a microcosmic manifestation of the macrocosmic rhythm to which the whole universe moves, in which world-creations and world-destructions follow each other like inhalations and exhalations in the human body.

Prāna, life, and spirit are virtually synonymous, for this supreme power is itself cosmic consciousness which informs all matter. Consciousness is veiled in dense, inorganic matter; less so, in varying degrees, in living bodies. It cannot be called mind, in the Western sense, but it functions as a mental principle in limiting, regulating, and controlling matter. When it directs the material energies toward building and sustaining breathing creatures, it is *prāna*.

If we of the Western world can accept this metaphysical Eastern doctrine, we can recognize in our breathing, in the movement of air from the "breathing of the continents" to the currents of psychic energy in the human body, a rhythm common throughout the entire universe. Alternative "moon breathing" through the left nostril and "sun breathing" through the right changes the course of subtle vital energy throughout the body. With the exhalation and inhalation of one breath of the supreme cosmic life-source, worlds appear and disappear. So, too, with each breath we take do our thoughts change, which are our perceptions of the world. The lives of a single cell, a man, a planet vary greatly on our time scale, but all follow the same cosmic rhythm of evolution and dissolution.

So it is that air affects us physically and psychically. It relates us externally and internally with the other three elements necessary for maintaining life on the earth, and to that one spirit which imbues all. It is not inexhaustible and enduring as it may seem. Nor is life on this planet, if we continue to violate it.

8

Spirits

This business of spirits is perplexing to most. One can't doubt that an invisible other-world impacted with unimaginable powers lies beyond our world of the senses. These powers seem often to be manifested by spirits—gods, demons, ghosts, spirits of the dead, guardians of sacred mountains. Whether they actually exist has never been settled to everyone's satisfaction, and there is a major divergence of opinion on their nature.

Two viewpoints are well expressed in W.Y. Evans-Wentz' Introductions to his own *The Tibetan Book of the Dead* and *The Tibetan Book of the Great Liberation*, and C.G. Jung's Psychological Commentaries in both books. Jung, expressing the general belief of Western psychology, asserts that all these spirits are projections of our own minds, archetypal thought-forms of our unconscious. Evans-Wentz, speaking for Eastern Buddhism, agrees with him that in reality there are no such other-world beings; they are all phenomena, transitory, illusory, and non-existent save in the *sangsaric* mind perceiving them. But he qualifies this by the word *sangsaric*, explaining the basic tenet of Mahayāmna Buddhism, which holds that the entire *Sangsara*, our universe of appearances, as well as *Nirvana*, the unmanifested state, are both phenomena. They exist—with their gods, spirits, and all entities *including our own selves*—only in the Universal Mind, the noumenal source of the cosmic whole which pervades all forms of life even to the atom and the cell. They are no less real for being phenomena once we accept that they, and we who perceive them, are alike phenomena in relation to the one Reality, the Universal Mind, the Dharma-Kāya. Recognition of this constitutes Enlightenment.

Concerning Jung's postulation that the Dharma-Kāya, or Universal Mind, is the Eastern equivalent of Western psychology's concept of the collective unconscious, Evans-Wentz simply stated that Jung's Commentaries served as a "bridge between the best thought of the Occident and the Orient."

Meanwhile, the "spirits of the dead," with other attendant phenomena appearing nowadays to an ever-increasing number of psychics, mediums, and people in all walks of life, are creating the new noetic science of parapsychology. The eminent Jungian psychologist, Marie Louise von Franz, records an interesting observation in her book *Number and Time.* "It is being more and more firmly established that parapsychological phenomena occur mainly in the surroundings of an individual whom the unconscious wants to take a step in the development of consciousness. . . . Creative personalities who must fulfill a new creative task intended by the unconscious also attract such phenomena, as do all people before the outbreak of a psychosis or in a state of nervous conflict which can only be overcome by an increase of consciousness."

If this is so, we might wonder whether in this setting sun of Western civilization we are on the verge of a collective psychosis. Or, is the Spirit of the Age nudging us into the realm of the paranormal, expanding our consciousness to embrace what the Nahuas and Mayas predicted long ago as the coming Sixth World?

To these learned interpretations of the nature of spirits, nothing can be added here. Yet a footnote may offer testimony to the belief in spirits long held by all Indian America.

The *kachina*, literally translated as "respected spirit," is the primary symbol of Hopi ceremonialism. Kachinas take many forms, as spirits of the dead, of mythical beings, of mineral, plant, and animal entities, of clouds and stars. They are the invisible forces of life—the inner spiritual components of the outer physical forms, which may be invoked to manifest their benign powers so that man may continue his never-ending journey.

The Hopi kachinas are said to live upon the San Francisco peaks to the west, although they come from farther away, from distant stars and mysterious spirit worlds. Each winter, they come down to visit the people, their arrival and departure in midsummer being marked by great ceremonials. They are personified by men wearing masks of abstract designs, of anthropomorphic creatures with horns, snouts, beaks, or of representations of human beings, animals, birds, insects. The masks are sacred. Each is ceremonially fed and carefully preserved; and when its owner dies, it is buried so that its supernatural power may return whence it came. The impersonators of the kachinas are likewise invested with their powers during the time they wear the masks. How many Hopi kachinas there are is not known, although some three hundred have been identified. Hence small wooden dolls, also called kachinas, are given children so that they may familiarize themselves with the masks and names of the real kachinas.

The "Kachina Cult," as anthropologists call it, may not have originated in historical time as has been claimed. The Hopis themselves assert that kachinas came up with them during their Emergence to this present world, and accompanied them throughout their migrations. The Kokopilau Kachina sings a song in a language so archaic that not a word of it is understood by contemporary Hopis. Almost certainly, the kachina concept was brought north long before the domination of Mexico by the Aztecs, probably from the great Toltec metropolis of Teotihuacan which was deserted when the Aztecs arrived.

According to Hyemeyohsts Storm, the Great Spirit or embodiment of the kachina spirit-power is known in the Cheyenne tongue as *Wakan-tonka*. Often abbreviated into *Wahkan*, it is spelled and pronounced *Huacan* in the ancient Nahuatl language. These syllables form the last part of the name of the prehistoric heart-center of the Toltecs, Teotihuacan. *Teo* is the Nahuatl name for "god"; *ti* is a preposition denoting "with," "upon," "near," as, for example, *xochi-ti* which means "with flowers"; and *huacan* means the "spiritual power" of the kachinas. Hence this ancient spiritual center of all Mesoamerica is popularly called the "City of the Gods." Brought north, kachina symbols appeared on the sacred shields of the Great Plains tribes, and a kachina figure is still mounted on the central pole of the Sun Dance lodge or wheel.

Whatever its origin may be, the belief in kachinas seems to have existed throughout Indian America since ancient times. The Hopi word and their striking masks and costumes, unique in the world, have grown so familiar—due to the popular sale of their doll-size images—that we tend to dissociate them from the abstract spirits they represent. Kachinas are not deities and worshipped as such. Rather, a kachina is a living symbol for that universal spirit, like the Hindu Self and the Dharma-Kāya of Tibet's Mahayāmna Buddhism, which embodies all living entities, and denotes that spiritual component within each of us, distinct from our outer physical forms. It would seem, then, that if spirits are projected from our dark unconscious into conscious-ness, as psychology puts it, we are but admitting into our small personal selves aspects of the vast universal Self also within us. The process and power evoked is not always unconscious. The many consciously structured rituals of the sixteen-day Snake-Antelope Ceremony bring rain. For thoughts are things called forth into visible shapes from the invisible forces of the universe.

The manifestations of kachinas among the Hopis is not re-stricted to their six-month sojourn on earth. All of the nine great annual ceremonials feature the role of one or more kachinas. Nor do they appear mechanically and chronologically at these scheduled times. For aside from their ritually invoked formal appearances, individual kachinas pop up at any time. Hopis tell of meeting spirits in the same offhand manner they mention living neighbors.

Spirits also commonly appear in dreams. This does not seem unusual. The archaic vision of life they represent has never been obliterated from the human mind. It still lives on in the shadows of the unconscious, rising into consciousness with a meaning still valid. Jung regarded this archaic vision as an impersonal force manifesting as archetypal images, usually in dreams. Contemporary Indians, as did most primitive peoples, usually regard it as a living, inner spirit-being. Whatever it is, the Dreamer serves as an intermediary between our worldly conscious ego and the supra-personal world beyond our sensory perception. Hence the Dreamer within us, whose dreams or visions come through the Singer, the medicine-man, or religious leader, fulfills a significant function in tribal ceremonialism.

During the three years I lived among the Hopis at Pumpkin Seed Point in Kiakochomovi, certain spirits manifested their presence in several paranormal incidents I experienced, and in a number of dreams during which they appeared to counsel me.

The palpable and often visible presence of spirits everywhere was taken for granted by the Hopis. There was hardly a well, spring, or cliff which was not the home of a guardian spirit. A pinch of cornmeal was always offered them by passersby; and prayer-feathers were deposited at the many secluded shrines, at the mouths of caves, beneath rocks and trees, and hung on the branches of fruit trees, on our trucks and cars, and in our homes.

This feeling of a land animated by spirit forces permeated all the three barren, sun-baked, rocky mesas and their villages. It gave a depth, meaning, and richness to the lives of the economically impoverished Hopis such as we materially affluent people do not experience.

This is not a primitive, animistic belief as so many of us regard it. There is a reality beyond the physical world of our sense perceptions which has been apperceived since past times by many other peoples the world over. It is still the core of religious belief among all tribes in Indian America. Their reverence for Mother Earth as a living body always has differentiated them from later European arrivals who exploited for material gain what they regarded as an inanimate earth. The difference is still apparent here among my neighbors. With few exceptions, neither the Anglos nor Spanish have the reverence for the land and its embodied spiritual forces shown by the Indians. The Southwest Pueblos are not the only tribes who possess this intuitive insight. Nor are the Hopi mesas the only places they regard as sanctuaries of spiritual power.

Our region here, dominated by the Sacred Mountain, was also recognized as a focus of spiritual forces by John Lansa, who made a prayer-offering of cornmeal when he visited me with his wife Mina, the Hopi *kikmongwi* and religious leader of Old Oraibi.

When Hyemeyohsts Storm and his wife Hmunhwohwah, a Cheyenne medicine-woman, visited me, they too were aware of the spirit forces around us. They talked to a sentinel tree, an aged, lofty cottonwood. They divined in field, pasture, and mountain slope other receptacles for spirits which I had not been aware of. To all of them, the spirits of mountains, trees, and streams, they offered tobacco, the customary offering among the Great Plains tribes as cornmeal is for the Southwest Pueblos. Like Mina and John Lansa, they had the eyes of the human spirit to see the spirits beyond our physical sight. And this vision, I think, is inherent in all of us when we open ourselves to it.

It is difficult to define the course of our relationship to the other-world of spirits. It seems to follow the same order of nature's physical evolution, the same psychological progression of the emergence of the contents of the unconscious into consciousness.

But where does it begin? Are we aware, in what Jung calls the collective unconscious, that in our primeval past our spiritual natures were a part of all the nature from which we have gradually alienated ourselves? Or is this the end result of our conscious searching to regain completeness after our expulsion from the Garden of Eden, as the Bible puts it? Which came first, the chicken or the egg?

In any case, our relationship with the other-world of spirits is progressive. Sakokwenonkwas, spiritual leader of the Mohawk Nation, tells us that we must first get in touch with our human spirits which are parts of the natural world. Then slowly, we begin to be sensitive to the spirits that do not have a material presence. Some persons have a "green thumb," a kinship with the plant kingdom, and can talk with a living tree. Then they can commune with the spirit of the mountain forest. Others establish a connection with the animal kingdom, through domestic horses and dogs, then with wild birds, deer, the small brown bear. And then of course great Orion, the Pleiades, and Sirius become speaking acquaintances.

Some time ago, the feeling that my own spirit self was dominating my conscious ego instigated a series of dreams of flying. How easy it was! I simply stood on an open place, on the lawn or driveway, bent my knees slightly, and pushed gently on the ground with my feet. I then rose without effort into the air to survey at leisure the earth below. The dream recurred frequently over a long period.

On several occasions, I showed off this facility to my neighbors with the exuberance of a boy on a bicycle shouting to his mother, "Look, Ma! No hands!" Rising into the air, I told them, "Look, there's nothing to it! Just bend your knees, push on the ground, and up you'll go!"

Hovering at tree-top level above them, I could see them squatting on the ground, arms outflung like wings, puffing and panting as they pushed the ground for a take-off. Nothing happened. Those poor earth-bound creatures! They couldn't get off the ground. "You just don't believe in the power of your own spirit, that's all!" I shouted, soaring away over the housetop.

Early mornings at dawn or sunup became the usual times for these dream excursions. I became bolder, rising to greater heights and venturing longer distances away. No effort was necessary to fly over town or the great gorge of the Rio Grande. I simply had to wish a destination to be there instantly.

But there came a day when I fell off the bicycle.

One early morning, I found myself hovering at ease high above my house. Down below, through the bedroom window, I could glimpse myself lying asleep in bed, one arm outflung. At the same time, I noticed beside me a small feather, the tiny fluffy feather from the down of an eagle which Indians call a "downy." Small and light as it was, it was not disturbed by earthly air currents or high altitude winds. It simply floated beside me, like a familiar companion.

Rising higher, I began to wonder why I had not ventured farther. Shouldn't I pick a really distant destination—such as the moon, the summit of the mythical Mount Meru, or even go close enough for a peek at the Pearly Gates themselves?

At this moment there sounded, as if coming from nowhere, a thunderous, commanding voice. "Stop it!" At its first sound the little downy quivered and shrank against my leg, as if clinging for protection. I myself felt a tremor of fear. "Cut out this monkey business!" the authoritative voice commanded. "Go where you're going and stay there, or go back to bed!"

Immediately I found myself back in bed.

My dreams of flying ended. I was grounded.

Rather than being disconcerted by the enforced cessation of my aerial dream flights, I felt somewhat relieved to be brought back to earth again.

PART TWO

1

The Sacred Mountains
of the World

My own home *tierra*, small and unique as it may seem, nevertheless reflects the indivisible life of the entire universe. Aware of this relation of the part to the whole, the ancient Chinese called it Tao, the undivided One, the Meaning of the World, the Way of Heaven and Earth; and from this rose their earliest religion, Taoism. Other peoples of the far distant past in India, Egypt, Tibet, Mexico, and Britain must have observed the same intimate relationship between the forces of nature around them, the forests and streams, the mountains and stars. From this transcendental unity of heaven, earth, and man, they evolved their own philosophical and religious systems; they built their great civilizations. Over and over again, we encounter in the records they have left us the same motif of sacred mountains, the universal theme of duality, the symbols of the circle and the square, which we find expressed in our own Indian America.

The scope and significance of sacred mountains throughout the world, I began to learn through the friendship of W.Y. Evans-Wentz. A great scholar, his lifelong devotion to psychic and spiritual matters spanned three continents.

Dr. Evans-Wentz was born in Trenton, New Jersey, in 1878, and spent his early years in La Mesa, California, near San Diego. Attending Stanford University, he then studied at

Oxford University in England, and at the University of Rennes in Brittany, receiving high degrees from all three.

For four years, he did psychic research among the Celtic peoples of Ireland, Wales, Cornwall, Scotland, and Brittany. This resulted in his first book, *The Fairy Faith in Celtic Countries*, published in 1911. He then spent three years of research in Egypt on the ancient funeral rites described in the *Egyptian Book of the Dead*. Following this work, he traveled throughout Ceylon, India, and Tibet, which led him into an intensive study of Tibetan Buddhism. On this, he became a world authority with the eventual publication of those now well-known, ancient treatises which he edited and annotated: *The Tibetan Book of the Dead, Tibet's Great Yogi Milarepa, Tibetan Yoga and Secret Doctrines*, and *The Tibetan Book of the Great Liberation.*

Dr. Evans-Wentz himself embraced the faith of Mahayāmna Buddhism and settled in India, buying property in Almora, Kumaon Province. Here he lived in an *ashram* at Kasar Devi, hoping to develop it into a research center for Eastern religious philosophies. The outbreak of World War II put an end to his efforts. He returned to the United States, settling in San Diego.

Our correspondence began in 1947, when I was studying the esoteric meanings of Southwest Indian ceremonialism. In Dr. Evans-Wentz' Tibetan Series, I discovered many Tibetan and Hindu parallels to the beliefs and rituals of the Navajos and Pueblos. He too found in my books *The Man Who Killed the Deer* and *Masked Gods: Navajo and Pueblo Ceremonialism* an astonishing fundamental similarity between the esoteric beliefs of the two religious systems.

He was then preparing the fourth and last volume of his Tibetan Series, after which he planned to return to India. Publication of the book was delayed, and his advancing age prevented him from leaving America. Meanwhile a new interest in the Red Man was engrossing him.

He had inherited a great ranch of some five thousand acres about twenty-five miles southeast of San Diego. Lying astride the international border of California and Baja California, it embraced Mount Tecate, known to the Cochimas, Yumas, and other Indian tribes as the sacred mountain of Cuchama, the "exalted high place" on whose summit young men had undergone initiation into the sacred rites of their people. From surviving members of the tribes, he began to collect the traditions concerning it.

As his research progressed, he wrote me in 1953 that he was undertaking a book on Cuchama, incorporating accounts of other sacred mountains throughout the world such as Kailas in Tibet, Omei in China, and Arunachala in India. He was not familiar with others in America, and asked for any information I could give him. Our correspondence increased as I sent him material, and I visited him in San Diego.

He was living in a cheap, downtown hotel as befitting a Pilgrim on the Noble Eight-Fold Path. He was then in his seventies, but looked twenty years younger—a tall, slimly built man with a reticence of manner, and warmth of character. Although I was not a Buddhist, he often addressed me in his letters as "Fellow Pilgrim," "Friend on the Path," and "Brother Waters," and now shared with me his vast experience and mystical insights.

Through him, I met in Los Angeles a close friend, George W. Bass, who had served in a British army detachment in India, and later studied pre-Columbian ruins in Yucatan. He was now preparing illustrations for Dr. Evans-Wentz' book.

Shortly thereafter, Dr. Evans-Wentz conducted a trip to Cuchama for Mr. Bass and his wife; Eddie, his young nephew, who was a psychic; and myself. I had seen Cuchama years before, when as a young engineer stationed in Imperial Valley, I rode the old San Diego and Arizona Railway line periodically to report to my boss in San Diego. The train passed through the Mexican village of Tecate. Above it loomed the chaparral-covered mountain whose Indian name and significance I did not then know. Now, by international agreement, a fire-lookout station had been built on the summit, and the road was opened for us.

On the summit, we stayed several hours looking at unusual rock formations. Young Eddie received the psychic impression that a certain flat area had been the rocky floor of a great cave long before a catastrophe of some kind had lowered the summit of Cuchama to its present height. He picked up two small stones which he believed had been part of the ancient floor. Dr. Evans-

Wentz also found a small artifact, from which he received the sensation of fire and smoke, which he drew in with his *praña*. We then offered prayers dedicating this "exalted high place" to the good of all mankind in the centuries to come.

When the Bass family and I returned to Los Angeles, Mr. Bass took the two small stones and an artifact to Charles F. Smith, a psychometrist, for a reading. He too believed one of the stones had once been part of a floor of an immense cave. The other stone showed ancient water marks. From them both, the psychometrist received impressions of smells, heat, and dripping water. Cuchama, he said, had been occupied during three culture periods. The first human beings were remnants of a migrating race already extinct in their original homeland. They were of gigantic size, with short legs and arms, but with enormous torsos developed from drawing in the vital forces of nature. Where they came from, and how long ago, he did not venture to say, save that when they arrived, Cuchama was a lofty beacon peak visible from far out in the Pacific. From the artifact found by Dr. Evans-Wentz, he received the picture of a tall woman wearing a tight headband. The larger piece it had broken from evidently had been a cooking tool or utensil used in comparatively recent times. This confirmed Dr. Evans-Wentz' sensation of fire and smoke.

It is interesting now, years later, to read the account of a recent overnight pilgrimage to Cuchama made by Philip S. Staniford, professor of anthropology at San Diego State University, and five companions. Their psychic impressions, together with drawings of the shape of the peak and its unusual rock formations, he records in an article published in the Summer 1977 issue of *Phoenix* magazine. His experience attests Dr. Evans-Wentz' belief that Cuchama was a sacred mountain of great spiritual power.

During the years that Dr. Evans-Wentz' book took shape, he sent Mr. Bass and me portions and drafts of the complete manuscript for review and whatever help we could give him. Unfortunately, neither of them lived to see it published. Mr. Bass died in Prescott, Arizona, in 1961, writing me a note on the day of his death. Four years later, in 1965, Dr. Evans-Wentz died in Encinitas, near San Diego.

At his death, he left his property in India to the Maha Bodhi Society to establish a Buddhist educational and religious center. The net income from most of his property in California was left to Stanford University for the purpose of providing a professorship and scholarships in Oriental philosophies and religions. Some 2,261 acres of his large ranch, including Cuchama, were deeded to the State of California, with the request that Cuchama itself be made a public property to be "maintained forever as a mighty monument to symbolize goodwill and fraternity between the races and faiths of the Occident and the Orient across the wide ocean of peace over which it looms."

Stanford University, at his bequest, also received a large collection of his Oriental manuscripts and private papers, including his manuscript of *Cuchama and Sacred Mountains.* It is a great pleasure to me now, so many years later, that it will finally be published; and that I have helped to edit and annotate this last work of such a devout and eminent scholar.

Buddhists always have deeply venerated mountains. Their metaphysical Mount Meru, they conceived as the axis of the cosmos, its material image being the great Mount Kailas of the lofty Himalayas. It was natural that Dr. Evans-Wentz' absorbing interest in sacred mountains was based on his own Buddhist faith and his long residence among and below the mighty Himalayas. His book, accordingly, is primarily devoted to the many mountains and their sacred traditions with which he was most familiar. There were innumerable others throughout the world he did not mention, but their functions and traditions were so similar that a few of them should be mentioned here.

When the Buddhists entered China in the first century, they designated four sacred mountains oriented to the cardinal directions. *Wu-t'ai-shan*, the North Mountain of Five Peaks, in Shansi Province. *P-u-t'o-shan*, the East Mountain, off the coast of Chekiang. *Chiu-hua-shan*, the South Mountain of Nine Flowers, in Anhwei. And *Omei-shan*, the West Mountain, in Szechuan.

Long before the introduction of Buddhism, the Taoists held five other preeminent mountains as sacred. *T'ai-shan* in Shantung Province, the Mountain of the East. *Heng-shan* in Shansi, the Mountain of the North. *Nan-yueh*, or *Heng-shan* in Hunan, the Mountain of the South. *Hua-shan*, or Flower Mountain of the West in Shensi. And *Sung-shan* at the center, in Honan Province.

There is a curious ancient belief that a gigantic divine man called P'an Ku, who existed before the world was created, gave shape to these five holy mountains. When he died, his head became the T'ai mountain in the east, his trunk the Sung mountain in the center, his right arm the Heng mountain of the north, his left arm the Nan mountain in the south, and his feet the Hua mountain of the west. Hence, this cosmic man appears in Chinese mythology as the creator of the land which bears his shape.

To these nine sacred mountains, pilgrims came for centuries to climb their steep, dangerous trails, praying and depositing offerings at their many temples, shrines, pagodas, and monasteries. Two resolute women, Mary Augusta Mulliken and Anna M. Hotchkis, made arduous pilgrimages to each of them in 1935 and 1936, just a year before the Japanese invasion of China. Their account, including a detailed description with sketches and paintings, was finally published as a remarkable book in Hong Kong in 1973.

In Japan, veneration of mountains since antiquity has been carefully documented in a recent study by H. Byron Earhart of Sophia University, Tokyo, provided me by my friend Bob Kostka. Early as the seventh century, it relates, there developed *Shugendō*—the "way" by which human beings could gain the religious powers inherent within sacred mountains by pilgrimages and rituals or by mountain retreats. The meaning and purpose of *Shugendō* are evident from the derivation of its name: *Shu*—beginning enlightenment of a pilgrim's inherent divine nature; *gen*—his innate realization; and *do*—his attainment of what Buddhists call *nirvāna* and the Japanese *nehan*.

Of the 134 sacred mountains of the *Shugendō* sect, Mount Haguro with 33 main temples was the most important. On it formalities were observed in each of the four seasons, or "four peaks," during which adepts or pilgrims were considered to be "entering the mountain," leaving this world for the "other world." The procession up the mountain and the many rituals symbolized the union of the mythical pair which created the human race; the five stages of gestation within the womb; and spiritual rebirth from the mountain. This also reflected the ancient Japanese belief that the spirits of the dead return to the mountains and are reborn from them.

Shugendō became infused with ritual elements of Buddhism, Taoism, and Shintoism, and new sites were later established. It was officially proscribed in 1872, but after 1945 new sects were formed on the long-rooted tradition.

A striking parallel to *Shugendō* existed in ancient Mexico where the Aztecs observed *Tepeilhuitl*, "The Feast of the Mountains," on the 29th of October. The two great peaks Popocatepetl, the "Smoking Mountain," and Iztaccihuatl, the "White Woman" (now popularly called "Sleeping Woman"), were specially honored. The sixteenth century Dominican friar Diego Durán describes the ceremonies in his *Book of the Gods and Rites and the Ancient Calendar*, now published in English translation.

In homes and sanctuaries, small images of amaranth seed and maize kernels were made to represent the principal mountains in the land. In the center was placed the dough image of Popocatepetl, with eyes and mouth, and dressed in native paper. Close to him was placed the image of Iztaccihuatl, regarded as his wife. Rich offerings were made to them, and many rites were observed. The little images were then decapitated as if they were alive, and the dough was eaten during a ceremony called *Nicteocua*, which means "I Eat God." Following this, children and slaves were sacrificed, and the people climbed to the tops of the hills to light fires and perform ceremonies.

An elaborate ceremony was also held to honor Iztaccihuatl. Two small boys and two small girls in Tenochtitlan, (now Mexico City), were richly dressed and carried in decorated litters up the mountain, accompanied by lords and nobles. Here the four children were sacrificed in a large cave where the image of the goddess was kept.

The astute Fray Durán adds a significant comment: "The principal aim in honoring these hills, in praying and pleading, was [not to honor] the hill itself. Nor should it be considered that [hills] were held to be gods or worshipped as such. The aim was another: to pray from that high place to the Almighty,

89

the Lord of Created Things, the Lord by Whom They Lived. These are the three epithets used by the Indians on pleading and crying out for peace in their time .... "

From this, it seems that beyond the exoteric rites honoring the mountains as living images, there lay the esoteric meaning of mountains as places of access to the divine power of all Creation, or as openings to higher consciousness.

There are still many ancient shrines on both Popocatepetl and Iztaccihuatl, at one of which a nocturnal ceremony is currently held on May 3rd. Reverence for mountains is common throughout all Mexico. It was not unusual for me, when traveling through the sierras by horseback years ago, to find sacrificed turkey cocks and fresh flowers deposited on mountains remote from any village.

The custom is most noticeable among the Chamulas and Zinacantecos of southern Mexico and Guatemala, descendants of the ancient Mayas. Wooden crosses are found everywhere throughout these highlands—at the foot and on the summit of sacred mountains, and at the openings of springs and caves on their sides. The most imposing I've seen was an array of twenty-one huge crosses, some twenty feet high, standing on top of a bare hill near the remote and primitive village of Romerillo, high in the mountains of Chiapas. At all these *Kalvarios* everywhere, the people come in procession to deposit offerings of pine boughs and flowers, rum and black chickens, and to light candles and burn incense. The cross, explains the anthropologist Evon Z. Vogt, has no Christian meaning to the Zinacantecos. It marks the meeting places of their ancestral Mayan gods, being the "doorway" of communication between them and man. So again, as in the *Shugendō* rites of Japan and the Aztec ceremony of *Tepeilhuitl* in ancient Mexico, we find sacred mountains serving as places of communication between the soul of man and the divine power of Creation, or as openings to higher consciousness.

When in 1935 Dr. Evans-Wentz visited the great sage of India, Sri Ramana Maharshi, he asked him if he had ever had a Guru, a teacher. The sage replied, as reported in *Talks with Sri Ramana Maharshi*, that a Guru is God or the Self, which appears to a seeker in some form, human or non-human, and his own

Guru took the form of the sacred hill of Arunachala nearby. Dr. Evans-Wentz, commenting that there were certain major psychic centers in the human body and corresponding centers in the world, then asked if there were any psychic effects in visiting such sacred places. Sri Maharshi affirmed this, replying what is in the world is in the body, and what is in the body is in the world also.

The beliefs of Indian America seem to confirm this Eastern teaching. A pyramid is a sacred mountain. So is the sweat lodge or vision lodge, whose frame is constructed of ten bent willows (the number given to endless time and space). So also is the body of man a pyramid, or sacred mountain. Hence, the processions up sacred mountains, observed in India, Tibet, China, Japan, Mexico, and in Indian America, were vision quests, as were the sweat lodge rituals. All adepts were seeking a holy vision, an opening to higher consciousness, either on the summit of a sacred mountain, at the apex of a man-made stone pyramid, or in the mind-center of the human pyramid. This belief is still held throughout the vast Andes in South America, where some thirty or more high peaks carry shrines on their summits.

In her study of spatial archetypes, Mimi Lobell equates the emergence of the mountain out of the sea of chaos with the rise of the ego and self-consciousness from the womb-cavern of the unconscious. There began in world history the era of mountain-worshipping and pyramid-building civilizations in which reverence for the Earth Mother gave way to that for the Sky Father, and patriarchal replaced matriarchal patterns. The movement was reflected in the social stratification of different castes, with a divine ruler at the apex of the social pyramid. Yet eventually, the ego in turn experienced a spiritual enlightenment, which again related it to the mother of all creation, the unconscious. Hence the religious function of the sacred mountain was to enable man to surmount his earthly existence at its summit and achieve unity with the transcendental universe.

In the religious cosmology of the Navajos in our own Southwest, five directional holy mountains marked their traditional homeland. *Tsoll-tsilth*, the Holy Mountain of the South with the directional color of blue, now identified as Mount Taylor in the San Mateo range in New Mexico. *Dogo-shee-ed*, the Holy Mountain of the West with the color yellow, now known as the San Francisco peaks in Arizona, *Debeh-entsah*, the Holy Mountain of the North with the color black, believed to be Hesperus Peak of the La Plata range in Colorado. And *Siss-na-jini*, the Holy Mountain of the East with the color white. Its location in modern times has never been accurately determined. Various authorities believe it to be Blanca Peak in Colorado, or Pelado Peak, Abiquiu or Pedernal Peak in New Mexico. The consensus identifies it as Wheeler Peak above Taos, the highest peak in New Mexico, and with this I agree for various reasons. Within these four directional, physical mountains there loomed at the time of the Navajos' Emergence the great axial core of the cosmos, *Tsilth-nah-ot-zithly*. This central Encircled Mountain, or Mountain Around Which Moving Was Done, was similar to the metaphysical axis of the Buddhist cosmos, Mt. Meru, and is invisible to human eyes. It has been identified as the present Huerfano Mountain above Chaco Canyon in New Mexico—a low hill which is merely the material image of its metaphysical reality.

There were countless other mountains once held sacred throughout the United States. Too few of them are known to us today for the simple reason that the indigenous Indian tribes have been decimated or uprooted, and the mountains themselves have been desecrated or destroyed.

Pike's Peak in Colorado, at whose foot I was born, was one of the most notable. The Ute Creation Myth centered upon it, and its mythical origin parallels stories of the Flood. Its psychic forces, like a great magnet, drew people to it for centuries. It was a mecca for Utes coming down from the Rockies, and for Arapahoes, Kiowas, and Cheyennes from the Great Plains to the east, who dropped votive offerings in the medicinal springs at its foot. When the White Men came, it was a beacon peak for the "Pike's Peak or Bust" wagon caravans of the gold-seekers. Years later, when I was a boy, it still exerted its spell, drawing train-loads of visitors from all over the world to jog up its canyons by burro, drink from its iron and soda springs, and gather wild-flowers at every turn of the trail. But neither its majestic snow-covered summit, nor the virginal beauty of its canyons, could alone account for the serenity and energy it exerted as a spiritual font. If there does exist for each of us a psychological archetype, or a Guru, manifested as a physical mountain, Pike's Peak is mine. I grew up with it, nurtured by its constant living presence.

Today its life-giving energy has been destroyed. There are both a cog-road train and a race-course highway to its summit. The front wall of the range has been stripped bare for gravel. Cheyenne Mountain, just south of the Peak, has been hollowed out to house the combat operations center of the North American Air Defense Command. The Air Force Academy has appropriated the slope of the Peak to the north, while an immense Army base covers the land to the south.

Mount Taylor, the Navajos' holy Mountain of the South, is the focus of the United States' uranium mining industry. Into its side is drilled the world's deepest uranium mine shaft. And on its eastern side, on land belonging to Laguna Pueblo, the largest open pit uranium mine is now in operation.

The San Francisco peaks comprise the Navajos' sacred Mountain of the West. It is also sacred to the Hopis, who carry prayer-feathers to deposit in its shrines and to bring back bunches of spruce for their ceremonies. Today both tribes are protesting through the courts plans to industrialize the mountain as a ski and recreation area.

These are but a few examples, here in the West, of the continuing military, industrial, and commercial onslaughts against the sacred mountains in America. Our destruction and desecration of the living land has made us the richest and most materialistic nation in history. But under our national ethic of economic progress at any price, we have been buying the physical energy derived from nature at the expense of the psychical energy so necessary for our survival as a spiritually healthy commonwealth. Today we are belatedly recognizing the role of physical ecology in our lives, but not that of psychical ecology. For all the living entities of the mineral, plant, animal, and human kingdoms possess an inherent psychical life, as well as a physical life, and all constitute one integrated life-system. Each helps to maintain the life of the whole; and when we do violence to any part, we injure ourselves.

If we can accept this concept, we might still endorse the premise that the sacred mountains of the world are repositories of psychic energy upon which mankind draws for its life and development. We may, I suppose, loosely regard them as psychic power plants analogous to our physical power plants. They might better be compared to *chakras*, the psychic centers in the human body that Dr. Evans-Wentz referred to during his talks with the Maharshi, for they serve as focal points or distribution centers located on all continents throughout the planet.

There is a growing belief that sacred mountains and other revered sites were located on a global grid of lines of force. Can we infer then that previous civilizations, and even so-called primitive societies, were aware of such psycho-physical centers positioned in the living earth so that their fields of energy could influence not only the life in their immediate areas, but that of the planet as a living whole? If so, we must belatedly recognize that the physical and psychic realms are but two complementary aspects of one transcendental whole.

2

Ley Lines

It has been suggested that the sacred mountains of the world might be connected in a vast global grid of invisible lines. We may call them "ley" lines after the mysterious "ley" lines that linked sacred sites in ancient Britain. The dictionary defines "ley," "lea," or "lay" as a field, or meadow. These ley lines traversing field, meadow, hill, and dale beneath their surface are believed to be such invisible lines of force.

Strangely enough, they were not discovered until 1922 when Alfred Watkins, standing on a hilltop near Hereford, saw them in a vision below the surface of the landscape. On this ley system of undeviating straight lines, the prehistoric Britains and Celts and later Druids had erected mounds, dolmens, stone circles, standing stones, and megaliths. Watkins marked out the sacred sites on an Ordnance Survey map, which showed that they stood in exact alignment on dead straight lines. He then wrote a book, *The Old Straight Track*, describing his discovery which was ridiculed. Nevertheless, additional discoveries during the fifty years since then have confirmed his findings. The extraordinary recent interest in Stonehenge and Avebury, the White Horse of Berkshire Downs, the Somerset Zodiac, Glastonbury Abbey, and Lichfield Cathedral, has revealed that these ancient megalithic monuments and later churches may have been laid out on ley line patterns.

Many of them reflect the symbol of the dragon as John Ivimy points out. Its celestial prototype was the great circumpolar constellation Draco, which, with Ursa Major and Ursa Minor, revolves around the Pole Star, formerly Draconis and now Polaris. Draco, as we know, writhes like a giant serpent between Ursa Major and Minor. It lent its symbolism to Avebury, the great "serpent temple," whose head was formed by two concentric ovals of huge upright stones, and whose tails were avenues of more standing stones. The Uffington White Horse is said to look much like a dragon, and is situated near Dragon Hills Mound where Uther Pendragon, "head of the dragon," is said to be buried. Carnac in Brittany was also a great serpent temple with rows of stones winding for miles. The symbolism of the sky dragon was perpetuated to the time of King Arthur. Myth ascribes to him a celestial birth. One version holds that he was born from Draco, whose dragon symbol he adopted as his ensign. Mrs. K. Maltwood, discoverer of the Glastonbury zodiac, postulates that a small area south of Glastonbury containing the earthworks which the megalithic peoples constructed as symbols of the zodiacal constellations can be identified as the Kingdom of Logres of the Arthurian tales; and that the adventures of the Round Table Knights were symbolic representations of the zodiacal movements of the planets and the Precession of the Equinoxes.

This supports the belief that the megalithic peoples were aware of the Precession, accepting the reality of a cyclical, circular flow of time. With the rise of medieval Christianity in later centuries, this belief was regarded as rank heresy by the Church, which asserted the dogma of an unchanging aspect of the heavens and a linear progression of history toward an eventual apocalypse. Nevertheless, the ancient teaching was still preserved orally into historical times by a "Dragon" cult.

The exact purpose of the great megaliths is yet unknown. It has been variously proposed that they were used to predict eclipses, were radiators of terrestrial energy, or as receiving stations for cosmic influences from the heavenly constellations. Whatever their object, it is becoming clear that they were employed by the megalithic peoples in their effort to achieve harmony with universal forces.

Curiously, these beliefs in both ley lines and dragon symbology were paralleled in ancient China. The ley lines in China have been widely discussed for a century or more by many writers including John Michell in his recent *The Earth Spirit*. They were known as *lung-mei*, "paths of the dragon," powerful, invisible lines of magnetic force. They were divined by geomancers employing the esoteric art of *fung-shui*, "wind and water," "that which cannot be seen and cannot be grasped." Along these dragon paths, they sited buildings and tombs.

The *lung-mei* were of two kinds: the Yin, or female, which followed along low hills, and the Yang, or male, which arched over steep mountains. The most auspicious locations, where the dragon pulse was highest, were where two streams met. Individual lines were associated with one of the five planets, and corresponded to the five materials, wood, fire, metal, water, and earth, and each had an affinity with a part of the human body. In determining the pattern of dragon influence, the geomancers first perceived the main paths of planetary influence, then the radiating *lung-mei* between them. By thus interpreting the occult geography of the region, they could relate man and his earth in one harmonious pattern.

When in Hong Kong, I was told an interesting story by a nun who had taught in a school there some years ago. A new hotel then being built was re-oriented in order to give it a better view of the bay. The Chinese workers predicted it would be a failure because the building did not adhere to the "wind-water" lines; and for several years after the hotel was opened, it was not a success.

Apperception of such a ley system was apparently common in ancient Mesoamerica. The geometrical precision of Copan, Palenque, Uaxactun, Tikal, Chichen Itza, Uxmal, and other great cities in Mexico and Guatemala, and the architectural beauty of their exquisite temples, ornate palaces, and lofty pyramids, have evoked the wonder of explorers and scholars for centuries. How the Mayas and Toltecs, a thousand years before Columbus arrived on one of the New World's offshore islands, could have achieved with stone tools such architectural harmony with their physical environment, we find difficult to imagine. But their comprehension of universal order, reflected in the inexpressible beauty and spiritual forces still evoked by their sublime ruins, attests their appeal to that in us which is attuned to the ever-enduring.

To account for this, Horst Hartung, a Mexican architect associated with the University of Guadalajara, postulated the use of a ley system, using the Spanish word "trazos" or "tra- zados," meaning plans or designs, for the English "leys." In a study prepared several years ago, he proposed that the Mayas constructed their great urban centers upon a basic pattern of rectangular leys or *trazos* formed by a dominant center line which was usually a north-south axis adjusted to an exact deviation according to the latitude of the site. This did not explain the many arbitrary non-rectilinear qualities of build- ings. Irregularities in the alignment of different parts of even a single building were common. This characteristic led many observers to conclude that the highly skilled Mayas were not capable of following a systematic building design or of con- structing a vertical right angle. But superimposed over this pattern was found another, similar system with a different orientation. As this pattern was extended over the site in zones, it implied that its use extended over time, and proved that the Mayas were indeed capable of delineating exactly a ninety-degree angle.

New light on this system has been cast by Falken Forshaw Kalin in a paper on Mayan archaeology prepared at the Univer- sity of Washington. He reviews Hartung's findings, adds his own original research, and includes ground plan maps of major Mayan centers, outlining the ley systems upon which they were built. His in-depth study, which he has kindly sent me, is too comprehensive to be quoted from here; it should be studied in detail whenever it is published.

The site plan of Palenque, for example, shows the placement of the Temple of the Cross, the Temple of the Foliated Cross, the Temple of the Sun, and the Temple of Bas Relief, on ley lines radiating from the pyramidal Temple of the Inscriptions beneath whose floor lay the tomb of the buried ruler-priest. Architectural edges, such as platforms, building facades, and *cenotes*, or reservoirs, and points, such as doorways and building corners, were clearly delineated by leys.

Kalin's conclusion is that the Mayan ley system was part of an intergalactic network of energy forms. It incorporated three levels of environment: the upper level of constellations and planets, the middle level of the earth's surface, and the lower level of underground streams and mineral deposits. The alignment of sites and buildings thus helped to align the lives of the people with the structure and nature of Creation, and the source of man's own consciousness.

Some years ago the Austrian mystic Rudolf Steiner also asserted that planetary influences affect not only the magnetic currents in the earth's surface, but the mineral deposits below. They, too, are charged with energy as they respond to the orbital cycles of the various planets. This energy they release into the soil stimulates the germination and growth of plant life. And here perhaps we have an answer to the question asked me by the little girl of my neighborhood, "How does this dirt make our gardens grow?"

The three ley systems in Britain, China, and Mesoamerica suggest the existence in the past of a common knowledge of forces and laws applicable on earth as in heaven: "As above, so below." It can be held that the earth is a living body with a nervous system related to its magnetic field, and traversed by a network of leys carrying energy. At their junctions are nodes of power comparable to the acupuncture points of a human body, and here apparently are located the sacred mountains of the world.

Esoteric religious philosophies long have pointed out that cultural and religious sites in the highlands always have had a special character; and that the evolution center in central Asia established by Manu, the mythical law-giver of humanity, lay at the longitude of ninety degrees east, while another prehistoric religious center in America was located at ninety degrees west.

Many years ago, I ran into a privately printed odd book which asserted that many ancient Indian mounds, shrines, mountains, and other sacred sites in the United States lay along the line of forty degrees north latitude, roughly from the shrine of Powhatan in Virginia to Pike's Peak. Other lines extended globally west across the Pacific from the effigy mounds in the

Ohio Valley to the Celestial Mountains in Asia. The author did not develop the subject beyond the sparse references.

Persuasive as these studies are, I don't feel comfortable with the assumption that a global ley system can be mapped, as with fixed Cartesian coordinates defined by latitudes and longitudes. The lines have been shown to follow the configurations of the constellations and planets, the earth's surface, and the underground streams and mineral deposits. The global pattern of such a system has not been mapped. Yet a grid form has been proposed since ancient times. Plato asserted that the earth, when viewed from above, would resemble a ball sewn from twelve pieces of skin. Three Russian scientists recently confirmed this belief, discovering faint magnetic lines around the planet, making of it a dodecahedron solid with twelve pentagonal slabs. The edges were defined by mid-oceanic ridges, core faults, and active volcanic zones; and at the nodes lay spots of originating hurricanes and vortices of oceanic currents. The Russians also found that the centers of ancient cultures lay on the energetic lines.

If the edges of this earth are ley lines, as they are called today, one must assume that the global ley system, if it is ever mapped, would include the areas throughout the length of the Americas, up through the Andes, the Sierra Madres, Sangre de Cristos, and the Rockies, along which were located sacred mountains and the cultural and religious centers of the New World.

If so, this entrancing conjecture must include a strange experience I had while living on the Hopi Reservation in northern Arizona. It has been recounted in detail elsewhere, but briefly, I awakened one night to see two men in my room. "Don't be alarmed," said one. "We're ghosts, and you should know that ghosts are just like you except that they live in a world invisible to you. In performance of our duties, we travel along a line between the two poles of the world's axis."

The other ghost was just as friendly, although more stern. "We've dropped by to tell you you're on the line. Mind what I say! Stay on the line now!"

Old Dan Katchongva, the chief religious leader, identified my two visitors as the Sacred Twins, Palongawhoya and Poqanghoya, one stationed at the north pole and the other at the south pole, who sent out messages as they traveled along the line connecting the energy centers of the earth. "See? You're on the line to receive their vibratory messages," said Dan. "You must stay on the line as they told you!"

This mysterious line, if it were a transworld line of energetic current, may throw some light on the clan boundaries of the Hopis' sacred land as marked on their ancient stone tablets, and the Hopis' resistance against federal attempts to partition the land by surveyed lines, for the boundaries seem to follow invisible "wind-water" lines. In many other original Indian lands one notices the same divisions of field and forest whose configurations follow natural lines.

More specific attempts to harmonize man's religious and social patterns with that of the universe are given in John Michell's *City of Revelation*. In it, he interprets the measurements, proportions, and sacred numbers of the ancient cosmic temples, including the Great Pyramid of Egypt, Solomon's Temple, the actual Temple of Jerusalem, the symbolic New Jerusalem, and Stonehenge in Britain. He finds that all of them are constructed on the universal pattern of the circle and the square; and that their units of measurement were related to each other, deriving from one original canon of cosmology which was common to the hermetic doctrines of Egypt, Babylonia and China, the Hebrew cabala, the Egyptian-Greek philosophy of Pythagoras, and the builders of Stonehenge.

Further insight into the structure and purpose of the Great Pyramid of Gizeh has been provided by the outstanding study of Livio Cetullo Steccini, an authority on metrology, featured in Peter Tompkins' exhaustive book *Secrets of the Great Pyramid*. Steccini concludes that the Great Pyramid is an exact scale model of the Northern Hemisphere and a highly developed scientific instrument incorporating the basic formulae of the universe. He drew no structural parallels with the pyramids in Mesoamerica since the metrology of the American continent had received meager attention, but the figures he established suggested that the American units agreed with those of the Old World.

It is a pity that Michell did not include the great structures of ancient Mesoamerica among the temples of the world. This lack of knowledge has now been expanded by maps and measurements made of the great ruins of Teotihuacan in Mexico, narrated by Peter Tompkins in his second comprehensive book, *Mysteries of the Great Pyramids*.

The ancient city of Teotihuacan, not far from present Mexico City, justifies the belief that it was constructed on a cosmic plan, and may have reproduced the astronomical pattern of the planets and constellations. Teotihuacan, as we know now, was the first and greatest metropolis in the New World, founded in the second century B.C. As revealed by a photogrammetric map made by René Millon, it covered an area of 38 square kilometers and contained a population of perhaps 200,000. It was divided into four quarters with temple complexes for priests and acolytes, residential palaces, and a general living area with grid pattern streets, hostels for traveling merchants, immense market places, canals and sewers.

Above all, it was a holy city whose religious ideology extended throughout all Mexico and Central America, exerting a spiritual dominance comparable to theocratic Buddhist Tibet, to other Holy Empires whose centers were Rome and Mecca, and to the Hellenistic commonwealth whose intellectual and religious capital was Alexandria in Egypt.

The heart of Teotihuacan was the majestic ceremonial complex dominated by the great Pyramid of the Sun. Past it ran the Street of the Dead. At one end rose the Pyramid of the Moon from a square courtyard surrounded by thirteen temples. At the other end lay the immense Ciudela or Citadel containing on each of three sides four pyramidal bases for more temples. In its center rose the great Temple of Quetzalcoatl, whose walls were decorated with huge sculptured stone heads of Quetzalcoatl alternating with those of Tlaloc, the god of water.

The enormity and massiveness of these immense structures are beyond belief. No other great ruins in all Mexico and Guatemala compare with them. Even today, two thousand years later when their smooth facing has been removed to show only their rough stone outlines, they reveal in their austerity and astronomical precision an insistent impersonality, a transcendent equation of immeasurable space and time.

Hugh Harleston, Jr., making precise measurements of the great structures, found a basic unit equivalent to 1.059 meters. This, he called a "hunab," after the Maya divinity Hunab Ku, who controlled all measures in the universe. The number 378 appears frequently in his measurements. The overall length of the walls of the Citadel was 378 hunabs; the length of the entire ceremonial zone was six times 378, the height of the Sun Pyramid; and the boundary buildings perpendicular to the north-south axis of the Street of the Dead ran 378 units both ways, equal to the distance between the Pyramids of the Sun and the Moon. Harleston determined that 378 times his basic unit multiplied by 100,000 gave the average spherical circumference of the earth, and that the 60-unit base of the Quetzalcoatl Pyramid multiplied by 100,000 gave the polar radius of the earth. Moreover, the 378 hunab length of the Citadel divided by the 60 hunabs of the Quetzalcoatl Pyramid represented the circumference of the earth divided by twice its radius, which gave the value of π or pi, 3.15. Another proportion in the Citadel gave the correct value of 1.62 for Φ or phi, the universal constant called by the ancient Greeks "the golden mean," used in the construction of the Cheops pyramid and Chartres Cathedral, and found to be related in nature to the spiral growth of seashells and other organisms.

Harleston then discovered that markers along the Processional represented the distances of planets from the sun, corresponding to the orbital values of Mercury, Venus, Earth, and Mars. He also found markers that suggested the possibility of two or more planets closer to the sun than Mercury, and still more outer planets beyond Pluto. This agrees with the assertion of Gurdjieff that we are already experiencing the influences of two planetary bodies beyond Pluto, yet undiscovered by modern science.

These are only a few of the measurements and mathematical studies of proportions made by Harleston and reported in voluminous detail by Tompkins. From them Harleston conjectured that Teotihuacan was a scale model of the earth, incorporating mathematical, astronomical, geodetic, and other data on the structure of the universe.

Unfortunately he did not develop the relationship of his own unit of measurement with those employed elsewhere in the ancient world. Tompkins, however, adds a brilliant commentary, pointing out that the Middle East had a basic unit of 40 "fingers" called a *bema*, equal to .77 of a meter. If Harleston's *hunab* is divided into 60 fingers, a unit of .01765 meters results. Hence the base of the Quetzalcoatl Pyramid becomes 90 *bemas*, instead of 60 *hunabs*, and the perimeter of the Pyramid of the Sun becomes 12,960 *bemas*, and its base length 1,296 fingers. The number 1,296 with its multiples and submultiples, says Tompkins, has been the numeric basis for astronomical measurements throughout all history, and is still in use. The measure of the Most Holy in Solomon's Temple was 1,296 inches, the Hebrew shekel weighs 129.6 grams, and the English guinea 129.6 grains. The number was employed in the construction of the Great Pyramid of Egypt and in the Babylonian ziggurats. When this full correlation is finally made, it may confirm the belief that all these ancient structures reflect a cosmic order common to the earth, the universe, and man.

The prodigious three-volume study of the Egyptian Temple of Luxor made by R.A. Schwaller de Lubicz, published in France more than twenty years ago, and now translated into an English abridgement as *The Temple in Man*, achieves such a synthesis. It is complemented by a detailed interpretation by John Anthony West, *Serpent in the Sky*. Schwaller's work demonstrates that this monumental temple of the Eighteenth Dynasty of Pharaonic Egypt was constructed to symbolize man, whose physical and psychic structures conform to the image of the universe. The Temple's architectural configuration included, for example, the location of man's physiological ductless glands and the astronomical orientations of heavenly bodies. Schwaller's thesis embraces the whole body of Egyptian wisdom, a "Sacred Science" of the relationships between constellations and planets, plants, animals, and parts of the human body, expressed in art, architecture, mathematics, astronomy, hieroglyphic writing, and symbology.

Comprehensive as it is, his work was achieved on a much higher level of consciousness than that of orthodox archaeologists and Egyptologists. On a mundane, historical level, it refutes their assumption that Egypt as a unified kingdom was established in 2750 B.C., by setting the date as 4240 B.C. This date, Schwaller establishes as the beginning of the first Sothic Year or New Year. These occur only every 1,461 years, when the helical rising of the star Sirius (Sothis) coincides with the summer solstice. For another thing, he concludes that the civilization of Egypt was founded as early as 36,000 B.C.; that it did not develop gradually, but was complete at its beginning; and that it was inherited from a still earlier, vanished civilization. The latter, of course, is understood to be Atlantis. The tedious research, which is the basis for this conclusion, is too detailed to give here. Nor does Schwaller comment on the controversial continent. It is wise he did not, for it might have caused his illuminated work to be regarded as suspect by those to whom any mention of the subject arouses antagonism. But if Atlantis did exist, as a growing number of other scholars now believe, it may account for the many religious and cultural correspondences between the civilizations of Egypt and Mesoamerica.

Schwaller's work is too encompassing and profound to be telescoped; it must be studied in its entirety. Its primary theme is that the various arts of Egypt were an evocative expression of a higher consciousness. Their aim was to stimulate the spiritual powers within man, rather than the mechanistic employment of the rational intellect for controlling the natural environment. Through rationalism man knows only what he perceives through the senses. Beyond this lies a knowledge perceived only by a higher consciousness when it is awakened. The one goal of all human existence is to attain this higher, universal consciousness, to return to its original wholeness. Each mineral, vegetable, animal, and human species also represents a stage in the evolution of this higher consciousness. Hence the function of Pharaonic Egypt's Sacred Science was to help further man's transition from corporeal life to spiritual existence. This, as we know, is the same great goal of the religious philosophies of India, Tibet, China, Britain, and Mesoamerica.

The significance of Sirius to Egypt has many wide ramifications. The Dogon tribe of Africa celebrates its most important religious rite, the Sigui, every fifty years. This period is the time required for a tiny, invisible star to orbit Sirius. The two French anthropologists, Marcel Griaule and G. Dieterlen, who have reported the ritual, state that the Dogon call it *po tolo* after a tiny cereal grain, the *Digitaria exilis.* Hence Griaule and Dieterlen call the star "Digitaria." The Dogon believe it is the smallest and the heaviest of all stars, and that it contains the germs of all things. It lies at the axis of the whole world, and its orbital movement upholds all creation in space.

The basis for this astounding belief is a mystery. The Dogons are a primitive tribe in central Africa. Without telescopes, how could they have perceived this tiny star so invisible that it was discovered only after the employment of modern astronomical instruments? By what means did they accurately determine its orbital period around Sirius, and its density? And how, above all, has it influenced their daily lives for undoubtedly many centuries?

As we know now, according to Rodney Collin, Sirius is the brightest star in the heavens beyond those in the solar system. Twenty-six times more brilliant than our own Sun, its distance from the Sun is one million times the distance from the earth to the Sun. Collin further reports that the double-star Sirius comprises this immense radiant sun whose mass is two-and-a-half times greater than our Sun, and a dwarf 5,000 times denser than lead. He asserts that no astronomical data contradict the possibility that our Solar System circles about Sirius in the latter's circuit of the Milky Way. In short, our Sun revolves around Sirius, the central sun of all suns. How curiously parallel this is to Dogon belief!

It is significant, indeed, that all beliefs ranging from the existence of ley lines through the structures of world temples, to the configurations of entire civilizations to cosmic, creative principles, are now appearing in this crucial period of change. It is as if the very earth is finally revealing its hidden secrets. But how far back can we project them? We can only conclude that there existed sometime a previous world civilization possessing the knowledge that the same order and precision with which all the business of the universe is conducted and can be observed in the psyche of man.

The inclusion of man's own consciousness among other manifestations of cosmic forces is wholly compatible with our expanding awareness of the nature of the universe. If it is true that every organ and cell within the living body of man, and every molecule of matter within the living body of the earth, is informed to some degree with consciousness, contributing to their composite consciousness, it is not too difficult to believe that all our planets contribute to the higher consciousness of the solar system, and it, in turn, to the consciousness of the living body of the galaxy which embraces it. Then, indeed, the one great goal of all the constituent and interconnected living systems, from cell to star, is the eventual attainment of universal consciousness.

We are not dependent upon the teachings of past civilizations or upon the discoveries of modern astro-astronomy to reveal this universal harmony and unity. It can be realized through nature itself, as affirmed by the vision of the great Sioux medicine-man Black Elk:

"Then I was standing on the highest mountain of them all, and round about beneath me was the whole hoop of the world. And while I stood there, I saw more than I can tell and I understood more than I saw; for I was seeing in a sacred manner the shapes of all things in the spirit, and the shape of all shapes as they must live together like one being. And I saw that the sacred hoop of my people was one of many hoops that made one circle, wide as daylight and as starlight, and in the center grew one mighty flowering tree to shelter all the children of one mother and one father. And I saw that it was holy."

3

Movement

Two of my friends were working with me in the yard one afternoon when a strange couple walked into the driveway. The man wore homemade moccasins and a feather stuck into his long hair, and we noticed a sheath knife belted around his waist. The woman behind him was barefooted, clad in a Mexican rebozo, and carried a small baby in a sling on her back.

"Jiggers! Here come the Apaches!" exclaimed one of my Indian friends, laying down his hammer.

Tired from their uphill walk, the couple sat down to rest a bit. Then they continued on up the mountain slope where they were living in a rude lean-to among the pines beneath El Cuchillo.

I should have realized then that their arrival signalled a momentous change in our life at Arroyo Seco, throughout all the country. They were emissaries of the great hippie movement then spreading throughout the nation. Footloose young people who had forsaken their homes and schools and jobs, unable to abide our excessively rational and materialistic culture, and seeking a simpler way of life. This young couple apparently had found it here. They were followed by a steady stream of others: dressing like Indians, building rude shelters and imitation tepees, establishing communes, and undergoing all the hardships of impoverished city-bred children trying to root themselves to the earth. While it is true that some of them were dirty, ignorant, lazy, and given to smoking pot, others were from affluent families, university-educated, and devoutly seeking new values. Their influx to Taos was militantly discouraged by the tourist-oriented Chamber of Commerce, and the hippie communes were soon largely abandoned by their inept members. Arroyo Seco, however, became a focal point for those who remained, and for the Long Hairs who came later. More and more of the latter, whose families could afford it, financed the purchase of land on the mountain slope above and the erection of new homes.

However much we may discount the hippie movement of the sixties, it was symptomatic of a great underground change taking place in America. It resulted in this small, rather backward village below the bare rock-walled El Cuchillo undergoing a change more drastic than it had experienced in its life of two centuries or more.

What can account for these seemingly sudden impulses to revolutionary movements in the hearts and minds of mankind, for the mass migrations of history, of the exodus of Flower Children from Haight Asbury to Taos? They cannot be fully explained rationally. Can it be that all human movement and change are impelled by the same mysterious, invisible forces that govern the migrations of swallows and wild geese, the rhythmic changes of the seasons, the movements of the stars above?

One of the most fascinating Nahuatl hieroglyphs is *Ollin*, Movement. It is the seventeenth of the twenty day-signs in the Sacred Calendar of the Nahuas and Mayas, the core of the great pre-Columbian calendar system perfected about the first century B.C. and used throughout all Mesoamerica.

The hieroglyph is basically simple, consisting of two entwined lines. There are many variations. The lines may be straight or curved, thin or blocked. One may be colored red, the other blue. One version is that of a serpent and a centipede entwined. But simple as the hieroglyph is, its meaning is profound. It symbolized the interlocked polarities of the cosmic dualities: earth and sky, light and darkness, male and female, good and evil. The tension between them was what gave movement, life, to man and the universe.

The concept of the tension between these dualities which resulted in movement was paramount in Nahuatl religious belief. According to tradition, there had been four successive previous worlds or suns, each designating a quadrant of the universe. The present fifth world, or sun, the Aztecs termed the Sun of Movement because it was the unifying center of the four previous directional suns which had preceded it. Its significance is shown on the monumental twenty-five-ton Stone of the Sun, commonly called the "Aztec Calendar Stone," where it holds the center place surrounded by symbols of the previous four suns and the twenty day-signs of the *tonalamatl,* or sacred calendar. Yet, within the Fifth Sun lay another synthesizing center, the soul of man. For only here in the movement taking place in man's heart could the opposite polarities be reconciled if man were to achieve his true role in the great pattern of Creation.

The hieroglyph *Ollin,* Movement, thus condenses in its deceptively simple, entwined lines the entire Nahuatl religious philosophy. The many ramifications of its full meaning can be traced only when we understand better the warp and weft of that great civilization whose spendor illumined America a thousand years before Columbus reached its shore. Still, I think all studied interpretations can be boiled down to the guiding principle of continuous movement, of perpetual change.

Perhaps it is not strange that these ancient people, barbarians as we used to think them, gave such importance to movement. Nothing in nature is static, still. The tides of the sea ebb and swell. Rivers are in constant movement. Even the earth beneath us pulsates with slow motion. We, ourselves, are gyrating on a planet that spins on its polar axis at the rate of 700 miles an hour, revolves around the sun at 70,000 miles an hour, and with the entire solar system moves around the galaxy at the phenomenal speed of 1,000,000 miles an hour. Beyond our own galaxy, the Milky Way, are millions of other galaxies revolving, contracting, and expanding in constant motion.

The universe of the infinitely small is like that of the infinitely large. Theoretical physicists exploring the sub-atomic world of matter have progressively found that the atom consists of nuclei and electrons, the nuclei consisting of protons and neutrons, and these nucleons composed of particles— all in a constant state of motion, like the planets and galaxies.

If we are not aware of these movements in matter and outer space, we are not too aware of the movements taking place within our own bodies, as the circulation of blood, of air. Nor are most of us conscious of the psychological changes taking place as a result; with every breath, for example, there is a change of thought.

There is no need to expound this idea if we can accept for the moment the Nahuatl premise of movement and change underlying all existence. A little difficult to understand is that movement itself is created by the interplay of the opposing cosmic forces. It is easy enough to grasp the idea when their forces are personalized by those two ancient Nahuatl gods, Quetzalcoatl and Tezcatlipoca. What a quarrelsome pair they were! Striving to become the sun and rule the world, one overcame the other and exerted his supremacy for the duration of a world and an era, achieving equilibrium. Then the other, overcoming him, initiated another world and era. So it continued throughout the four previous worlds whose existence and meaning lie embalmed in the nebulous realm of myth. What battles they had, in the vast quadrants of the universe, these two sons of the one supreme godhead, Ometéotl, who embodied both dualities! They remind us of the Zarathustran accounts in ancient Iran of the struggles between Ormuzd and Ahriman, representing the antithesis between the light and dark powers of life.

Yet these Nahuatl gods, like all gods, merely impersonated abstractions with which men since ancient times have tried to grapple. It is curious how similar to the Nahuatl symbol of *Ollin* is the still more ancient Chinese T'ai-Chi Tu symbol. It is formed by a circle divided into halves, one dark, the other light. The meaning of this symbol is profoundly similar. The circle represents the "supreme ultimate" or "primal beginning." The light half, the Yang, and the dark, the Yin, designate the two polar forces of the universe: the positive and negative, male and female, light and darkness, earth and heaven. These opposite powers are never static and at rest. Between them exists a state of tension that keeps them in motion, constantly generating change.

Although the Nahuas viewed the dual powers as being in immortal conflict, they believed in their eventual reconciliation. The Chinese, too, saw in their motion a tendency to unite. Each principle contained a small measure of the other, as shown in the symbol by a small light Yang spot in the dark, and a small dark Yin spot in the light. Their meaning in terms of change was fully developed in the three-thousand-year-old classic *I Ching*, the *Book of Changes,* whose origin goes back to mythical antiquity. It is based solely on the polarity of the positive Yang and negative Yin principles, its theme being the continuous change through movement underlying all existence.

Full comprehension of this book of profound wisdom seems impossible. In it were rooted both branches of Chinese philosophy, Taoism and Confucianism. Chinese scholars and marketplace soothsayers consulted it for centuries. A plethora of European books have attempted to analyze and interpret it. From it, C.G. Jung largely developed his theory of synchronicity. Today, thanks to its modern translation and interpretation by the noted late sinologist Richard Wilhelm, the *I Ching* has attained wide attention and common usage.

The bases of the *Book of Changes* are eight symbols conceived, as Wilhelm tells us, as images of all that happens in heaven and on earth. They are expressed in trigrams of three lines, solid or broken. They may represent the forces of nature: heaven, earth, thunder, water, mountain, wind, fire, and lake. Or they may represent a family consisting of father, mother, three sons, and three daughters. Or again, they may represent the governing officials of the state: sovereign, prince, prime minister, and so on. More precisely, the eight images or trigrams represent not these objective things, but their relationships which are constantly undergoing change. Hence the trigrams are symbols expressing their tendencies in movements.

These trigrams are combined with one another into hexagrams of six lines, either solid or broken, positive or negative. This results in a total of sixty-four hexagrams, and on these the *I Ching*'s oracles are based.

The usual method of consultation is briefly this. One throws three coins on the floor. If two of them come up heads, draw a straight, solid line on a piece of paper to denote a firm or Yang line. If two coins come up tails, draw a broken or yielding Yin line. Then one turns to the *Book of Changes* to read the interpretation of the hexagram.

But no relationships are permanently static. Nothing, says Wilhelm, is absolutely at rest; rest is but an intermediate state of movement, and there are points shown in the hexagram when one throws the coins and all come up heads, denoting a firm, unbroken Yang line; or else all three coins turn tail up, indicating a broken, yielding Yin line. These are moving or changing lines— the Yang line changing into a Yin line or the Yin line into a Yang line. This of course results in a second hexagram rising out of the first, for whose interpretation one must again consult the text. As it is possible for each line to change or move, each of the hexagrams can change into another for a total (64 x 64) of 4,096 transitional stages, representing every possible situation. The hexagrams thus give images of conditions and relationships existing in the world, while the individual lines treat particular situations within these general conditions.

The *I Ching* is generally used as a book of divination, as I use it. My introduction to it, more than thirty years ago, I well remember. While I was living in Mora, Mabel and Tony Luhan invited me to have lunch, and for something to do, Mabel got out a copy of the *I Ching*, translated by James Legge, and published in 1889. This early translation simply showed the six lines of the hexagrams not separated into their two trigrams. To represent the six lines someone had made for her six small sticks, three of which had been marked with a dividing line, and three unmarked. These Mabel threw after silently asking a question. Then I, in turn, threw the sticks and obtained the same hexagram. What the oracular pronoucement meant, I had no idea, the text was so full of archaic Chinese allusions. But this was irrelevant. What was vastly significant was that I had thrown the same hexagram as Mabel against the odds of 4,096 to 1. Today I would give a buffalo nickel to know which hexagram we both obtained, what image and relationship it represented, and the psychological meaning of this extraordinary coincidence. Certainly it was oracular, for it led to my move to Taos, and to a close friendship with her and Tony that existed until their deaths.

Not until 1950, upon the publication of the new version of the *I Ching* translated and annotated by Wilhelm, did I begin to realize the universal significance of this remarkable book. Through him there opened a view of its psychological basis.

The ancient sage Ta Chuan, in his *Great Commentary*, points out that the conscious and the unconscious are both evolved in the oracular pronouncement. The conscious process stops with the formulation of the question, and the unconscious process begins with the division of yarrow stalks (or the throwing of the coins). The hexagram obtained reflects two images or events, the situation in a person's life on earth at that moment, and the suprasensible image in heaven.

The foundation of Chinese philosophy, asserts Wilhelm, rests on the belief that the world is a system of homogenous relationships—a cosmos, not a chaos. Every event in the visible world is the effect of a pre-existent image or idea in the unseen world; everything that happens on earth is a corporeal reproduction of this archetypal image. The changing or moving lines in a hexagram serve as a connection to a new situation. Hence the oracle guides one to proper action in the future.

Nothing happens by chance. All movement and change take place according to the same immutable laws. Is it by mere chance that a throw of the coins reflects the observer's situation at the moment, his psychic condition, and the hexagram he obtains? According to Jung, neither of these has a causal influence on the other. In his Foreword to the *I Ching*, he postulated his theory of synchronicity, asserting that "synchronicity takes the coincidence of events in time and place as meaning something more than mere chance, namely, a peculiar interdependence of objective events among themselves as well as with the subjective (psychic) state of the observer or observers." In his many writings on synchronicity he develops more fully the non-causal but meaningful relationships between separate, objective events, and the subjective element, the consciousness of the observer.

The simple basic meaning, then, of both the Nahuatl symbol of *Ollin* and the Chinese T'ai-chi Tu is that the cosmic opposites are in a state of cyclic transition, one changing into the other. This is reflected in all the phenomena in heaven and on earth. Day gives way to night. Winter follows summer, wakefulness changes into sleep, death succeeds birth, fortune changes into misfortune, good evokes evil and evil grows out of good. A continuous transformation of opposites through movement.

Do we dare to suppose that only our little world is susceptible to the law of movement and change? Or are our neighboring planets and outer stars obeying the same law, being like our earth organic, living entities on a similar journey of transformation? All life seems to follow a circular, cyclical movement. It is said that the heavenly bodies in outer space are moving away from us at unimaginable speed into infinity. But their path, if we accept this law of movement, is not a straight line, and it does not recede into infinity. It curves in a great circle enclosing dimensions of space and time we have yet to fathom.

All this may seem to be straying too far from my own Father and Mother mountains. Yet, if the universal law of movement dictates the changes of polarity on great cosmic scales, certainly the changes must also take place on the lesser scales of nature. I suspect this is so here. El Cuchillo del Medio and the Sacred Mountain are not static manifestations of the male Yang and female Yin polarities. They have begun to lose their predominant influences.

With the arrival of the first Flower Children and later Long Hairs, the little village below and the mountain slope above began to change. Young couples began to buy land, fell pines. Deer no longer came down to my aspen grove on moonlit nights. The bear vanished from their dens in the cliff wall on the trail to El Salto cave. Cars and pickups rumbled past my house in swirls of dust. A community water system is already underway; no more dipping water out of the stream or even digging individual wells. The immense water tank looms out of Emilio Fernandez' high mountain meadow, and from it the community water line will be tapped by every family down to the village.

These changes are forebodings of the immediate future. It won't be long until the road from Arroyo Seco is paved to the foot of El Cuchillo. The mountain slope will be shaved of its stately pine and spruce. A grid of streets will be laid out, and along them will rise a conglomeration of homes far different from my old adobe, some of them with solar heating.

Will this new suburb be known as El Cuchillo, or El Salto? Certainly, it will lie wholly within the domain of the presently forbidding El Cuchillo. Dollars to doughnuts, its new residents will be unaware of its negative reputation, the tradition of El Salto cave, its alleged ghosts and *brujas*. Will this mean that the influx of new people will change El Cuchillo's present masculine Yang polarity to that of the feminine Yin? Or does it reflect the fact that El Cuchillo's polarity is already changing?

What about the Yin influence of the pueblo's Sacred Mountain? Is it conversely changing into Yang? The Indians themselves are showing another side of their dual nature, becoming militantly independent. Since regaining title to their Blue Lake wilderness, they have asserted exclusive possessiveness to all their land. All entrance roads into the Reservation are closed to outsiders. No more horseback trips to Blue Lake. No more picnics at the mouth of the Lucero. Even the gates across the road from my house, through which I rode so freely on horseback, are padlocked. Townspeople and visitors must pay an admittance fee to enter the pueblo, even for the great ceremonial dances on Christmas and San Geronimo. In the thrust toward tribal self-government and the management of their own affairs, the tribal council has hired a professional administrator and two consultants to supervise the pueblo's financial and personnel matters, and several projected programs. These include housing, health, social welfare, and irrigation projects. How different now is this business-oriented structure from the simple, devoutly religious pueblo of a few years ago!

Let's not carry this idea of a change in polarity too far. Else we'll be led into current popular and scientific predictions that another shift in the global axis is due soon, with a reversal of the magnetic polarity of the earth's north and south poles, causing a change in climate, volcanic activity, earthquakes, tidal waves, and other geological catastrophes.

My speculations here extend no farther than my own *tierra*. Yet it seems obvious that all pueblos, all America, is undergoing the same change. Beyond all reasoning, beyond all economic and political programs, despite the seemingly impregnable fortress of our present Western civilization, something is transforming our guiding principle into its antithesis. The spirit of our time is imbued with the need for change.

What pattern of life, of world civilization, is indicated, we don't know. Whatever it may be, we can only be assured that it will conform in some way to the universal law of movement towards the complete pattern of all Creation.

4

The Hopi Prophecy

It is curious how an odd idea from an obscure source, long unknown, ignored, or considered irrelevant, suddenly emerges to general public notice. The idea itself cannot alone account for its sudden spread and wide acceptance. Nor can the media of books, magazines, and newspapers which report it. Relevant though it may be, an idea first requires a fertile ground in which to take root and grow. And this must be the unconscious level of those who at last find in it something akin to their own deeper feelings.

The Hopi Prophecy is such a phenomenon. When I recounted it in the *Book of the Hopi* published some years ago, it was as generally unknown as the Hopis themselves. Today the Hopis are prominent in the news, and their prophecy has caught the imagination of people everywhere.

The Hopis, when I lived among them for three years, were a small tribe of five thousand people confined to a desert Reservation of four thousand square miles in northern Arizona. They lived in nine ancient villages built on top of three high mesas, with a tenth some fifty miles away. Oraibi on Third Mesa, dating from 1200 A.D. or earlier, was the oldest continuously occupied settlement in the United States. Just below it lay Kiakochomovi, New Oraibi, historically a new village without tradition, a "government town." The nearest modern towns on the transcontinental highway—Flagstaff, Holbrook, and Winslow—lay a hundred miles south by narrow dirt roads. Impoverished farmers, the Hopis subsisted mainly on the sparse patches of corn they grew in the sandy desert below their mesas. Isolated and neglected, they were but a fragment of the nation's ignored Indian minority.

The Hopis themselves, however, maintained an inner life as rich and meaningful as their outer life seemed shabby and meaningless. They perpetuated the tradition of a mythological past and a prophecy of the impending future. The fecundant past was embodied in their Creation myth and migration legends, and dramatized in their nine great annual ceremonials, the only true Mystery Plays indigenous to America.

These recount that the Hopis had lived in three previous worlds which were successively destroyed when mankind ceased to follow the plan of all Creation, depending instead upon materialistic desires and technical inventions. Yet there was always a small minority who adhered to the divine plan, and escaped to the next world. Such were the Hopis who emerged from the annihilation of the Third World into our present Fourth World, reaching the shores of southern Mexico or Central America. Here, they were directed by its caretaker and guardian, Massau, to make ordered migrations by clans to the four directions—*pasos* to the north and south, to the Atlantic on the east and the Pacific on the west—before they settled in their permanent home, Túwanasavi, the Center of the World. Túwanasavi was not the geographic center of the continent, but the spiritual or magnetic center at the junction of the north-south and east-west routes of their migrations. The area corresponds generally with what we today call the Four Corners region, the only place where four states touch—New Mexico, Arizona, Colorado, and Utah. Here in this harsh desert heartland they would have to depend upon nature for their simple livelihood, and so maintain the Creator's divine pattern of life instead of becoming profane and materialistic.

This is the difference between the world view of the Hopis who would preserve nature, and the later pragmatic arrivals who would destroy nature for material gain. When the destruction by the latter reaches a climax, the Hopis believe a cataclysmic rupture takes place to restore the balance of forces. A new world is created to replace the old, and to it emerge those devout Hopis who seek to re-establish the sacred plan of Creation. Each such Emergence of man to a new world is thus a new step of human consciousness sanctioned by the enduring moral laws which govern the revolutionary process. This pattern had been followed three times before, and would be followed again.

This continuity of life throughout the previous worlds, whose events, although contents of the unconscious, are still felt as consciously immediate, reflects the Hopi conception of time. The past and the future are too entwined in the present to be separated into tidy compartments as they are in our own rational White culture.

Benjamin Lee Whorf, in his perceptive *Language, Thought, and Reality*, calls the Hopi language a "timeless language." It has no three-tense system like our own. Our "length of time" is expressed not as a linear division of past, present, and future, but as a relationship between two events. Hopi time, says Whorf, is a true psychological time. "For, if we inspect consciousness, we find no past, present, future; everything is in consciousness, and everything in consciousness *is*, and is together." Hence, Hopi time is not a motion. It is a duration, a storing up of change, of power, that holds over into later events. A constant anticipation and preparation that becomes realization.

In this mode of thought lies the power and validity of the nine great, interlocked, annual Hopi ceremonials. They re-enact the Emergence from the three previous worlds as if they were in the immediate present. And in preparation for a fourth Emergence to another new world, the Hopis pray and hold good thoughts during each of the nine to twenty-day ceremonies. For thought is power. It is the seed planted to bear fruit in durational time, the anticipation that will become realization. The immediate purpose of their collective effort during ritual after ritual is to help maintain the balance of all the forces of nature. What a cosmic scope it covers! A vast web of relationships that includes not only human beings but the sub-orders of the mineral, plant, and animal kingdoms, the super-orders of the kachinas, those spirit beings, and the living planetary bodies above. All are interrelated in the spiritual ecology of one universal pattern which supersedes that of the human will.

But the Hopi Prophecy is not as simple as this bone-bare skeleton might suggest. It is fleshed with an intricate maze of symbols, archetypal images, and ceremonial interpretations that we must try to understand in light of the historical events which it projected.

It relates that when the first Hopis first arrived on this new Fourth World, three stone tablets were given to the leading Bear Clan. The cryptic markings outlined the boundaries of the Hopis' sacred land, the areas to be apportioned to the various clans, and the figures of six men representing the leading clans. One of these ancient stones was still in the custody of Mina Lansa, the *kikmongwi*, or village chief, of Old Oraibi, who showed it to me some years ago.

The time would come, however, when the Hopis would be overcome by a strange people who would take much of their land and try to force them into a new way of life which deviated from the sacred path. If the Hopis did not comply, they would be treated as criminals and punished. The Hopis—a People of Peace, as their name implies—were not to resist. Help would come, as shown by a fourth stone tablet given to the Fire Clan by Massau, its deity. On one side were engraven a swastika and a sun. On the other side was the figure of a man without a head, and the *nakwach* symbol of the brotherhood of man. One corner was broken off. Massau explained that the missing fragment had been given to the Hopis' elder brother, Pahána (derived from *pásu*, "salt water"), who had been directed to go in the direction of the rising sun. Eventually he would return to his younger brother, the Hopis, carrying the missing corner of the tablet to identify him as the Lost White Brother. Some of the Hopis would have been contaminated by the materialistic way of life of their conquerors. On the Day of Purification they, with all the world, would be destroyed. Only those people who still adhered to the divine plan would be saved. With them,

121

Pahána would initiate a new universal brotherhood of man, beginning a new cycle and mankind's Emergence into the Fifth World.

The Hopis interpreted the events of recorded history as confirmations of Prophecy, and confirmed the difference between the world views of the Hopis and Whites. The westward march of empire by the Whites bore out the prediction of a conquering race whose members usurped much of their land and confined them on a government Reservation. American soldiers broke into Hopi homes, captured their children, and sent them to distant schools to learn a new language and a new way of life. The People of Peace offered no armed resistance, as did their neighbors, the 8,491 Navajos who were finally defeated and marched into a captivity which lasted four years.

The sacred Fire Clan tablet showing the figure of a man without a head indicated how these evils could be dispelled. If a Hopi leader assented to having his head cut off, he would save his people. The two tribal leaders at the turn of the century, Lololma—friendly to the Whites—and Yukioma of the Hostiles, both declined to fulfill the Prophecy.

When Lololma, shamed in front of his people, died of a broken heart in 1901, he was succeeded as village chief of Oraibi by Tewaquaptewa, his sister's son. Tewaquaptewa adopted Christianity, established good relations with the Whites, and became leader of the Friendlies. Armed conflict between the two factions was averted by a "push of war" on September 8, 1906. A line was marked across the rocky top of Third Mesa. The two forces massed on each side. It was agreed that the faction which was pushed over the line would leave Oraibi forever. The bloodless struggle of the People of Peace ended when the Friendlies of Tewaquaptewa pushed Yukioma's Hostiles across the line. That night, Yukioma and his followers packed their belongings and trudged north to camp at a spring, founding the village of Hotevilla.

The Hopis' way of life had withstood three hundred years of Spanish and Mexican rule, and fifty years of United States aggression. This Oraibi Split was more than a social schism between factions friendly or hostile to the encroaching Whites. It constellated the psychological split in the Hopi soul between good and evil, and the cultural rupture between the old way of life and the new.

Now in 1934 came the passage in Congress of the far-reaching Indian Reorganization Act, also known as the Wheeler-Howard Act. It announced a new era in the relationship between the federal government and Indians. The Act, as it was explained to the Hopis, offered economic aid and federal support through their adoption of a Hopi Constitution and the establishment of a Tribal Council which would function as the sole representative of all the Hopi villages. Acceptance or rejection of the proposed system was to be decided by popular vote.

The man engaged by the Bureau of Indian Affairs to campaign for Hopi approval was Oliver LaFarge, the well-known anthropologist and author of the Navajo novel *Laughing Boy*, which had won a Pulitzer Prize. From the start, he ran into trouble. The *kikmongwis*, religious and clan leaders, saw no reason why their traditional form of self-government should be replaced by one devised and controlled by the federal government under the BIA. The general mass of Hopis showed their ingrown habit of shying away from anything that smelled of government control. Hence they did not attend the meetings called by LaFarge, in village after village, to organize them into a federation under a new Constitution and Tribal Council. Their abstention from all meetings and discussions, rather than participating in argument, clearly expressed their opposition in the traditional Hopi manner.

The final election was held on October 24, 1936. In the traditionalist stronghold of Hotevilla, only thirteen persons voted out of a population of two hundred—twelve votes for, one vote against. This vote was federally reported as a landslide victory for the proposed IRA-BIA system, ignoring the two hundred and thirty-seven persons who had showed their opposition by staying away in their fields.

The overall vote throughout all villages showed only 755 votes cast by the 4,500 Hopis—651 for acceptance and 104

123

for rejection. This total of 755 votes from 4,500 people represented only sixteen percent of the people. Yet the BIA and the Department of Interior expressed satisfaction that it reflected the will of the people. The vote was officially approved in December 1936, and the Hopi Tribal Council established.

The Tribal Council, as set up, was to comprise one member from each of the villages. This White concept of "democracy" was utterly foreign to the Hopis. For ages, each village had existed as an independent sovereignity headed by its spiritual leader, the *kikmongwi*. He and other religious clan leaders governed not only the religious but the secular life of the villages. Property rights were determined by clans in a hierarchical order in a system of matrilineal descent. Yet property rights of clans were regarded as communal rights; no Hopi land could be alienated or expropriated by foreign powers.

In one sweep, the Tribal Council erased this traditional system by negating the function of the *kikmongwis*, the ancient structure of the clans. Hence the leading traditionalist villages, viewing it as merely rubber-stamping the dictate of the Bureau of Indian Affairs, thereafter refused to send representatives from their villages. This, in effect, made the Council illegal, for it was not representative. A few progressives, however, supported it in order to gain prestige, favor with the government, and whatever benefits they might receive.

Still the Redeemer, Pahána, the Lost White Brother, did not return. But there were hopeful signs when World War II broke out.

On the gourd rattle used by kachinas in their ceremonies are painted two prime Hopi symbols, the swastika, surrounded by a red circle representing the sun. The significance of the swastika was accentuated when the Nazis adopted it as their emblem. For a time, some Hopis believed the Germans were the people who would return with Pahána. Then, with the defeat of the Hitler regime, came Japan's drive for world power, climaxed by the bombing of Pearl Harbor. The national emblem of Japan was the rising sun, the other primary Hopi symbol. So now the Hopis transferred their hopes to the Japanese.

These two beliefs were mentioned in my *Book of the Hopi*, but they were editorially deleted. And wisely, I think, for the references clearly implied a political disloyalty to the United States when it was hoped the book would help to better the Hopis' relations with the government and their economic conditions.

The dropping of atomic bombs on Hiroshima and Nagasaki confirmed another phase of the Hopi Prophecy which related that a gourd full of ashes would be dropped from the sky, bringing destruction to man and earth. In a letter datelined "Hopi Indian Empire, March 28, 1949," and signed by six chiefs, four interpreters, and sixteen other Hopis, these spokesmen wrote the President of the United States. They warned him that the Hopis and White men now stood face to face at the crossroads of their respective lives, at the most critical time in the history of mankind. "What we decide now and do hereafter will be the fate of our respective peoples . . . . We are talking now about the judgement day. In light of our Hopi Prophecy it is going to take place here in the Hopi Empire."

No answer was received, nothing was done. Events marched on toward the final Day of Purification.

Immense deposits of coal were discovered beneath the surface of Black Mesa. This great tableland of 3,300 square miles lay partly within the Hopi Reservation and partly within the immense Navajo Reservation which surrounded it on all sides, and was considered sacred by both tribes. Lease of the Hopi land to the Peabody Coal Company, a member of the consortium of the country's twenty-two greatest power companies which had already devastated Appalachia, was granted by the Department of the Interior without Congressional or public hearings. Neither the traditionalist leaders, nor the Hopi people, were generally informed of the terms of the contract which was signed on May 16, 1966, by the Tribal Council, acting through its Interior-approved tribal lawyer, John S. Boyden of Salt Lake City.

Three weeks later, on June 6, a similar contract was signed by the Navajo Tribal Council for a thirty-five-year lease on the

Navajos' portion of Black Mesa. The contracts provided royalty payments of twenty-five cents a ton for the coal. The Hopis would eventually receive an estimated $14.5 million, the Navajos $58.5 million, while the Peabody Coal Company profits would amount to about $750 million.

Strip-mining of 45,000 tons a day of Black Mesa coal by Peabody Coal began immediately. Its colossal, coal-fired Four Corners power plant spewed daily 1,300 tons of gases, pollutants, and particulate matter into the air, covering 10,000 square miles. The five million tons of pulverized coal a year were mixed with water and pumped through a slurry line to the Mohave Plant, near Bullhead, Nevada, 273 miles away. The water for this—between 2,000 and 4,500 gallons per minute—was pumped from the underground water table upon which the Hopis depended to supply their springs and sparse corn patches. A third great power plant, the Navajo Plant, was erected near Page and Glen Canyon Dam in Arizona. The 8 to 10 million tons of Black Mesa coal it required yearly were shipped by a new railroad 78 miles across Indian land; and the plant's 70-story smokestacks poured still more pollutants into the air.

This colossal "Rape of Black Mesa," with its devastation of the land, depletion of water resources, and pollution of the air, in order to promote the sale of power to Las Vegas, Los Angeles, Phoenix, and Tucson, was widely publicized. Public resentment against the great power companies and the federal bureaus supporting them was voiced by the Native American Rights Fund, the Environmental Defense Fund, the Sierra Club, the National Wildlife Federation, and the Black Mesa Defense Club. "Save Black Mesa" posters appeared everywhere. The National Environmental Policy Act of 1969 was enacted, requiring the preparation of environmental impact statements. Yet despite attempts to impose emission standards, nothing stopped the extension of still more strip-mining and plans to erect still more power plants by private interests backed by the federal government.

The lease of Black Mesa land now precipitated a century-old dispute between the Hopis and Navajos.

In 1882, the government had set aside a large desert wilderness of 4,000 square miles, some 2,500,000 acres, for the "Hopis and other Indians as the Secretary of the Interior may see fit to settle thereon." This tract, nominally the Hopi Reservation, lay in the center of the immense Navajo Reservation of 25,000 square miles. The 5,000 Hopis were a sedentary people living in their mesa-top pueblos and growing corn in sparse desert patches below. The Navajos were pastoral grazers of sheep. As they increased to more than 100,000 people, and their flocks overgrazed the land, more and more families drifted into the Hopi Reservation.

The federal government now designated a small central area of 631,306 acres (about 2,500 square miles), known as District 6, for exclusive grazing by the Hopis. Nevertheless, Navajo encroachment upon the Hopi land outside its boundaries kept increasing; fights between Hopis and Navajos grew more bitter.

In 1962, three federal judges then ruled that the Hopis still had exclusive right to the District 6 area of 631,306 acres; and that the remaining 1,800,000 acres or more, designated as the Joint Use Area, were to be used jointly by both tribes. There was little "joint use," for the ever-increasing Navajo sheepherders kept encroaching on the area. The federal government was finally forced to pass legislation in 1974 partitioning the area, each tribe getting 911,000 acres. Out of this decision came lawsuits between the two tribes and against the government; and the still pending problem of where to relocate 3,500 Navajos and some Hopis. The net result was a reduction of 911,000 acres from the original 2,500,000 acres established for the Hopis in 1882.

The Hopis' last hope of ever regaining the sacred land granted them by Massau was extinguished when they were offered $5 million in payment for all original or aboriginal lands they had lost. Application for the settlement had been made to the Indian Claims Commission by the Interior-approved Hopi attorney. In approving the claim, the Commission held that the United States took the Hopi lands when it created the Hopi Reservation in 1882; and that the Reservation constituted all the aboriginal Hopi lands. The Hopis, however, asserted that the land had been taken from them in 1848 when the United States took over the country from Mexico; and that their boundaries then included an area more than twice the size of the 1882 Reservation.

Nevertheless, a vote on the offered settlement was pushed through, according to traditionalists, by Boyden, the tribal attorney, in order to collect a ten-percent commission of $500,000, after having obtained a $1 million commission for arranging the lease of Black Mesa for strip-mining. The referendum took place in October 1976. On that day nearly 2,500 Hopis were attending a ceremonial dance at Shongopovi and did not show up at the polls. Nor did many others. All manifested their opposition by their abstention, in accordance with Hopi tradition. Only 229 votes approving the settlement, and 21 votes against it, were cast from among 7,500 Hopis.

The traditionalists immediately drew up a petition to the Commission signed by 1,000 Hopis, protesting the relinquishment of all rights and claims to the aboriginal lands. The Commission disregarded their appeal, and the Attorney General approved acceptance of the vote.

The issue involved many legal ramifications, and also personalities. Former Secretary of the Interior Stewart Udall, who had granted Peabody Coal Company the Black Mesa lease, was a Mormon. The Hopi tribal attorney, John S. Boyden of Salt Lake City who had formerly run for governor of Utah and had been a candidate for the Commissioner of Indian Affairs, was a Mormon. The Chairman of the Hopi Tribal Council, Abbott Sekaquaptewa, was a member of a staunch Mormon family. His brother Wayne was a Mormon Church leader, publisher of the weekly newspaper *Qua' Toqti*, head of a construction firm, and operator of the craft guild, motel, and restaurant in the Tribal Council's Hopi Cultural Center.

The Tribal Council then granted the Church of Jesus Christ of Latter Day Saints a long lease on 200 acres just north of Old Oraibi for the establishment of a Mormon church.

By now, old Oraibi was a crumbling archaeological ruin occupied by only a handful of traditionalists. The new center of life was Kiakochomovi, New Oraibi, site of the tribal offices promoting modern developments. A White town in effect, it was not a true Hopi village following a ritual cycle under the direction of a *kikmongwi*, or village chief. Its affairs were managed, White-fashion, by a governor and a board of directors.

Construction of a large modern Civic Center was begun with a $1.3 million government grant. Its site was claimed to belong to the Sand Clan by a member of the clan with priest-hood rights who immediately instituted suit against the Tribal Council. His claim was disputed on the grounds that his priest-hood was no longer functional, and that no clan lands remained. Hence Kiakochomovi had annexed the land and deeded the construction site to the Tribal Council.

The cumulative effects of the tragic course of events briefly outlined here were now evident. Few Hopis depended solely upon the earth for a simple existence. They had government and commercial jobs. Children were not taught the meanings of the ceremonials. More and more Hopis were adopting Christian-ity, especially the Mormon faith, and were entering the main-stream of modern American life.

Yet this change of orientation had brought forth problems never before encountered. Dissension and quarrels between the two factions rent all villages. Murders were not uncommon. Alcoholism was a serious problem. An intangible feeling of spiritual bankruptcy permeated all three mesas, despite modern innovations.

The traditionalist minority still stood firm against what they considered this moral and social disintegration. They opposed every issue with mass meetings, appeals to both Hopis and Navajos, letters to the President and Congress. Members gave talks throughout the country. Delegations vainly sought hearings at the United Nations. And one member attended a special U.N. Committee on Human Rights Conference in Geneva, Switzer-land, in September 1977 to hear documentation on "Discrim-ination Against the Indigenous Peoples of the Americas"— which was not reported by the American press. This was fol-lowed in October by a letter to President Jimmy Carter, im-ploring him to stop the violation of their religious, land, and basic human rights. According to a White support group, "Friends of the Hopis," more than 30,000 telegrams and letters supporting the Hopi statement were sent to President Carter. There was no response.

The leader of this stubborn resistance was small, aging, and ill Mina Lansa, the adopted daughter of Chief Tewaquaptewa of Old Oraibi, and custodian of the ancient Bear Clan tablets. When the old chief died in 1960, leaving no Bear Clan successor, his position of *kikmongwi* normally reverted to the Parrot Clan by right of clan succession. The first man in line was his eldest son, Myron, who opposed his father. Next in line was his adopted son, Stanley Bahnimtewa, who was living in Los Angeles, California, and who agreed to let Mina, his sister, act for him. So, in 1964, Mina became the *kikmongwi* of Old Oraibi, the leader of all traditionalists, and the symbolic mother of the Hopis. She was aided by her husband, John, head of the Badger Clan and chief of the important Powamu Society. Both of them had been friends of mine for twenty years, and I sympathized with their indomitable fight against overwhelming odds. Mina's illness was more serious than we thought when Dan Budnik brought her and John here to Taos in November 1977, hoping that a rest and a healing ceremony by Joe Sun Hawk of Taos Pueblo would be beneficial. Taken then to a hospital in Phoenix, Arizona, she died on January 8, 1978, at the age of 75. She was a great spirit, embodying the ancient traditions and religious beliefs of her people.

Her death deprived the Hopis of their symbolic mother, as Tewaquaptewa's passing had removed their symbolic father. The weekly newspaper *Qua' Toqti*, "The Eagle's Cry," always had ridiculed Mina as the "self-appointed Chieftess of Old Oraibi"; and cautioned in its editorials that her outmoded religious beliefs only reinforced superstition. In Hotevilla, after the death of old Dan Katchongva, there remained a hard core of traditionalists—a "quarrelsome, dissident faction" called by *Qua' Toqti* "Grandfather David and his Gang." Aging "Grandfather" David Monongva was not the recognized *kikmongwi* of Hotevilla, being of a minor clan which had no traditional standing. Nevertheless, he was accepted as a nominal, though ineffectual leader without authority or influence.

Backing them was the white organization characterized by the progressives as the "shoeless and long-haired radical left of the blue-eyed so-called 'Friends of the Hopis.'"

Ostensibly, the progressive Tribal Council faction, which looked to the technological future rather than to the traditions of the past, had affairs well in hand.

Economically oriented, the Tribal Council administration was concerned with managing the complex business of the tribe through an imposing number of departments and committees.

There were more than 400 permanently employed members of the staff. This meant that of the total population of 8,000 Hopis, one out of twenty was employed by the tribal administration. The total wages paid all employees, including construction workers, had trebled from less than $1 million in 1973 to $3 million in 1977.

The total assets of the tribe amounted to more than $13 million. The yearly income from Hopi resources, excluding government grants, ranged from $1.5 to $2 million, most of it coming from Peabody Coal royalty payments.

More new construction projects were under way, including another $1 million tribal administration building and the huge $1.3 million Civic Center. Projected for the future were a new high school, a new hospital, and a new highway bisecting the reservation which would increase tourist travel. Moreover, the Tribal Council, politically subservient to the Bureau of Indian Affairs, was attempting to convert the Hopi social structure into the pattern of White communities. Following the lease of Sand Clan land for a new Mormon church, it proposed the establishment of a New Village Community within the ancestral clan holdings of the Badger Clan.

Despite this bright economic future, the Indian Law Resource Center in Washington, D.C., a leading law firm in asserting the rights of Native Americans, undertook legal support of the Hopi traditionalists in 1977. In a lengthy report, it documented the fraudulent means by which the federal government deliberately sabotaged the traditional leadership of the Hopi *kikmongwis* by establishing the B.I.A.-controlled Tribal Council. A second issue concerned the B.I.A. lease of Hopi land for coal strip-mining, and the $5 million settlement for Hopi relinquishment of all Hopi lands. A third primary issue involved John S. Boyden, the B.I.A.-approved legal counsel for the Hopi Tribal Council. The report alleged that Boyden was working for the Peabody Coal Company interests during the time it was strip-mining Black Mesa, and hence revealed a conflict of interest calling for immediate governmental investigation.

Meanwhile, there were growing misgivings even among the progressives. The Peabody Coal Company was pumping water from mile-deep wells at the rate of 3,000 gallons a minute or 40,000 acre feet a year. The water pressure head already had been decreased 10 feet and was being decreased 1.5 feet a year. Moreover, Peabody Coal was not adhering to the rules for pumping water prescribed by the U.S. Geological Survey.

It now appeared that, when the Peabody lease expired, the coal deposits would be exhausted, the land irretrievably ruined, and the water resources depleted. What then would happen to the Hopi bureaucracy, to the people themselves who had forsaken the sacred path and succumbed to materialism?

There remains the Hopi Prophecy.

Copies of it have been distributed throughout the United States and foreign countries; newspapers, magazines, and books have published accounts of it. The accounts vary greatly, and some White commentators have not been reluctant to add their own interpretations. Among them has developed a syndrome of "Prophecy Worship" which insists that the Prophecy be taken literally; that Pahána is an actual person, a coming Messiah; and that the world will be destroyed, save for those people who still adhere to the divine plan.

Our phenomenal interest in this dire Prophecy demands a close look. Why does it coincide so closely with our unconscious fears today? What are its hidden meanings?

Profoundly religious, the Prophecy is a mythic structure of our collective unconscious, the deep substratum of our psyche attuned to all the invisible forces of the living universe. It is differentiated from the conscious pattern of our pragmatic White intellect, built on the rationally limited premise that man is the supreme achievement of Creation, destined to control all the forces of nature.

The ancient Prophecy contains many variations and a multitude of symbols and archetypal images. The clearest exposition was given me in great detail in 1970 by the late Chief Dan Katchongva of Hotevilla, the son of the historic Yukioma. Briefly, Pahána will wear a Red Cap or Red Cloak when he returns. Bringing the sacred stone tablet (or the missing corner) he will be "not one, but many, large in population." With him will be two powerful helpers. One of them will bear the symbol of the swastika, representing the male and purity. The other will bear the symbol of the sun, representing the female and purity. They will shake the earth in warning. Then all three, as one, will bring on the Day of Purification. If they fail in their mission, One from the West will come like a storm. He too will be many people and unmerciful, covering the land like ants. If he, in turn, is not successful in arousing the people to awareness of their misdeeds, the Great Spirit will bring destruction to the earth. But if only a few Hopis remain faithful to their ancient teachings, Pahána and his two helpers will lay out a new life plan leading to everlasting life, in which all people will have one religion, one tongue, and share everything equally.

The swastika and the sun are the two prime symbols in Hopi ceremonialism, still painted on the gourd rattles carried by kachinas during ceremonies. Each carries a profound, esoteric meaning.

The swastika is a form of the universal symbol of the cross. The symbolic meaning is clear. For if the extensions of the four arms of the cross in opposite directions represent division and conflict, their point of intersection signifies reconciliation and unification, the meeting point of the conscious and unconscious.

Looked at another way, mindful of the Hopi concept of time, the horizontal arms of the cross represent our linear concept of time divided into past, present, and future. The vertical arms represent the durational time of the Hopis. And here at their intersection, they merge into one unbroken timeless line.

The swastika form of the cross is equally fecundant in symbolic meaning.

The earliest Hopis, as we remember, made ordered migrations to the four directions. Upon reaching their extremities where the land meets the sea, the leading clans turned right, forming a swastika rotating counter-clockwise to symbolize the earth which they were claiming for their people. The other clans turned left, describing a swastika rotating clockwise with the sun, which symbolized their faithfulness to this supreme creative force.

Having completed their migrations, all clans returned to the center point of intersection. That is to say, after they had made psychological journeys to the limits of consciousness at the vast ocean of the collective unconscious—where the land meets the sea, they found their sacred homeland, the spiritual center of their own inner universe.

Geographically represented by Túwanasavi, the Center of the World, it bears out today both literal and mythical truths. It is a focal point of conflict between two ways of life, the Indian and the White, between the immeasurable past and the impending future. And in their conflict, it may also be a focus of reconciliation.

The symbolic meaning of Pahána, the Lost White Brother, does not carry the literal interpretation so often given it. As related in Katchongva's account of the Prophecy, he is "not one but many." Personifying the original, undefiled, pure spiritual nature of man, he is within us all. He is indeed both one and many, the divine, universal Self embodying all our lesser worldly selves. Slowly but surely, it will manifest itself as our consciousness expands toward a perception of our inherent unity.

This Self, the one universal, eternal Beingness, is known to Tibetan Buddhists as Dharma-Kāya, the essence of Buddhahood. It is curious that when a group of them visited the Hopi mesas they wore the red hats and yellow-red cloaks of their order, similar to the garb of the predicted Pahána, and found many Hopi parallels to their own beliefs.

To place the Hopi Prophecy in larger perspective, we must remember that the ancient Mayas also predicted with astrological and mathematical precision that this present fifth world would end with a cataclysmic destruction in A.D. 2011. How closely this prediction coincides with the Hopi Prophecy and our own growing fears of widespread earthquakes and a shift of the world's axis!

My own interpretations of this ancient Maya prediction, in my book *Mexico Mystique*, may apply to the Hopi Prophecy. The mythical previous worlds of the Mayas, Navajos, Hopis, and Buddhists may not have been actual geographic land masses, although changing configurations in the global landscape have periodically taken place. More important, they were dramatic allegories for the successive stages in the evolution of consciousness in enduring mankind. Hence I have termed the predicted sixth world of the Mayas as the "Coming Sixth World of Consciousness."

The present materialistic phase of Hopi life may appear negative indeed. But if we accept the ancient Nahuatl and Chinese concepts of cyclic changes from one polarity to its opposite, we may view the Hopis as conforming also to the universal law of movement and change, experiencing a painful transition to a new evolutionary stage.

We all stand today on the threshold of a new era, a new cyclical change in world history. Yet this glimpse into the future from the immeasurable past of a people who may be the oldest inhabitants of America also carries a warning. If we are to avert a cataclysmic rupture between the spiritual and material, between our own hearts and minds, we must reestablish our relationship with all the forms of living nature.

5

The Circle of the Law Belt

The circle in its many forms—the Medicine Wheel, the Sacred Hoop, and the Sun Dance—embraces the ceremonialism of the Great Plains tribes, the Cheyennes, Arapahoes, Pawnees, Crows, Sioux, and others. It symbolizes the "Way of the People" towards achieving completeness of being and harmony with the universe.

The two-volume study *Sweet Medicine*, compiled by Peter J. Powell during fourteen years of research, is the definitive tribally approved record of Cheyenne ceremonialism. Hyemeyohsts Storm, a Northern Cheyenne, has given many interpretations of the meaning of the Medicine Wheel in his beautiful book *Seven Arrows*. It makes no mention of the two ritual observances of traditional Cheyenne spiritual belief, the Sacred Arrows and Sun Dance ceremonies, based on the revered symbols of the Four Sacred Arrows and the Sacred Buffalo Hat, so authentically recorded by Father Powell. Nevertheless, Storm's warmly appealing book offers revealing interpretations of the wide applications of Cheyenne symbolism. These were expanded when he and his wife Hmunhwohwah visited here, introducing me to the Circle of the Law Belt.

Whether its origin is Cheyenne, if it derives from one of many other tribes, is common to all, or a composite of many variations, I don't know. Nor do I think it matters. The Circle's meanings are intricate and profound, but expressed in earthy images known to us all. They have as many ancient and modern, intertribal, and controversial interpretations as the Hopi Prophecy. Hence I'm somewhat reluctant to attempt an explanation of its many wheels within wheels, although I have the permission of the Storms to do so. The one great value of its profound concept, despite the question of its origin, is its universality. We can take from it just what we bring to it. This interpretation, then, however incomplete it might be, is a brief outline of its structure and meaning as I see it.

Hmunhwohwah, as she conducted me into the great Circle, explained that it may be simply viewed at first as an actual circle of Plains people sitting on the prairie. There are eight groups placed at directional positions around the circle. On the Southeast are the Peace Chiefs, on the South the War Chiefs, the Singers and Medicine People at the Southwest, the Women at the West, the Council at the Northwest, the Hunters at the North, and the Dog Soldiers on the Northeast. The position at the East is the place of movement. It is the Doorway to Awakening, guarded by the Contraries, the No Names or Mirrors. Through this Open Door we enter and leave the Circle.

If one enters this actual circle with a perplexing question or problem, he must make the complete round, sunwise, to obtain a conclusive answer. The Peace Chiefs may advise a peaceful solution, the War Chiefs outright combat. Introspection will be counselled by the Women, and wisdom by the Hunters. . . . All these separate answers are partial and often contradictory. A comprehensive solution based on every aspect of the problem can be reached only by making a complete round of the circle.

The Circle has another, symbolic aspect. Each directional point on its circumference designates, among other things, a special quality or attribute of our composite nature. The South designates trust and innocence, the warm emotions of the heart, while the North denotes the cool wisdom of the mind. The West is the place of introspection and dreams; and directly opposite, the East symbolizes spiritual awakening. So, too, all other directional points with their attributes are counterbalanced by their opposites. Hyemeyohsts emphasized that a symbolic journey to all points of our psychological compass must be taken by each of us before we attain full maturity.

A still larger perspective of the Circle was offered by Hmunh-wohwah. It is the great wheel of life we all follow from birth. In progressively more intricate symbolism, more wheels within wheels, there is a smaller circle at each of the eight major directional points. Each represents and measures the duration of a span of our individual life. The first is the Children's Circle on the Southeast, which mirrors a child's life from his gestation period of nine months in the womb. His progression from birth is carefully measured as he too journeys to its four directions. Nine months in the south, nine months in the west, nine months in the north, and nine months in the east. At the age of three years, he then goes from the south to the west of the Children's Circle for three years, to the north for three years, and to the east for three years, making at each the same four directional journeys. Now at the age of twelve years, the time of puberty, he is ready for his Vision Quest.

From the Children's Circle, he enters the Camp Circle on the South of the great Law Belt, followed by the Learning of the Hunt Circle, the Providers Circle, the Power Circle, and the Teaching of the Hunt Circle. In each, he spends twelve years, developing by the same process. He is now a man of 72; and if he has learned the wisdom of all the circles during his round, he is able to view life and its problems from all aspects.

There are many of us, of course, who reach this age without attaining full maturity. A man may be fixed, psychologically, in one of the circles, viewing life emotionally or mentally; he may be introspective and lacking practicality, or he may be obsessed with the urge to power, wealth, or worldly fame. How many such men we meet today! It is interesting to place such men—and ourselves—on the great Law Belt according to their ambitions and driving powers, and see at what age they stopped progressing.

But if a man successfully makes the round to full completeness, he enters at age 72 the Teaching of the Law Circle on the Northeast. He is now capable of teaching the wisdom its name implies. The duration of this circle is a symbolic period of nine years, nine being a significant number in the numbering system closely allied with the great Law Belt itself.

And now in his later years, the man enters the last circle on the East. As previously recounted, it is the place of Movement, the universal law that dictates the movement of life around the great Law Belt. It is the Doorway to Awakening, to a larger life beyond; and it lies directly opposite the circle on the West which symbolizes earth, death, and the past. The symbolism is at once apparent, for life does not end with earthly death. It continues its movement on a greater circle. Hence the Eastern Doorway is both a transcendent entrance and exit for this present Wheel of Life, as Buddhism calls it. The matured man leaves it by superseding the worldly dualities, the opposites, symbolized by the guardian Contraries. The fully awakened or illumined man, at this late stage of his worldly life, thus loses his individuality and becomes a No Name, a Mirror of all the wisdom he has acquired. He is a sage, a seer.

The task of those making this great round is to achieve a balance of all its forces, and this balance the Law Belt itself teaches us. For the upper northern half, variously symbolized by water, the mind, and the future, is counterbalanced by the lower southern half symbolizing fire, the heart, and the present. And the western half, designating earth, death, and the past, is counterbalanced by the eastern half, symbolizing air, awakening to a life beyond worldly past, present, and future, and the movement in, around, and out of the Circle itself.

This great Circle to me seems comparable to the spatial archetype of the Great Round posited by Mimi Lobell, which appeared in the civilizations of the Near East as early as 1500 B.C., and which still exists today in many forms. The Great Round developed from the chaos of the undifferentiated unconscious, the maternal womb-cavern from which man emerged as a human being. It gave time to the timeless, following the cycles of vegetation, gestation, and the periods of solar, lunar, and stellar movements. It laid the foundations for civilization. The Great Round derived its power not only from the unconscious, Lobell tells us, but from the integration of its creative forces with the conscious, intellectual qualities of the mind. Like the archetype of the Great Round, the Circle of the Law Belt attunes us to the rhythms of the cosmos and to the eternal continuity.

The Numbering System

The Indian numbering system complements the Circle of the Law Belt. Like all such systems, it attests that numbers have held special meanings for mankind since earliest times, being integral parts of the one composite mystery of the universe.

Pythagoras in the sixth century B.C. asserted that the natural integers are not merely objective symbols used to denote quantitative properties, but that they possess dynamic individual characters of their own, and represent attributes of both matter and kind. Jungian psychology defines numbers as "archetypal structural constituents of the collective unconscious"; and Jung asserts that the first ten natural numbers represent an abstract cosmogeny derived from the first integer, the monad.

The Indian numbering system helps us to understand this cosmogeny and the meanings of the first ten numbers. Their symbols are listed below; and with their individual meanings are given comparative interpretations from other hermetic and modern scientific sources:

1. Sun
2. Earth
3. Plants
4. Animals
5. Human Beings
6. Grandfathers and Grandmothers
7. Spirits
8. The "Dance" of All
9. The Law Belt
10. Measure—Time and Space

1. The Sun

To Indians, as well as to most early peoples, throughout the world, and to most branches of modern science, the sun is the source of all life on this planet. It is easy to understand the assumption that it represented the mysterious powers of all

Creation. Hence Number 1 expressed it all—the all-embracing Oneness, the cosmic Unity, the one creative force of all life.

2. The Earth

From Mother Earth all living entities are born. She is the matrix of all Indian ceremonialism. Contrary to popular belief, she embodies both feminine and masculine principles.

Most world religions perceive that the basic Oneness manifests itself in diversity, in opposite polarities. This gave rise to early man's conception of duality. Number 2 expressed this dualistic world of darkness and light, masculine and feminine, good and evil. There arose what anthropology calls the Cult of the Halves, symbolized by the ancient Chinese symbol and doctrine of Yang and Yin, the basis of Taoistic thought. Hence most world cosmologies begin with the world creation by Creator-Twins. This great expansion of perspective has been called the first "pausing point" in mankind's mental evolution.

3. Plants

From Earth first came plant life, the grasses, the shrubs, the trees. Hence plant life is allied with water, the basic element of all life. The universal Tree of Life is represented by the forked pole in the Sun Dance ritual, which still symbolizes the opposite polarities.

But out of the paired Number 2, representing the dualism of world and god, there emerged, according to modern psychology, the triadic beliefs associated with Number 3—the Christian Holy Trinity of the Father, Son, and Holy Ghost; the folklore figures of the three Fates, three Graces, and three Witches; and the three lines in the trigrams of the Chinese *I Ching*. All were connected with time and fate; and 3 itself became the first counting number, beginning the linear succession in the numbering system. With Number 3, man strode forward into objectivity and knowledge. But Marie Louise von Franz points out in her difficult study *Number and Time*, that Trinitarian thinking, as she calls it, was largely intellectual and encouraged absolute declarations of ego consciousness. This was why Jung maintained throughout his writings a feud with the Christian ethic of the Holy Trinity; it lacked the feminine, and hence the unconscious, factor in the equation of life.

This lack was supplied by the emergence of the so-called anthropological Cult of the Quarters—the recognition that the universe had a quaternary structure. The evidence was everywhere: in the four primary directions; the four elements of earth, air, fire, and water; in the successive positions of the circumpolar constellations, which suggested the symbols of the square and circle, and the cross and swastika; and which resulted, as Zelia Nuttall pointed out, in the four-fold structure of society and religion throughout the world. The mandala, symbol of many races, expressed it fully.

4. Animals

In the Indian numbering system, the symbol of Number 4 is Animals. For animal life follows 3, plant life, in the natural succession of living entities born from Sun 1, and Earth 2. The appearance of animals signifies a great turning point, for it heralds among the Four-Legged children of Mother Earth the appearance of the Two-Legged animal, the human being, Man.

In progressing in number conception from 3 to 4, man is said to have taken his greatest conscious step towards understanding his original, primitive, and unconscious perception of the Oneness, Wholeness, and Unity of the Universe symbolized by Number 1. For if 1 was geometrically associated with the point, 2 with the line, and 3 with the plane, 4 now reflected the complete body in space and time. All models of the universe are said today to have a four-fold structure, including Einstein's dimensional model. Moreover, psychology posits that the structure of the human psyche, as well as the physical universe, has a four-fold structure.

Such was the evolution of the simple number system among primitive societies as posited by the anthropologist W.J. McGee. Recognition of the meaning of 4, he considered the second "pausing point," beyond which many numbering systems never advanced.

Multiple variations of the tetramorph exist in all religions: the four-armed cross, the four gospels, evangelists, sons of Horus, seasons, cardinal points, primary elements, and so on. Moreover, a psychic quality was attached to the quaternity, which exerted great influence over religion, ritual, and architecture. The immense power it exerted was emphasized by a center point within the four field forces of the quaternity.

5. Human Beings

Indians assign 5 as the symbolic number of man.

The attribute or quality which distinguishes man from the rest of his animal brothers is consciousness. And this consciousness of the self, the consciousness of his relationship to his surroundings, gave rise to conception of a center point within the quaternary symbol which reconciled the forces of the four quarters.

The quaternary symbol thus developed into a quincunx, the most frequently occurring hieroglyph throughout ancient Mesoamerica. It took many shapes: four points placed about a center point; the points being circles or petals enclosed within a square or a circle; or it showed the form of a cross. Fray Diego Durán, a Dominican missionary in the sixteenth century, described the image of the Aztec god Huitzilopochtli holding a shield whose insignia was a quincunx. The hieroglyph appears on the headdress of the old Fire God, on the image of Tlaloc, god of water, on the cheeks of Coyolxauhqui, who was Huitzilopochtli's sister, and on the Aztec Sun Eagle. The great Stone of the Sun, now popularly known as the Aztec Calendar Stone previously described, was a quincunx, the head in the center being the fifth point. Moreover, the symbol marks the facial structure of the image of the deity of the planet Venus. Mme. Laurette Séjourné, an. archaeologist who has made major excavations at Teotihuacan, reminds us that the synodical revolutions of Venus occur in a series of five, hence Number 5 is a symbol for Venus. It also symbolizes the great figure of all Mesoamerican religious belief, Quetzalcoatl, who by penitence and self-sacrifice reconciled the bi-polar opposites and made the final ascent out of matter into spirit, being transformed into Venus. His transfiguration objectifies the Aztecs' belief that reconciliation of the opposite polarities must eventually take place in the human heart.

This supports the Mesoamerican concept of four previous worlds succeeded by the present Fifth World, in which we are endeavoring like Quetzalcoatl to reconcile the opposite polarities of matter and spirit. So too does Navajo ceremonialism assert that "Man is made from everything," containing all the attributes of the preceding four worlds.

The importance given by Indians to Number 5 is confirmed by the Hebrew cabala and the Greek philosophy of Pythagoras, both of which are said to have derived from Egyptian and Babylonian cosmology. Pythagoras, as is well known, illustrated his teachings with a system of geometry corresponding to the prime numbers, positing five sacred solids. These solids are the only regular polyhedra which have equal angles and equal faces, and whose points touch the edge of an invisible, enveloping sphere. Each was associated with one of the primary elements, earth, air, water, and fire, plus a fifth, the ether which represented the element of the enveloping sphere.

The assignment of 5 as the number of the human microcosm, man, is reflected mathematically by the fact that 5 lies at the center of the Pythagorean decad, 0-10, between the Absolute Below and the Absolute Above. We stand between Heaven and Earth, at the mid-point of our Road of Life.

6. Grandfathers and Grandmothers

Literally, I suppose, the symbol was chosen because of the great importance given to Indian tribal elders who were revered for their power and wisdom. These medicine-men and medicine-women had completed the Circle of the Law Belt, and so had attained the capacity to pass on its teachings. Their wisdom and power embodied not only traditional tribal ceremonialism, but the magic or esoteric influence reflected from the stars. That the stars influence life-forms in nature is attested by the hexagonal shapes of flowers, snowflakes, crystals, the cells of a honeycomb, and of plankton in the seas.

Much is said about 6 in other arcane teachings. It was regarded as the mediator between the visible and invisible worlds; and was symbolized by the *I Ching* hexagram, the lower trigram signifying Earth, the upper trigram Heaven. Mathematically, 6 was held to be a perfect number, for it was both the sum and product of all its factors. In sacred geometry the hexagram represented the macrocosm, as the pentagon represented the human microcosm. Hence 6 was the number of all material things, of matter, God having created the world in six days.

7. Spirits

If Number 6 symbolized the influence from the stars, Number 7 symbolized the reflection of influence from the earth to the stars. For Indian ceremonialism, unlike some other religious philosophies, does not restrict man to this one planet; he is a citizen of the entire universe. He is influenced by all its invisible, outer forces; and at the same time he affects them by his life, his rituals. Like the Hopis, he brings rain.

In Indian ceremonialism, notably that of the Hopis, spirits are synonymous with kachinas, literally "respected spirits" of all the forces of the universe. According to Nahuatl mythology, the Aztecs came forth from seven caves, in seven migrating tribes, to found their capital of Tenochtitlan. And deep in the heart of the great Pyramid of the Sun at Teotihuacan, built by the far earlier Toltecs, there has lately been discovered a complex of seven caverns.

Number 7 is especially sacred in all ancient Mysteries. Biblical references are too numerous to mention: 7 churches, 7 seals, 7 candlesticks, 7 plagues, 7 spirits of God, the beast in Revelations with 7 heads, etc. The ancient astrologers knew 7 planets, and 7 stars in the Great Bear. As Michell points out, 7 has no gender, for 3 is the first odd number and 4 the first even number, and these two make 7; therefore, the Holy Ghost was often given this number. Mathematically, 7 is neither the product nor the factor of any other number. In geometry no one can draw a mathematically perfect heptagon. Nor is it often found in the shapes of nature.

In short, Number 7 is associated with spiritual and esoteric things, as 6 with the mortal and material.

8. The Dance of All

By "dancing," Indians mean exploring meanings, relating values, equating worldly and spiritual conceptions. Hence Number 8 signifies the balancing of all the inner and outer powers designated by the previous seven numbers and their personalized symbols.

One cannot help observing the correspondence between the simple octagonal Navajo *hogan* of cedar logs roofed with dirt and whose door faces east, and the eight directional small circles around the perimeter of the great Law Circle, with its Open Door toward the east. Structurally and symbolically, both reflect the same inherent pattern.

9. The Circle of the Law Belt

The balancing and combining of all the powers—as the human microcosm 5, the macrocosmos 6, and the spiritual 7—result in the Circle of the Law Belt, Number 9. Upon it, each force assumes its proper place. But eventually, all its symbols "dance" with the power of the moon, with Death, whose position on the West also symbolizes the earth and the past. So man dies, his worldly life becomes the past. Yet directly opposite on the East lies Movement, The Doorway to Awakening, whose interpretation already has been given. For life does not end with temporal death. It continues its movement on a greater circle, the Eastern doorway being both the transcendent exit and entrance as dictated by the law of movement.

Hence other esoteric numerical systems also consider 9 the number of judgement and finality, marking the climax of microcosmic man's spiritual attainment.

10. Measure—Time and Space

Number 10 is formed by 1 to which is added 0, or zero, which signifies endless time and endless space, the ocean, the void, the birthplace of all life, and the measure of all things.

Man, then, returns to Number 1, but with fully illumined consciousness to proclaim at last the completely realized all-embracing Oneness, the cosmic Unity, and the one Creative life force.

How simple and sensible this Indian numbering system seems! No less profound than Old World symbology, Pythagorean geometry, gematria, cabalistic abstractions, modern computations of theoretical physicists, and the interpretations of depth psychology, it adheres to the basic progression of life forms emerging from the earth. Mother Earth is impregnated by Father Sun, giving birth to plants, to animals, and to man. The human animal develops consciousness, and this at the mid-point of his life-journey marks the shift of his polarity from matter to spirit.

There are indications that interpretations are given to other numbers beyond 10. Apparently 13, for example, is equated with the thirteenth house of the ancient Mayan zodiac. A surviving remnant of the *Codice Peresianos* reveals that the Mayas had a zodiac of thirteen houses, and it is believed that the thirteenth symbolized the "Great Door," the entrance to the celestial realm beyond the known planets.

Modern astrologers use the zodiac of twelve houses originated by the ancient Sumerians and Chaldeans. The zodiac as we know it today is the Great Circle of the Ecliptic, an imaginary belt sixteen degrees wide whose center line, the ecliptic, is the apparent path of the sun, moon, and constellations. It is arbitrarily divided into twelve sections or houses of thirty degrees each, designated by a sign named from the shapes of the constellations within it.

It may not be too preposterous to conjecture here that the Circle of the Law Belt may be equated with the great Circle of the Ecliptic. The Chaldeans in Mesopotamia called the route of the sun the Path of Anu, which coincided with man's Road of Life. Along this path lay twelve "chiefs" of the constellations it passed through. The later Greeks gave to the Path of Anu the name of "Zodiac," which means the "Road of Life." The course of a seeker following the Circle of the Law Belt to the Eastern Door may thus be compared to the Road of Life marked by the circle of the Zodiac, whose Mayan thirteenth house also symbolized the Great Door to the celestial realm and to the expanded consciousness it implied.

This simple and profound numbering system, so closely allied with the Circle of the Law Belt, stands on its own as an original expression of ancient American philosophy. That it corresponds so closely with other numbering systems in the ancient East, and with the West's modern psychological interpretations, validates the intuitive soundness of its conception.

Hence this brief review can't be concluded without a brief outline of the esoteric system expounded by the late mystic of Central Asia, Georges Ivanovitch Gurdjieff. His notable theories of the "Ray of Creation" and "Reciprocal Maintenance" assert that all life-energies and modes of existence in the universe can be grouped into a series of "essences." There are ten of these—corresponding remarkably to the symbols of the numbering system of Indian America. They range upward from the primary creative energy of the earth itself, through planets, invertebrates, vertebrates, man, demi-urges (or kachinas), to the Divine Will which corresponds with fully illumined cosmic consciousness symbolized by the Number 10. Each of these essences feeds on the energy of the essence below, and in turn feeds energy to the essence above—as plants feed on the energy of the earth, animals feed on plants, man feeds on the energies of vegetable and animal life, and in turn supplies the psychic energy for higher forms of consciousness.

To these two categories Gurdjieff adds two more, which are seen as representing the spiritual workings of Creation, and finally that Endlessness symbolizing the supreme creative force of all life. This series has been regarded as synonymous with the "chain of the worlds" linking our earth, moon, sun, and planets with the Absolute. And more specifically they have been equated with the physical and psychical influences we on Earth are receiving from the various planets in our Solar System, including two more yet undiscovered bodies from which we are already receiving influences.

The symbolism of all these various numbering systems seems to show that the entire universe is structured on one cosmic principle from the galactic to the sub-atomic worlds of matter, which is duplicated by the structural system of man's own ever-expanding consciousness. If indeed our planet Earth, solar system, and galaxy are all living bodies imbued with a distinctive consciousness, is it beyond our imagination to believe that each is progressing through stages of development symbolized by man's psychical movement around the great Circle of the Law Belt?

6

The Four-Fold Structure
of Mind and Matter

Most ancient concepts of the structure of the world in space and time seem to be based on the number four. If this structure reflects universal harmony, as it must, it is perhaps best expressed by one of the oldest symbols known to man—the square inscribed within a circle or a circle within a square.

Although the symbol was not referred to directly, its origin was clearly suggested by a woman archaeologist in Mexico, Zelia Nuttall, in a comprehensive archaeo-astronomical study published in 1901 under the title *The Fundamental Principles of Old and New World Civilizations*. Pertinent as her voluminous study was, it was generally ignored by academicians of the time and only lately is it receiving the attention it deserves.

Her theory was simple. The ancient, world-wide symbol of the cross or swastika, often pictured within a circle or square, was derived from the pattern formed by the great circumpolar constellations Ursa Major and Ursa Minor in their annual circuits around the Pole Star, formerly Draconis and now Polaris. As we can see on any star chart, an imaginary line drawn between Merak and Dubhe, the two principal stars in Ursa Major (the Big Dipper), points directly to the North Star. Wheeling in a circuit around this one fixed point in the heavens, the constellation described the four arms of the cross, dividing the circle into four quarters or quadrants. From this prototypal pattern man developed his concept of the Four Quarters of heavenly space, and the quadruplicate division of his earthly domain with a central governing power whose rule, controlled by the heavens, extended in four directions.

Nuttall meticulously developed how the Aztecs of Mexico established their social and religious structures on this four-fold pattern. Their capital, Tenochtitlan, was laid out in four quarters, each with four wards; the entire nation was divided into four provinces with four districts; and the army into four divisions.

The great Stone of the Sun, commonly known as the Aztec Calendar Stone, and said to be one of the most important documents in the history of the human race, she believed to be a reproduction of the wheel of sinistral revolutions described by the circumpolar constellations, and an image of the Aztec territorial state modelled upon the harmonious order of the heavens. The head in the center represented the divine central power. And the square compartments represented the four past eras of air and water, fire and earth; also the four positions of Ursa Major as it revolved about the Pole Star.

In equal detail, Nuttall then described how the same pattern was followed in Guatemala, with its four nations, four provinces, and four capitals; in Yucatan, whose ruler, "the Divine Four," had sub-rulers governing the four quarters; in the four provinces of Peru, governed by the "Four in One" under the Creator of "Earth, Air, Fire, and Water in One"; and by the social systems in Egypt, Babylonia, and India.

The same pattern is still reflected today in almost all small villages throughout Mexico. Each traditionally has a square central plaza with a circular bandstand in the center around which people parade during weekly concerts, the women and girls one way, men and boys in the opposite direction. In the old Indian pueblos of the Southwest, the pattern is also evident—circular kivas within square house structures surrounded in turn by remnants of a circular wall. All have a fixed center, a sociological and psychological focal point, in contrast to our modern Anglo towns and cities spreading out to remote shopping areas.

The circle and square form the numinous symbol known in ancient Sanskrit as a mandala, denoting the fullness of divine Creation, the immeasurable infinitude of all space and time. Its shape is any combination of a circle and a square, but always with four as a basis of its pattern. To the ancient Mayas, it symbolized the divine Hunab Ku, the source of all movement and measure, the circle representing the infinite and eternal, the square the worldly and material. In the ancient Chinese *I Ching*, the circle also symbolized heaven, the square the earth. Hence the harmonic relationship of earth and heaven through the cyclic interplay of positive and negative, the Yang and Yin. Mandalas have been found everywhere, in all ages. Egyptian mandalas show Horus in the center with his four sons at the cardinal points, as later Christian mandalas place Christ at the center surrounded by the four Evangelists. The mandalas of Tibetan Buddhism are superlative examples, as those of ancient Mexico, and those of the sand-paintings of Navajos and Pueblos. C.G. Jung believed the mandala reflected the psychic structure of man himself, and encouraged his mentally disturbed patients to unconsciously draw their own as an aid to their recovery.

The concept reflects the meaning given the number 4 by the Pythagorean philosophy of mathematics in the fifth century B.C. Pythagoras held that four contained the perfect harmonious proportion. Asserting that "things are numbers," he based his philosophy on the pattern known as the *tetraktys*—an equilateral triangle of ten dots or points arranged in symmetrical relationship with four points on each side, adding up to the perfect number, 10. The supreme oath of the Pythagoreans was, "By him who gave the fourness to the soul," their aim being to govern their lives on the same law and measure that governed the cosmos.

Herbert Weaver, in his *Divining the Primary Sense,* develops the influence projected on nature by the number 4. He recounts modern experiments conducted with a device resembling a dowsing or divining rod. The theory behind its use is that prehistoric and primitive man was able to sense directly the radiations emitted by plants and animals. The force-field detector, invented by Lawrence Veale, recaptured this sensorial endowment lost to modern man. The instrument recorded the locations of organic, as well as inorganic matter, such as birds' nests and human cave dwellings. But a simple sign interposed between the instrument and the organism would suppress its paramagnetic radiations. The sign always comprised a pattern of four: four dots, four parallel lines, a four-armed cross, a square.

From this, Weaver traced these radiation-suppressing signs to the patterns on a leaf or feather, which protected bird or plant from predators. The signs were scratched on paleolithic and mesolithic cave walls, inscribed on shrines, temples, and cathedrals of later civilizations, and can still be found in the universal symbol of the cross. The number 4, then, seems to radiate a distinctive force-field in the structures of nature and man.

Most of us regard the "flat earth" idea, which supposedly terrified Columbus' sailors, as a superstition we have long outgrown. I must confess that I was bothered for some time by the Mayan assertion that the earth was flat, "four-pointed, four-sided, four-bordered," as told in the *Chilam Balam of Mani*. It did not seem that the ancient Mayas, brilliant astronomers, astrologers, and mathematicians that they were, could believe in such a cosmography. But what else might they have meant?

In their erudite *Hamlet's Mill*, Giorgio de Santillana and Hertha von Dechend offer an explanation. To ancient peoples, the "earth" was not the global planet. It was the ideal plane passing through the band of the Zodiac, whose center line was the Ecliptic. This plane was marked by four points, the two solstices and two equinoxes, which made the four corners of what was called the "quadrangular earth." Since constellations ruled these four corners only temporarily, the quadrangular earth was believed to be drowned when they vanished, and a new "earth" arose with four new constellations rising at its corners.

This explanation confirms not only the Mayas' extraordinary knowledge of astronomy, but illustrates the belief of ancient peoples in a cosmography we have discounted and replaced by modern terrestrial geography. The element of time which must be included will be discussed shortly.

The concept of the quadruplicate structure of the world has left its imprint on all peoples. The Aztecs conceived the universe to be divided into four quadrants extending from the earth at its center. The quadrants represented the cosmic forces of the four directions which successively created "worlds," or "suns," constituted of the four primary elements: earth, air, fire, and water. They did not exist concurrently; one followed another as the reigning cosmic forces moved in cyclic order around the circle like a great revolving wheel. For the duration of their cyclic era, there was rest. At the end, there was a cataclysm; the world was destroyed. The wheel turned and the forces of the succeeding quadrant created a new world. With dynamic movement, this informed an otherwise stable cosmography. It was precisely ordered, for the destruction of each world, and the creation of another, occurred on a calendar day carrying the numeral 4.

The idea of four successive worlds is expounded in great detail by Tibetan Buddhism which traces the evolution of man through the mineral, vegetable, animal, and human kingdoms with the derivative elements of fire, air, water, and earth. Both Zoroasterism of Persia and Greek mythology maintained the existence of four previous worlds. In ancient Egyptian thought, manifestation of the unmanifest took place in gradations of crystallization called "worlds"; hence four main creation myths. The Hebrew cabala posits in its creation myths four Adams corresponding to four worlds, or *Olāms*, of descending spiritual power. The first *Ōlām* is called the "World of Junction," the abode of Adam Qadom, the Heavenly Adam, androgyn and archetype for the three lower Adams. The second *Ōlām* is the "World of Production" or creation. From this issues the third *Ōlām*, the "World of Formation" of still greater materiality. It served as a model for the fourth "World of Making," inhabited by the Fourth Adam "After the Fall," our earthly sexual humanity.

In the Americas, the Andean Incas maintained a tradition of four previous *runas*, worlds, races or humanity, culminating in the peoples of our time. According to the Zunis of New Mexico there were four successive worlds. The first world or "underworld" was considered the "Mountain of Generation." The second cave-world to which mankind emerged was called the "Umbilical Womb or Place of Gestation." Here beings separated to become fathers of the six kinds of men: yellow, red, white, black, grey, and mingled. The third cave-world was lighter, "like a valley in starlight." It was named the "Vaginal Womb or Place of Sex-Generation," for here people began to multiply in kind. In the fourth, the "Womb of Parturition," it was "light like dawning," and men began to perceive according to their natures. Finally, into the present, upper "World of Disseminated Light and Knowledge of Seeing" mankind emerged, blinded at first by the light and glory of the Sun Father.

Contemporary Navajos still relate in their creation myths, and depict in sandpaintings, these previous four worlds. The Hopis observe, best of all present tribes, the tradition of four worlds, although they believe the present world is the fourth rather than the fifth. Among their religious orders is the Two Horn Society, whose symbol of two horns worn on the masks of their members designates ritually-remembered knowledge of the three previous worlds. The One Horn Society, on the contrary, has knowledge only of their present fourth world. The most dramatic portrayal is given in the great Niman Kachina ceremonial when the chronology of the four worlds is reflected in the four appearances of the masked kachina dancers during the day by their dancing patterns on the various sides of the plaza, and in the four sections of the song they sing.

The most complete development of this successive four-world concept was made by the Mayas. Perhaps no other people on earth were so obsessed with the idea of time; and because the previous four worlds evolved successively, they included the factor of time, mathematically computing the astronomical dates and durations of each, and predicting those of the present fifth world.

Before we can understand this astounding prediction, we must try to understand the time-reckoning system on which it was based—the phenomenal calendrical system which the Mayas introduced to all Mesoamerica about the first century B.C. And with this, their unique numbering system, in which they used the symbol of zero, or nought, for the first time in history.

The great calendrical system comprised three interlocked calendars—the Sacred Calendar of 260 days, the 360-day Solar Calendar, and the Venus Calendar based on the 584-day synodi-

cal period of the planet Venus; there was also a Lunar Calendar.
So precise were the Mayan calculations that the Sacred Calendar
enmeshed with the Solar Calendar every Calendar Round of 52
years, and the cycles of the three calendars—the Sacred, Solar,
and Venus—coincided every 104 years, or two Calendar Rounds
of 52 years. Thus 52 was a significant number in the measurement of time, 5,200 years being regarded as a Great Cycle. This
astounding calendrical system, as we shall see, synthesized
mathematics, geometry, astronomy, and astrology with religious
and philosophic principles in one great unified concept.

How far back into measureless, eternal time the Mayas projected their calculations is not known. Inscriptions carved on
their stelae record dates of 90 million and 400 million years ago.

Nonetheless, it is generally accepted that the Mayas regarded
the Great Cycles of approximately 5,200 years as representing
the duration of each of the four preceding and the present
worlds. The overall duration of these five worlds total 26,000
years. This closely approximates the 25,920-year cycle of the
Precession—the time it takes for the Vernal Equinox to move
through the twelve space-and-time zodiacal houses, each of
2,160 years duration, and now called an "age."

Their last Great Cycle is regarded as the duration of the
present Fifth World. Its beginning was projected by the Mayas
back to 3113 B.C., according to the accepted correlation of the
Mayan and present Gregorian calendars by three authorities,
Goodman, Martinez, and Thompson. And its end was projected
to 2011 A.D., at which time the present Fifth World would be
destroyed by another catastrophe and superseded by a coming
Sixth World.

The inventor of the snorkel and guided missile rocket, German
scientist Otto Muck, offers alternate dates. He states that the
phenomenal Mayan calendar was begun in 8498 B.C. with the
conjunctions of the Sun, Moon, and Venus. Some 5,127 years
later, in 3375 B.C., began the present Great Cycle. By his calculations, it and the end of the Fifth World would occur in 1750
A.D. Muck, however, used in his calculations the correlation of
Herbert Spinden which was 260 years earlier than the Goodman-
Martinez-Thompson correlation. So if we add the difference of
260 years to his figure, the date comes out to 2010 A.D. which

closely approximates the more accepted correlation date of 2011 A.D. The multiples and sub-multiples of 260 are significant in Mayan calculations.

The 260-day Sacred Calendar, the Mayan *tzolkin* and the Nahuatl *tonalmatl*, was the cornerstone of the Mesoamerican calendar system. Its origin, purpose, and meaning are unknown, for it measures no natural time span. Its 260-day cycle comprises groups of 20 days, each bearing a name or day-sign combined with a number progressing from 1 to 13. Thus to the first day-sign, *cipactl*, or "crocodile," was assigned the number 1, and so on down to the thirteenth day-sign *acatl*, "reed," which bore the number 13. The fourteenth day-sign, *ocelotl*, took the number 1 again. What are we to make of this curious combination of 20 day-signs with numbers ranging from 1 to 13?

The problem has never been solved. Eduard Seler, the noted Americanist scholar, stated in his two-volume commentary on the *Borgia Codex*, in 1904, that he believed the Sacred Calendar was constructed upon the relation of the five synodical revolutions of Venus to the eight revolutions of Earth. Since then, many other theories have been offered, none of them conclusive, and the mystery is attracting the attention of scholars in many fields.

Alan W. Harris, a computer specialist, has outlined in a letter to me his mathematical speculations. He believes the purpose of the Sacred Calendar was to link the 365-day solar cycle to the great 26,000-year Precession of the Equinoxes. He points out that five 5,200-year Great Cycles (eras or suns) comprise one Precessional cycle of 26,000 years; and that a 52-year Calendar Round is 1/100th of a Great Cycle and 1/500th of a Precessional cycle. The factors of 26,000, $12 \times 5^3 \times 2^4$, reveal many other cycles and recurring numbers such as 4, 5, 13, and 400 which are significant and sacred numbers to the Mayans.

In the factors of 260—$13 \times 5 \times 2^2$ and $73 \times 5 = 365$—there is no 3. But the factors of 360 are $5 \times 3^2 \times 2^3$, so Mr. Harris includes the 360-day solar calendar. Using 104 cycles of 360 days, or degrees, meshed with the Sacred Calendar of 260 days, all the synodic periods of the visible planets can be synthesized into one continuous "phase" relationship. The use of 25,920 instead of 26,000 years in the Precession permits division evenly by 12 instead of the Mayan 13. Imbedded here, between the Mayan and European systems 13/12, 73/72, 65/64, and 26,000/25,920 was another code Mr. Harris did not have time to investigate. His observations and conclusion, without detailing his mathematical computations, are extremely pertinent.

Another friend of mine, Jack L. Ryan, has been working on the same problem for many years. He believes that a world catastrophe changed the length of the antediluvian solar year from 360 to 365 days and necessitated a reformation of the calendar. To make the transition, the Sacred Calendar was introduced, as he explains below:

"The Mesoamerican Calendar is a curious relic of antediluvian times when the earth experienced a faster-moving primordial year approximately 360 days long, called a *"tun"* by the Maya. The present year of 365+ days was inaugurated when the catastrophe that triggered the Deluge also caused a slight but crucial acceleration in the earth's angular velocity (axial spin).

"Then, as now, there existed a phenomenon caused by a wobble in the earth's polar axis known as the Precession of the Equinoxes. The earth's cycle from vernal equinox to vernal equinox takes about 20 minutes less time than its complete orbit around the sun. This discrepancy shows as a very gradual change in the position of the stars on the celestial sphere. Consequently the North Pole describes a small, slow circle among the stars about every 26,000 years.

"The Mayan astronomer priests knew that the two points where the equator intersects the ecliptic shifted in a westerly direction by a trifle more than one degree every 72 *tuns* or 360-day years. Thus, the elapsed time for one rotation of the terrestrial axis around the pole of the ecliptic was computed at exactly 26,000 *tuns*–9,360,000 days. This was the Great Celestial Lub, or Resting Place, the time taken by all planets in the solar system to return to their original positions.

"It is to this vast precessional time-span that we must look for the clue to solve the enigmatic origin of the *tzolkin*, the 260-day cycle known as the Sacred Calendar. The Mesoamerican astronomer-priests were no doubt sorely dismayed to find that one degree measured not 72 tuns but 72.222. So, those ingenious chrono-metricians simply invented the 260-day cycle to provide a Sacred Calendar, 36,000 of which would equal a planetary precessional period of 9,360,000 days. This was the equation they developed: 360 x 26,000 = 260 x 36,000 = 9,360,000.

"They also adopted 25,920 *tuns* instead of 26,000 so that every 72 turns the arc of the ecliptic moved exactly one degree. But this adjustment totalled 9,331,200 days instead of 9,360,000. Hence, to solve this dilemma, they inaugurated the 365-day year or *tun*. Each of the 12 periods in the Precession was 2,160 years (12 x 2,160 = 25,920), and is still regarded as a zodiacal 'age.' This reformation of the antediluvian calendar solved many problems. For the 18,720-year (52 x 360) period of one calendar, and the 25,920-year (72 x 360) period of the other, converged at the end of 336,960 days.

Ryan's long, mathematical and astronomical study embraces a universal scope. It reveals planetary cycles extending from the basic Calendar Round of 52 years up to a projected, phenomenal period of nearly one-half million years. Ryan also computes the convergences of the cycles of all the planets in the Solar System. His study, more comprehensive than any yet attempted, shows an awesome order of the universe apperceived by the Mayas whose mathematical and astronomical genius has not yet been fully understood.

A pragmatic use of the Sacred Calendar has been sent me by Rarihokwats of the Mohawk tribe in New York, founder and previous editor of the national Indian newspaper *Akwesasne Notes*. His explanation is geometrical rather than mathematical, and illustrated by simple graphic drawings. They are not reproduced here, and I hope they will later be published. Rarihokwats' interpretation is based on the graphic relationship of the circle and the square. His series of drawings result in the figure of the Sacred Calendar within the Solar Calendar, showing a grid which can serve as a computer for rapid addition and subtraction, multiplication and division, extracting square and cube roots, and more importantly for measuring the great cycles of 5,200 years.

Venus was particularly significant in the astronomy and religion of both the Mayas and Nahuas. Seler, as already mentioned, perceived this in his study of the esoteric *Borgia Codex*. Many modern scholars have tackled the same problem in investigating the function of the well-known Caracol in Chichen Itza, Yucatan. "Caracol" in Spanish means "snail"; and this curious ruin, whose circular tower contains a winding staircase to apertures above, suggests the spirals of a snail. The circular tower is unique in Mesoamerica; only the tower in the ruins of Casa Grande, Arizona, compares with it. Modern investigators believe the

Caracol was used as an astronomical observatory, chiefly of Venus.

The structure is now under study by Falken Forshaw Kalin, already mentioned. He suggests in a letter to me that it may represent the resolution of the square with circle, for the tower itself rises from a square base of steps. This suggests another, psychical function beyond his archaeological and astronomical observations.

For the square, as we know, symbolizes the earth, the circle heaven. In them exist different times. Earth-bound man goes by linear time, which has a beginning and an end. Heavenly time is circular, cyclical, spiral. It has no beginning or end, simply duration. Hence man in his religious strivings to supersede the temporal and achieve the eternal aspires to emerge from earth-bound linear time into eternal cyclical time. So it seems to me that the complete structure of the Caracol may symbolize such a ceremonial ascent from the square to the circle, from linear time into circular time.

The astounding prediction of the end of the Fifth World coincides with our present Age of the Fish, now ending, the twelfth and last age in our zodiacal circle; and it also marks the end of the Precessional period of 25,920 years. Just when this great transition to a new period will be made has not been determined exactly by our calculations, but certainly world-wide changes will accompany it. The dire Mayan prediction of global catastrophe is echoed by the current Hopi Prophecy which has now attained wide notoriety, and it is repeated by popular predictions in the public press.

There seems to be a sound basis for our uneasy feelings in the correspondence between the zodiacal and precessional cycles, and the changes in earth and man. As de Lubicz records, a new period is always preceded by preparatory events—seismic movement, climatic changes, and finally by the spirit that animates man, giving birth to a new state of thought, and expansion of consciousness. This may be the only true meaning of successive cosmic cycles, the evolution of consciousness.

So it seems to me, that the previous four or five worlds, suns, *runas, Ōlāms*, however they are called, are allegories for the successive states of man's ever-expanding consciousness. They are symbols of cosmic changes taking place in great rhythmic cycles which relate the inner world of man to his material outer world. If this is true, we are already beginning to experience those events preparatory to the advent of the Mayas' predicted sixth world of expanded consciousness.

This interjection of the Mesoamerican concept of five worlds is not an unnecessary detour from the theme of the quaternary structure of matter and mind. The full significance of this structural pattern, however, must include the center point within, which converts the quaternity into the quincunx. For the center point, as previously noted, reconciles the force fields of the four quarters. As 5 in the numbering system, it is the number of man, in whom the reconciliation of the opposite polarities must take place.

Worlds, planets, suns, matter and essences, and stages of human development—they are all synonymous, fashioned of matter and spirit, all imbued with one consciousness in varying degrees. We perceive, as we are progressively able, mere glimpses of the mighty transcendent edifice. Yet as the fifth integer in the natural numbering system, and as a constituent part of the present Fifth World (as the Mayas termed it), we stand at the mid-point of our evolutionary journey, able to look back through the stages we have passed and to anticipate those now to come.

PART THREE

1

Jung and Maharshi —
On the Nature
and Meaning of Man

In a six-line *I Ching* hexagram, the two top lines denote heaven, the two lower lines earth, and the two middle lines man. Hence between heaven and earth stands man, inherently imbuing, connecting, and reconciling their two forces. But man today is not generally conscious of his cosmic role, who, or what, he really is. And so we must ask, just what is his nature and meaning? Two conflicting views are held on opposite sides of the world. Their most significant spokesmen are Carl Gustav Jung of Switzerland and Bhagavan Sri Maharshi of India. No two men could have been more different, both in their lives and the principles they expounded. Contradictory as they were, each of them has influenced me so greatly that I wonder if, like my signal peaks, they were complementary sides of the same coin.

Their difference is mirrored on a greater scale by the opposite polarities of the world's two hemispheres. The long conjectured meeting of the East and West has taken place only in the outer confrontations of international war, politics, and economics— effects, not causes, of the deeply rooted, conflicting views of the nature and meaning of man. Their eventual reconciliation can be achieved only on an inner level, between Eastern metaphysics and Western psychology, whose principles are so clearly set forth by Jung and Maharshi.

The religiosity of the East, as opposed to the materialism of the West, has nearly become a cliché. Yet for three thousand years, it has stood as an intuitive edifice against the repeated tremors of rational doubt. From it have led all the broad high-ways of world faiths, with all their branches and by-ways, their blind alleys. According to the *Vedic Conglomerate* and *Veda Inquiry*, both studies compiled by my friend, Sanskrit scholar Dr. Allan H. Fry, the ancient *Vedas* (meaning "knowledge") comprise the ultimate and basic scripture of India, the birth-place of the East's major religions. The *Vedas* are believed to have been revealed to sages of remote antiquity and were com-posed in archaic language as early as 1200 B.C. From them derived the *Brahmanas* treatises which formed the basis of Brahmanism. The *Upanisadas* represent the development of the profound philosophical questing of the *Brahmanas*, embody-ing the insight of *rishis* (sages), and a distillation of the highest wisdom of the *Vedas*. The word "Upanisad" means "sitting down, near, devotedly," particularly at the feet of a master who imparts esoteric and secret doctrines. No one knows who or when they were composed "in the dark abyss of time," but they are believed to have been written down about 600 B.C. They may comprise the most profound philosophy yet achieved. The basic truths of the ten most important of the 108 Upani-sadas were later systematized in the *Vedanta*, the core of India's religious philosophy. Eleven major seers and sages have interpreted and expounded Vedantism from the seventh cen-tury up to the present time.

My friend, Dr. Fry, with his fluency in Sanskrit and his deep perception of Hindu thought, does not include Sri Ramana Maharshi in the direct line of major seers and sages. He regards the Maharshi as "one of those birds the Hindus called *laimsas,* 'wild geese,' who ever renew the perpetual and ineffable quest of humanity for an answer to the question 'Who am I?' The Maharshi, by his own life, answered the question by carrying out the release of his own human potentiality by fulfilling the ages-long search for the Self." And that may be why his impact has been so marked; his personal example speaks more clearly than abstract expositions.

The traditional "holy man" like Maharshi, who died in 1950, is no longer the norm in India, but an oddity. The entire East is infected with Western materialism; embroiled in hot and cold wars, concerned with political stability, economic reforms, and industrialization; while millions of people in Viet Nam and Cambodia are suffering from the applied teachings of Christianity received from our B-52 bombing planes.

But while the East is importing Western plumbing, autos, and TV sets, it is exporting its metaphysical ideas. America is currently beset with an influx of Swamis, Gurus, Yogis, and occultists of all kinds. Some of them are authentic. Others are American opportunists who have grown beards, assumed new Eastern names, and are "adjusting" their teachings to popular tastes and pocketbooks. Classes and mail courses in cosmic wisdom, astral projections, mind control, practical yoga for health, wealth, or power, black and white sorcery, are widely advertised with Do-It-Yourself kits of crystal balls, Tarot cards, palm-reading manuals, and color charts of auric emanations. Early authentic texts known only to scholars a few years ago—like the primary source books on Tibetan Buddhism by W.Y. Evans-Wentz—are now published in mass paperback editions, crowding the shelves of news stands, drugstores, and supermarkets.

In this confusing outcry of the printed and shouted word, the quiet teachings of Sri Ramana Maharshi seem to be ignored. Yet, many allegedly new and original teachings of lesser Maharshis paraphrase or are patterned after them, and they form a hard core for the beliefs of a slowly but steadily growing minority of earnest seekers.

Meanwhile, in the West has arisen Jung's "analytical psychology." Its phenomenal acceptance as a new basis for Western religious beliefs is easily understood. Western Christianity with its own devout tradition of two thousand years has degenerated into a factionalism comparable to that of the East. Protestantism alone has split into some four hundred squabbling denominations, creeds, and sects; and the parent Roman Catholic Church maintains its control over millions of members by secular means, not spiritual. Little wonder that modern Christianity has lost its numinous appeal to the soul of man.

Western psychology is a relatively new science. Most psychiatrists in America still belong to the original camp of Freud, the pioneer, but there are many new factions and leaders: left-wing

Freudians Herbert Marcuse and Norman O. Brown; radical Freudian Wilhelm Reich upholding the pleasure principle instead of the sexual; Alfred Adler's stress on the inferiority feeling and power drive; Fritz Perl's Gestalt Therapy; and William Glasser's Reality Therapy. Of all these mushrooming new shoots, Jung's analytical psychology has emerged as the dominant school.

The first Jungian training school was founded in Zurich scarcely twenty years ago, and there were few Jungian psychologists to be found in the United States. Today, analysts are practicing in most large cities, and millions of people who never set foot in an analyst's office are avidly reading Jung. The phenomenal growth of Jung's analytical psychology, however, is due less to its applied treatment of individual psychotherapy, as is Freud's psychoanalysis, than to its much wider and popular appeal as a new Western religious-philosophy that transcends orthodox Christianity. As such, it comes into conflict with the ages-old religious-philosophy enunciated by Maharshi.

They show many similarities and parallels. Jung, one of those "wild geese" like Maharshi, based his beliefs on his own personal experience, admonishing us to seek alone within ourselves the truth of our essential being instead of depending upon sermons, treatises, and analyses. His search, like that of Maharshi, led into that realm which cannot be reached by the rational mind, and in which we may discover another dimension of our earth-dimensional beings, the player of all our worldly roles, the dreamer of our dreams, the secret observer of our surface selves.

How similar seem their goals. Yet how different are their paths toward achieving that totality of being which embraces the material and ethereal, the divine and profane, in one transcendental, unified whole. Only our own eventual comprehension of the nature and meaning of man will decide whether they are contradictory or complementary.

Bhagavan Sri Ramana Maharshi was born of simple peasant parents in 1879, in the small south India village of Tirucculi. His father died when he was twelve years old; and with his widowed mother, two brothers and a sister, he moved to Madura to live with his uncle and aunt. An indifferent student, he gave up his schooling and sat alone in meditation.

In 1896, when he was seventeen years old, he began to suffer inexpressible spiritual anguish which was manifested in severe headaches. Discarding his clothes for a *koupina*, or loin cloth, he left home and went to Tiruvannamalai, near the sacred "Red Hill" of Arunachala, some one hundred miles to the south. Here his anguish and headaches left him.

At the sacred hill of Arunachala, dedicated to Siva, "the Auspicious One," the "Source of Beatitude," he lived for many years in different places: in the underground confines of the great temple Páthala Lingam, in the shrine and mango grove at Gurumurtan, Pachiamman Koil, Virupaksha Cave, and the Mango Tree Cave. Nothing interrupted his constant meditation, save the daily visits of attendants bringing him milk and morsels of food. The attacks of ants and insects he did not notice. He never bathed. On winter nights, he folded up his legs, placed his head between them, and remained without moving. Early in the morning, the layer of dirt on his body was soaked with dew and appeared white. One morning when he was meditating, hands folded on his breast as a protection against the cold, a visitor broke a coconut and poured the milk over his head as an *abhisheka*, believing he was a statue. Finally in 1922, after twenty-six years, he moved to the southern slope of Arunachala where an *Asramam* was established for him as an acknowledged self-realized sage. Here he stayed until his death in 1950.

Maharshi did not object to it, but denied all responsibility for its management. "If I find it disagreeable, I will go away. That is all." He accepted no gifts, founded no school nor system, composed only a number of hymns and verses. Many devotees attached themselves to him, calling themselves his disciples, but he did not consider anyone to be his disciple. The mere reading of books he considered useless. Queried how he could quote *Bhagavad Gita*, he replied, "It is due to hearsay. I have not read 'Gita' nor waded through commentaries for its meaning. When I hear a *sloka*, I think that its meaning is clear and I say it. That is all and nothing more. Similarly with my other quotations. They come out naturally . . . . Truth is beyond speech and intellect."

Sitting or reclining on a couch in the hall, he was content simply to answer questions from visitors. They included people of all kinds and faiths, Maharajah and peasant, families from throughout India who had come simply, as was the custom, for *darshan*—the spiritual benefit of being in the presence of a holy man. Others came from Europe and America, from over all the world. Sri Bhagavan's answers were recorded by Sri Mungala S. Venkataramiah, who like Maharshi spoke Tamil, Telegu, English, and Sanskrit. These answers, or talks, covering the period of four years from 1935 to 1939, were published in *Talks With Sri Ramana Maharshi*, used here for reference.

They cover the whole range of religious ideology and practices. Maharshi did not discount the approaches of other disciplines; all, if conscientiously followed, led to the same goal. Asked by Dr. Evans-Wentz if solitude is necessary, he replied, "Solitude is not to be found in forests only, but in towns and in the thick of worldly occupations. Solitude is in the mind. A man attached to desire cannot get solitude wherever he may be; a detached man is always in solitude."[1] Another visitor asked which Yoga posture was best for meditation. "Posture really means location and steadfastness in the Self," Maharshi replied. "It is internal. External positions are immaterial. The internal posture of the mind is needed."[2]

Unschooled as he was, he could on occasion reply to involved theological questions with specific answers. Yet to many he remained silent. For *mouna*, silence, transcends speech and thought. Deep meditation is eternal speech. "Which is better, to preach loudly without effect or to sit silently sending forth intuitive forces to play on others? A remote saint in the forest can benefit the world. For realization of the Self is the greatest help that can be rendered to humanity, although the latter may not be aware of it."[3]

As Jungian psychology might put it, he worked through the collective unconscious, the universal substratum of mankind, rather than the conscious mind. This may help to explain why

---

[1] *Talks With Sri Ramana Maharshi*, 3rd ed. (Madras, India: The Jupiter Press, Privated Limited, 1963), par. 20.

[2] *Ibid.*, par. 17.

[3] *Ibid.*, par. 285.

a mere "naked fakir," as Churchill would have called Maharshi, in a remote *Asramam* in India and still largely unknown throughout the world, exerts an influence constantly spreading today.

What was the goal to be sought by his process of *vichara*, self-questioning and self-searching? "Who am I?" Simply realizing the Reality—eternal existence without beginning or end; infinite existence everywhere; existence underlying all forms, all changes, all forces, all matter and all spirit.[4] Simply realization of the Self which is Reality. "What is not the Self? There is nothing but the Self," constantly asserted the Maharshi.

The generally accepted Hindu explanation of the Self, the Irreducible Real as a logical God or alogical Godhead, is fully defined by Sir John Woodroffe by the terms *Chit, Sat,* and *Ananda*. There is no equivalent in English for the Sanskrit term *Chit*, consciousness. It is embodied in all entities of the universe—stones, trees, plants, animals, man, the heavenly bodies—in different degrees. There is no inorganic "dead" matter, as held by the West. Even a stone is alive, possessing consciousness on a low threshold. *Sat*, pure Being, and *Ananda*, Bliss, are likewise inexplicable in Western terms. For wholeness and fullness as perfect Being-Consciousness is perfect Bliss, proceeding from the expansion of conscious life towards freedom and fullness of being. The Self, then, is the one eternal and universal Absolute or Irreducible Real, considered as Being-Consciousness-Bliss, of which every entity is an undivided part. As such, it is beyond our concept of duality, beyond the forms of Space, Time, and Causality by which it manifests itself as the Reducible Real. It is in us as we are in it.

There is a great difference between the Eastern and Western concepts of consciousness. What the West calls consciousness is the faculty by which man's so-called conscious mind observes objects beyond it. But to the East this consciousness in reality is only unconscious, because it in turn is the object of the one Absolute Consciousness, the Self.

We do not easily realize Reality because a phantom, the Ego, arises in man between his gross body and the transcendental

---

[4] *Ibid.*, par. 28.

Self. Functioning as mind, intellect, and memory, it projects itself as the spurious "I" thought, the personal individuality, the little self. It identifies itself with objects, and cannot remain independent of such association. This association Maharshi called Ignorance. If it is dispelled by killing the Ego's objectifying tendency, the Ego merges into its source, the Self.

Stated otherwise, "the mind is a bundle of thoughts" which arise because there is a thinker. The thinker is the Ego, the root-source from which all other thoughts arise. Seek, therefore, the origin of the spurious "I" and other thoughts, and the Ego will disappear. Only the Self will remain.[5]

There is an exhaustive body of Hindu literature on the structure and functioning of the Ego. Some sources assert there are five inner organs or *antahkaranas*: Knowledge–*Jnāna*, Mind–*Manas*, Intellect–*Buddhi*, Memory–*Chitta*, and the Ego–*Ahankāra*. Others say only two: *Manas*–Mind and *Antahkāra*–Ego. Still others say the *Antahkarana* is only one: the organ which arises between the insentient body and the eternal and self-luminous Self, namely the Ego, whose different functions make it appear differently under many names. In all cases the operation of these functions is as carefully detailed as the physiological and psychological processes recorded by Western science. Comments Maharshi: "The intricate maze of philosophy of different schools is said to clarify matters and reveal the Truth. But in fact, they create confusion where no confusion need exist. Why should confusion be created and then explained away? To understand anything there must be the Self. The Self is obvious. Why not remain as the Self? What need to explain the non-self?"[6]

The word "Yoga" means simply "to join" the small personal self with the greater Self in order to achieve liberation from the limiting world of phenomenal existence. There are many Yoga systems or techniques for controlling body, breath, and mind. All are helpful aids, but no more than aids. One must even-

---

[5] *Ibid.*, par. 347.

[6] *Ibid.*, par. 392.

tually dive inward by self-questioning, self-searching to achieve realization of the Self.

But Self-Realization is not something new to be gained. For whatever may be gained may be lost. The Self, eternal and ever-present, is already in each of us; we are the Self. We have only to dispel the ignorance imposed by the Ego to realize it.

"I want to help bring America and India closer. I want to help bring unity to the world. How?" an American lady asked Maharshi.

To such questions, he always replied, "Let the world alone. A Higher Power is guiding the destinies of nations. Look to yourself."

Many of his talks dealt with consciousness in the waking and sleep states. There are three states, according to him: deep slumber when the Self is in pure consciousness, the dream state, and the waking state. Man exists in all three states. Deep sleep, dream, and waking are only modes passing before the Self, like images on a cinema screen. Wakeful consciousness is not knowledge, but ignorance. The dream creations are purposeful; they serve the dream-purpose. There is a fire on the screen in a cinema show. Does it burn the screen? There is a cascade of water. Does it wet the screen? The dream creation, however, is contradicted in the waking state. The waking creation is contradicted in the other two states. What is not continuous cannot be real. If real, the thing must ever be real—and not real for a short time and unreal at other times.[7]

In deep slumber, man has no cognizance of the world. A scientist in the waking state may mathematically prove the world is round, yet in deep slumber he has no cognizance of the world. Not until he emerges into the conscious waking state do the world and its forms reappear.

"Does the world then not exist?"

"Realization of the Self, which lies beyond knowledge and ignorance, will answer the question."

"So it is just an experiment in somnambulism . . . or in day-dreaming?"

The Maharshi smiled.

---

[7] *Ibid.*, par. 315.

Reincarnation was a problem posed by many visitors. Maharshi answered in many ways. To one questioner he said, "Do you know the present life so well that you wish to know the past? Find out the present life, then the rest will follow. Why do you wish to burden yourself with more knowledge and suffer more?"[8]

He quoted the words of the lord Krishna to Arjuna in the *Bhagavad Gita*: "Many have been my births and re-births, O Prince—and many also have been thine own. But between us lies this difference—I am conscious of all my many lives, but thou lackest remembrance of thine." Then he explained them by saying, "The ego remains the same. New bodies appear and hold it. See what happens even to your gross body. Suppose you go to London. You take a conveyance, go to the docks, board a steamer, and reach London in a few days. What has happened? The conveyances have moved, but not your body. The movements of the conveyances have been superimposed on your body. Similarly also with your ego. The reincarnations are superimpositions."[9]

Again he quoted from the *Bhagavad Gita*: "Know thou, O Prince of Pandu, that there never was a time when I, nor thou, nor any of these princes of earth *was not*; nor shall there ever come a time, hereafter, when any of us shall cease to be."

The apparent contradiction is resolved by understanding that reincarnations of the Ego continue unendingly until they are transcended by realization of the eternal Self.

Over and over, Maharshi kept repeating the same advice. "You are not the body. You are not the mind. You are nothing but the Self. So *be* the Self here and now. Carry on with your activities, but free yourself from the doer of them. You are not the Doer. The Self is the witness."

What is needed for gaining the highest goal is loss of individuality.[10] The absorption of the temporary Ego into the Absolute Self as a drop of water is adsorbed into the ocean of the Infinite,

---

[8] *Ibid.*, par. 171.

[9] *Ibid.*, par. 311.

[10] *Ibid.*, par 502.

the complete obliteration of the personal "I," the individual consciousness—this is the summation of the Maharshi's teachings.

How different in his outer life was Jung. Well-educated, the father of five children, and a successful psychiatrist, he founded the school of analytical psychology and attained world-wide fame. He traveled widely: throughout Europe, to Africa, America, and India. As an imposing record of his great achievement he has left eighteen volumes in his Collected Works,[11] together with his autobiography,[12] miscellaneous books, talks, letters, and continuing writings about him.

Yet in his inner life he was remarkably similar. Outward events he considered inconsequential, and in his autobiography he chiefly records only his inner experiences. The first sentence in it states: "My life is a story of the self-realization of the unconscious." How similar this seems to Maharshi's goal of realization of the Self!

Son of an orthodox Lutheran minister, he was born in Switzerland and lived in Germany for a time. Like Maharshi, he had a curious religious experience in early childhood. It was expressed in a dream of an underground chamber containing a golden throne on which was standing a huge, ritual phallus—a subterranean God "not to be named." Thereafter, Lord Jesus never became real for him, as he thought of His underground counterpart. Some years later, more disturbed about the purity of the Church as his father conceived it, and the possibility that God and Sin were related in some mysterious way, he had another vision. This one of a great cathedral, above which sat God on his golden throne. And then from it fell an enormous turd, shattering the roof, and breaking the walls of the cathedral asunder. Jung felt "enormous, indescribable relief, and unutterable bliss."

During his boyhood and youth, church became a place of torment to him. He could not reconcile his father's sermons

---

[11] *The Collected Works of C.G. Jung*, vols. I–XVIII, Bollingen Series XX (New York: Princeton University Press, 1958).

[12] C.G. Jung, *Memories, Dreams, Reflections,* ed. Aniela Jaffé (New York: Random House, 1961).

about the "good" God with the terrible God of his dreams. Nor could he discuss his doubts with his father who always said, "Oh nonsense, you always want to think. One ought not to think, but believe." There grew up in him the conviction that he must solve his problem alone, in his deepest self.

During this time, Jung became conscious that he was two persons, which he simply named No. 1 and No. 2. The first was the schoolboy, concerned with the daily manifestations of life about him. Personality No. 2 was remote from the world of men, but close to all nature, to dreams; a realm wherein dwelt God as a hidden, personal, and at the same time a supra-personal secret. The counterplay between these two personalities ran through Jung's whole life, and always No. 2 was of primary importance. This duality is present in every man. As Maharshi would have said, No. 1 was the little personal self, the Ego; No. 2 was the impersonal, universal, absolute Self.

Jung, unable to become a theologian like his parson father from whom he felt alienated, entered the University of Basel for medical training. In 1900, he became an assistant at the Burgholzli Mental Hospital in Zurich, Switzerland. Five years later, he became senior physician at the Psychiatric Clinic, a post he then resigned in order to keep up with his increasing private practices as a psychiatrist.

During these years, he became familiar with Freud's work. In 1907, he met Freud in Vienna, beginning a close friendship and collaboration which lasted five years. Dr. Sigmund Freud, with his technique of dream analysis, had opened a new path of investigation of the unconscious, becoming the great pioneer and founder of modern psychology. What he had discovered was the upper level of the unconscious, distinct to every individual, now known as the personal unconscious. He conceived this as a reservoir of repressed sexuality. Any expression of spirituality was a consequence of repressed sexuality.

"My dear Jung," he said, "promise me never to abandon the sexual theory. That is the most essential thing of all. We must make a dogma of it. An unshakable bulwark of it against the black tide of mud—of occultism."

What Freud seemed to mean by "occultism," of which he seemed deathly afraid, included "virtually everything that philosophy and religion, including the rising contemporary science of parapsychology, had learned about the psyche."

Jung could not accept this premise. Hence his celebrated break with Freud to establish his own school of analytical psychology in opposition to Freud's psychoanalysis. This was based on his investigations into a deeper level of the unconscious common to all mankind, impersonal and universal, which he termed the "collective unconscious." It contained the psychical record of man's entire history expressed in the form of universal images that have existed from the remotest times. These "primeval images," as Jung first called them and later termed "archetypes," were released into consciousness, as through dreams. During this process, the forms were modified according to the cultural background of the dreamer, but their meanings remained the same.

Throughout his life, Jung sought the meaning of these archetypes. As an empirical psychologist, he did not rely solely on his own and his patients' dreams, but sought for their confirmation in the myths and techniques of previous cultures. It is more accurate to say that he confirmed their previous experience, which long had been known to primitive man and modern man, to great painters and writers of every race and nation who unconsciously perceived their forms and meanings. This led him to an exhaustive study of alchemy, on which he became an authority. The alchemists of medieval Europe, beyond the belief that they were exoterically attempting to transmute gross matter into gold, were esoterically concerned with the transmutation of matter into spirit. In psychological terms, they were attempting to bridge the unconscious and conscious—a goal parallel to that of the Eastern discipline of Yoga which attempted "to join or to unite" the personal self with the universal Self. And this historical premise basically coincided with the aims of both Jung and Maharshi to supersede the human duality that plagues mankind in all its manifestations—light and dark, good and evil, male and female, cause and effect, matter and spirit—with the tensions and conflicts they perpetually engender.

Jung, as all scientists and pioneers, was a great coiner of new words and new meanings for old words to express his findings: *archetype, anima* and *animus, centroversion, individuation, synchronicity*, and the like. They constitute a technical jargon as confusing to the general public, still largely dependent upon Freud's sexual symbology, as the traditional religious terms of the East like *chit, sat, ananda*, and *ahankāra*. Unfortunately, he adopted for his own use the Eastern term "self" but gave it an entirely different meaning from the Unborn, Unmade, and Eternal totality of Being, Consciousness, and Bliss which the Maharshi termed the "Self." It is necessary here, at the outset, to grapple with the difference between them.

To Jung, the Unconscious was simply all that was non-conscious. His various definitions of the self are confusing for he does not differentiate between the individual "self" and the impersonal, higher "Self" (in whose existence he did not believe). In one instance, he views it as the central archetype, the archetype of order, the totality of the personality. He says (in *Psychology and Alchemy*, Volume 12 of his Collected Works) that "The self is not only the centre but also the whole circumference which embraces both conscious and unconscious; it is the centre of this totality, just as the ego is the center of the conscious mind . . . the completest expression of that fateful combination we call individuality."

And again he writes, "I believe that the thing which I call the Self is an ideal centre, equi-distant between the Ego and the Unconscious, and it is probably equivalent to the maximum natural expression of individuality, in a state of fulfillment or totality. . . . It is therefore an ideal centre, something created."[13]

Realization of this Self was achieved by Centroversion and Individuation. Centroversion was a process of working toward this center, as elucidated by Erich Neumann, the most creative of Jung's pupils. Expansion of consciousness and achievement of the wholeness of personality was brought about by the Ego reflecting upon itself, acting as a symbol uniting the conscious and unconscious. This marked the end of the self-development of the Psyche, which manifested itself first as the Ego, and then

---

[13] Miguel Serrano, *C.G. Jung and Hermann Hesse* (London: Routledge & Kegan Paul, 1966), Jung to Serrano.

was experienced by this Ego as the Self.[14] "The Self," he asserts, "proves to be the golden core of the sublimated Uroboros, combining in itself masculine and feminine, conscious and unconscious elements, a unity in which the Ego does not perish but experiences itself, in the Self, as the uniting symbol."[15]

Individuation was defined by Jung as "the process by which one becomes a psychological 'in-dividual,' that is, a separate, individual unity or whole."[16] "We could therefore translate Individuation as 'coming to selfhood' or 'self-realization'."[17] This was a theory, ethic, or discipline which maintained the constant preservation of the individual, conscious Ego.

More light on the unconscious and the two selves has been cast by the Italian psychologist Roberto Assagioli's *Psychosynthesis*. In his synthesis of Western psychology and metaphysics, he posits three layers of the Unconscious. The lower region contains the elementary psychological activities which direct the bodily functions and various pathological manifestations. The middle region contains the field of Consciousness, the flow of sensations, images, thoughts, and feelings. Its center is the conscious self, or "I," the point of pure self-awareness. From the upper unconscious, or superconscious, we receive our higher intuitions and inspirations—artistic, scientific, philosophical, and humanitarian; it is the source of the states of contemplation and illumination, psychic functions and energies. In this region may be apperceived the existence of the impersonal, universal Self, whose reality can be realized, as the Maharshi demon-

---

[14] Erich Neumann, *The Origins and History of Consciousness* (New York: Bollingen, 1954).

[15] Erich Neumann, "Mystical Man," *Spring*, 1961. Erich Neumann, *Depth Psychology and a New Ethic*, Trans. Eugene Rolfe (New York: G.P. Putnam's Sons, 1969).

[16] Collected Works, *The Archetypes and the Collective Unconscious*, Vol. IX, p. 275.

[17] Collected Works, *Two Essays on Analytical Psychology*, Vol. VII, p. 171.

strated, by prolonged meditation or in unsought paranormal experiences.

How different is this concept from that of Jung. To Assagioli, the Unconscious is not one nebulous realm of all that is non-Conscious. He divides it into three regions, as described, and defines their separate characteristics and functions. The abysmal lower level has been partially investigated, but it has yet to be fully plumbed. The existence of an upper or subconscious level Western psychology ignores or denies. The great difference, of course, lies in the field of Consciousness in the middle region, which contains the conscious, individual self or "I." Jung and Neumann, quoted above, postulate that it does not perish but experiences itself as the Self. The Maharshi, to the contrary, maintains that the individual self, the personal "I," is but a manifestation of the universal Self, reflecting its light, and by which it is eventually absorbed.

Clearly, Assagioli accepted the teachings of Maharshi. Jung did not. During his visit to India in 1938, he studiously avoided "all so-called 'holy men,' Swamis or Gurus." "I didn't even go to see Ramana Maharshi, who had so interested Somerset Maugham, because I felt it was not necessary to do so. I knew what a Swami was; I had an exact idea of his archetype; and that was enough to know them all, especially in a world where extreme personal differentiation doesn't exist as it does in the west."[18]

No, he was not ready to accept India's archetypes; he was confirmed to those of Europe, particularly those of medieval alchemy. "Shall we be able to put on, like a new suit of clothes, ready-made symbols grown on foreign soil, saturated with foreign blood, spoken in a foreign tongue, nourished by a foreign culture, interwoven with foreign history, and so resemble a beggar who wraps himself in kingly raiment, a king who disguises himself as a beggar? Or is there something in ourselves that commands us to go in for no mummeries, but perhaps even to sew our garments for ourselves?"[19]

---

[18] Serrano.

[19] Collected Works, *The Archetypes and the Collective Unconscious*, Vol. IX, par. 27, part 1.

Jung had not visited India on his own initiative, but at the invitation of the British Government to participate in the celebration of the twenty-fifth anniversary of the University of Calcutta. Also at the time, he was preoccupied with his study of medieval alchemical philosophy, which he continued during his voyage. In India, he was awarded three doctorates, from Allaha-bad, Benares, and Calcutta—representatives of Islam, Hinduism, and British-Indian medicine and science. In Calcutta, he came down with dysentery and spent ten days in the hospital. Upon recovering, he had a European dream associated with the quest for the Holy Grail, which wiped away all his impressions of India and swept him back to the Occident. It was as though the dream asked him, "What are you doing in India? Rather seek for yourself and your fellows the healing vessel, the *servator mundi*, which you urgently need. For your state is perilous; you are all in imminent danger of destroying all that centuries have built up."[20]

He therefore departed from India without leaving the ship to see Bombay, burying himself in his Latin alchemical texts.

It may seem strange that Jung refused to see the Maharshi while in India, although he visited native *shamans* in Africa and the *cacique*, or religious leader, of the Indian Pueblo of Taos, New Mexico, during one of his trips to America. The latter made such a great impression upon him that he recorded it several times.[21] What a historic confrontation their meeting would have been, during the very period when the Maharshi's talks were being recorded!

One hesitates to accentuate this too strongly, save that Jung himself made such a point of it. For, six years afterward, he wrote an Introduction to his friend Heinrich Zimmer's *Der Weg zum Selbst*, a book about Sri Ramana Maharshi's teachings. "I do not know," he wrote, "whether my friend found it an unforgivable or an incomprehensible sin on my part that I had not sought out Shri Ramana. . . . Yet I fear that if I journeyed

---

[20] Jung, *Memories, Dreams, Reflections*, p. 283.

[21] "The Symbolic Life," seminar talk, April 5, 1939, London: The Guild of Pastoral Psychology, Guild Lecture No. 80. Letter to Serrano, September 14, 1960. Collected Works.

to India a second time to make up for my omission, it would fare with me just the same: I simply could not, despite the uniqueness of the occasion, bring myself to visit this undoubtedly distinguished man personally . . . Shri Ramana's thoughts are beautiful to read. What we find here is purest India, the breath of eternity . . . the song of the ages. This melody is built up on the one great theme . . . which everlastingly rejuvenates itself in the Indian spirit, whose youngest incarnation is Shri Ramana himself. It is the drama of *shankara*, the 'I-maker' or ego-consciousness, in opposition and indissoluble bondage to the atman, the self or non-ego."[22]

This melody, theme, or teaching Jung could not bring himself to listen to; his mind was already made up. Throughout the Introduction and his future writings, he pointedly refuted the Eastern premise with the attitude so clearly described in the *Bhagavad Gita*: "The Real Self is the friend of him in whom the Personality hath yielded mastery; but in him whose personality is defiant, and which will not acknowledge the mastery of the Real Self, it appeareth as if the Real Self were its bitterest foe . . . Thus, through the smoke of illusion and error, the True Friend is seen as the Bitter Enemy."

Nevertheless, there was something heroic in Jung's new and solitary stand against the ages-long metaphysical tradition of the East. It required absolute honesty, an extraordinary analytical mind, and an indomitable ego that brooked no opposition, even as early as his stormy break with Freud. Jung was quite right in asserting there was no evidence for, and no possibility of proving, the validity of a metaphysical postulate such as an impersonal "Universal Mind" which seemed to him a relic of the original human "soul." To maintain such a postulate, faith was required; and faith he considered a primitive mental condition unwilling to give up a childlike relationship to a mind-created and hypostatized supreme principle of reality, whatever it may be called.[23] Throughout his work, he studiously avoided taking

---

[22] Collected Works, *Psychology and Religion: West and East*, Vol. XI.

[23] Collected Works, Vol. XI, pars. 760, 763.

a religious viewpoint, adhering strictly to that of psychology which treats all metaphysical claims as mental phenomena. A prospective meeting with Maharshi brought out in him, a thoroughly rational Western man, a deeply rooted fear, or aversion to an unknown he was not prepared to face. This, too, must have had a psychological base. Personally, I am inclined to believe he was unconsciously frightened by an intimation of a spiritual depth below his hypothesized level of the collective unconscious, just as Freud before him had been frightened by the so-called black tide of occultism or spirituality below the level of the personal unconscious.

He continued to build that great edifice culminating in individuation, "the process by which one becomes a psychological 'in-dividual,' that is, a separate, individual unity or whole."[24] "We could therefore translate Individuation as 'coming to selfhood' or 'self-realization.'"[25] It did not shut out the world of objects, but gathered it into itself. Unlike the Maharshi's avowed absorption of the Ego by the universal Self, it postulated the personal Ego's experiencing itself as the Self—an experience which still maintained the preservation of the individual, conscious Ego.

Jung's somewhat blanket refutation of India's archetypes as foreign-made symbols "like a new suit of clothes" seems rather inconsistent. For if archetypes are primeval images common to all mankind, there is not one separate suit for each race, nationality, and culture. The meanings of all are the same. One Eastern archetype especially he did accept, the *mandala*. The word in Sanskrit means a magic circle, a symbol of the center, the goal, or the Self as a psychic totality. Symbolically represented as any combination of the circle and the square, it had been immemorially used in Lamism and Tantric Buddhism as an instrument of contemplation. Egyptian mandalas date from the ancient past, and Christian mandalas from the early Middle Ages. Some of the most beautiful are those of Tibetan Budd-

---

[24] Collected Works, Vol. IX, par. 490.

[25] Collected Works, Vol. VII, p. 171.

hism. Navajo and Pueblo sandpaintings in the Southwest, and the gorgeous skin paintings of the pre-Columbian codices of Mexico, with which Jung was not familiar, are exquisite mandalas. Jung encouraged his patients to draw their own as aids to their mental recovery; and he himself painted a notable series of them during his own journey into the interior.

One must be impressed by his wide knowledge of the East's teachings. It came from his study of the ancient texts which provided the historical antecedents he was always seeking, rather than from direct personal encounters with their contemporary adherents like Maharshi. For these texts—two of Evans-Wentz' Tibetan Buddhist series, Wilhelm's presentation of two ancient Chinese texts, Zimmer's book on the Maharshi, Susuki's exposition of Japan's Zen Buddhism, and others—he wrote expository introductions, commentaries, and forewords which interpreted them from his own psychological premise. Yet despite his bias, these Eastern teachings exerted a profound influence upon him: a yeast that began working without his conscious knowledge, for he still stuck to his Western premise.

In his commentary to *The Tibetan Book of the Dead*, or *Bardo Thodol*, he states that "giving up the supremacy of the Ego means the end of all conscious, rational, morally responsible conduct of life, and a voluntary surrender to what the *Bardo Thodol* calls 'karmic illusion'." And to him "Karma implies a psychic theory based on a hypothesis of reincarnation—an hypothesis of the supra-temporality of the soul. Neither our scientific knowledge nor our reason can keep step with this idea."

Moreover, he believed it was impossible to get rid of the idea of the Ego or of consciousness even in the deepest state of *samadi*. For if one were able to get rid of his consciousness completely in moments of profound ecstasy, then these moments would be non-existent; one could never remember or record them. "Since the Unconscious really means the not-conscious, nobody can gain that state while he is still alive, and be able to remember it afterwards, as the Hindus claim. In order to remember, one must have a conscious spectator, who is the Self, or the conscious being."[26] This, of course, expresses his dis-

---

[26] Serrano, Jung to Serrano, 1959.

belief that Maharshi, as many other saints and sages before him, had achieved Self-Realization and still carried on the activities of his worldly conscious self.

Here again Jung equates consciousness with what he calls the Self–that hypothesized ideal center created between the Ego and the Unconscious which is equivalent to the "maximum natural expression of individuality." How different this is from the East's unborn, uncreated, universal, and absolute Self which is not a theorized center but includes both the conscious and unconscious and permeates every organic and so-called inorganic entity in the universe.

Jung could not accept the existence of a pure spirituality that lay beyond and included the consciousness of the individual Ego, the personal unconscious of Freud, and his own hypothesized collective unconscious, in an ultimate cosmic consciousness beyond comprehension by the human mind.

He believed the identification of the Self with God would shock all Europeans. "It is a specifically oriental Realization, as expressed in Sri Ramana's utterances. Psychology cannot contribute anything further to it, except that it lies far beyond its scope to propose such a thing. However, it is clear to the Indian that the Self as a spiritual source is not different from God; and in so far as man abides in his Self, he is not only contained in God but is God himself. Sri Ramana is quite clear in this respect."[27]

Furthermore, he points out the danger of confusing Individuation with becoming a god-man or superman: the result of one who identifies his Ego with the contents of the unconscious he terms inflation. "The self in its divinity (i.e., the archetype) . . . can become conscious only within our consciousness. And it can do that only if the Ego stands firm. The self must become small as, and yet smaller than the Ego, although it is the ocean of divinity."[28]

There are many paradoxes in these statements, always bearing in mind the difference between Jung's and Maharshi's concep-

---

[27] Heinrich Zimmer, *Der Weg zum Selbst,* Introduction.

[28] Aniela Jaffé, *The Myth of Meaning,* trans. R.F.C. Hull (New York: G.P. Putnam's Sons, 1971).

tion of the Self. Jung considered the Self, to be experienced by the Ego, as the essence of individuality. Yet in alluding to it as an archetype of wholeness he considered it as a God-image, universal and eternal, comparing it with the dogmatic figure of Christ.[29] The conflict between these functioning opposites, the antithetical natures of the Ego-personality and the transpersonal Self, Jung does not resolve in what Jaffé calls his drama of Individuation.

Maharshi's realized conception of the Self transcends this duality. Clearly explained by Woodroffe,[30] there is but one consciousness, the Absolute Consciousness *Chit*, which is one of the attributes of the Self. Individual consciousness, being but a function of the temporal Ego, only reflects the light of the Self, playing it solely upon a small fact-section of the whole spectrum of life. What the West calls consciousness, then, is really unconscious because it is the object of the one Absolute Consciousness and functions only as the limited reasoning faculty of the transient, limited Ego.

Chit, as unlimited consciousness, is dissociated from mind and matter; whereas empirical consciousness is associated with the psycho-physical body, and is the limited consciousness of the individual finite self, or Ego. *Chit* is the alogical Reality-Whole, the spiritual principle in man in which his universe of experience lives, moves, and has its being.

But *Chit* as Being (*Sat*), and Bliss (*Ananda*), is also the Power to *Be* and *Become*. Infinite, static, and eternal, it finitizes itself in the universe of Shape (*Rupa*), and Name (*Nama*), remaining itself unchanged. This power of the Irreducible Real (the Supreme Self, the alogical Godhead, or *Chit*) to evolve as the Reducible Real (the universe of limited selves), and to involve it again, seems alogical to the West. This explains the Eastern belief that a finite stone, for example, is also infinite *Chit*

---

[29] *Ibid.*

[30] Sir John Woodroffe and Pramatha Natha Mukhyopadhyaya, *Mahamaya: The World as Power: Power as Consciousness (Chit-Shakti)* (Madras, India: Ganesh & Co., Ltd., 1954).

limiting and defining itself in matter, just as it limits and defines itself in pragmatic consciousness. Both man and stone have supreme Consciousness in varying degrees, limited to one aspect of experience as determined by its karma.

This principle is carried even farther. The smallest particle of organic and inorganic matter also is, or embodies, the infinite Consciousness and Power to Become, as shown by the potency of the living germ and cell to expand and multiply, and by the immense power of the material atom when released. The ultimate limit or point beyond which Power cannot be contracted for creative evolution the East terms *Bindu*. This, as the Veda says, is "smaller than the smallest" as the other pole is "greater than the greatest."[31]

If we accept the foregoing, it is apparent that this power to infinitely expand and contract applies only to the supreme Self; not to that self which can be experienced by the limited Ego, which can become conscious only within our consciousness, and which is equivalent to the maximum natural expression of individuality.

We are aware of the danger of using quotations out of context from the enormous volume of Jung's writings to represent his ethic. Yet they are spread so insistently throughout his work of many years, one may safely accept them as expressing the Ego-dominated Western world's indomitable insistence upon the perpetuation of its cult of individuality. It seems impossible for the West to concede the timeless belief of the East that the nature, meaning, and final goal of man is to lose his individual identity and personal consciousness and merge into that one universal and eternal consciousness of the supreme Self.

To break through the barrier of the conscious, rational, limited mind; to confront the frightening unknown; and finally to experience through Enlightenment or Illumination the transcendent light of the Self! We cannot doubt that there have been many mystics, saints, and sages like Maharshi who have achieved it, but without exception all of them have refused to

---

[31] *Ibid.*, p. 188.

attempt to describe their experience. And the very good reason, they say, is that it is rationally indescribable. The process of Self-discovery is wholly subjective, not intellectual.

Yet, if consciousness and the intellect evolve out of the unconscious, what is its purpose? The sole purpose of the intellect, says Maharshi, is to realize its dependence upon the Supreme Power and its inability to function after a certain stage. Then, as a necessary tool to be discarded when it has accomplished its task, it is annihilated. That is Realization; that is the finality; that is the goal.[32]

Perhaps the East would have said Jung was, as the individual self, using his intellect to further the demand of the greater Self to realize itself.

More and more, Jung's work took on a mystical tinge as he became more concerned with religious ideas and abstract principles. The influence of Eastern metaphysics made itself felt. And his conclusions tended more and more to take an Eastern direction.

It is curious that Jung rejected the teachings of India as expounded by Maharshi, but accepted one of ancient China. He was introduced to it by the noted sinologist Richard Wilhelm, who translated and explained *The Secret of the Golden Flower*, the *Book of Life*, and the more ancient *I Ching*, or *Book of Changes*. Long fascinated by the phenomena of coincidence which he and his patients had experienced, Jung believed there might be another factor in nature besides the connection between cause and effect. The *I Ching* confirmed his belief in an acausal principle as well as causality; and from it he largely developed his theory of synchronicity: that archetypal energy could be manifested both in internal imagery and external events.

The idea had been broached by Kammerer's Law of Seriality in 1919, which postulated "a recurrence of the same or similar things or events in time and space which are not connected by the same acting cause." Wolfgang Pauli, the nuclear physicist, later had developed in his Exclusion Principle the same belief as

---

[32] *Talks With Sri Ramana Maharshi*, par. 502.

it applied to theoretical physics: that coincidences are manifestations of a universal principle in nature which operates independently from physical causation. So Jung and Pauli collaborated on a common approach to the problem. Pauli's essay, "The Influence of Archetypal Ideas on the Scientific Theories of Kepler," and Jung's paper, "Synchronicity: An Acausal Connecting Principle," were both published in one volume by the Jung Institute in 1952.

Jung defined "synchronism" as simply a "simultaneous occurrence of two meaningfully but not causally connected events," or "a coincidence in time of two or more causally unrelated events which have the same or a similar meaning." He laid stress on their common meaning which rested on an archetypal foundation; that is, the coincidence of a psychic state and a physical event was connected with archetypal processes. The *I Ching*, for which he wrote the Foreword and so helped to make it immensely popular, illustrated his theory.

In a lecture to the English Society for Psychical Research, in 1919, Jung explained apparitions, spirits, ghosts, and other materializations as unconscious projections, regarding this whole territory as an appendix of psychology. When the lecture was reprinted in his Collected Works in 1947, he appended a footnote stating that he no longer felt as certain as he had previously, and he doubted whether an exclusively psychological approach could do justice to the phenomena in question.

He also considered the possible meaningful coincidence of planetary aspects and positions with the existing psychic state of the questioner, although he was inclined to believe astrological correspondence was not a matter of synchronicity but of causal relationship. To test astrological tradition, he and a co-worker made a statistical investigation of the horoscopes of a number of married couples. Apparently no firm conclusion was drawn.

Jung's interest was now drawn more closely into physics— into the relationship of the psyche to matter. Early in his career he called the myth motifs of the collective unconscious "primordial images" that had existed in man since the earliest times. In 1919, for the first time, he had applied to them the term "archetypes" because they were not actual images, being irrepresentable until they had risen into consciousness. Finally, in 1946, he began to describe them as "psychoid archetypes," being both psychic and non-psychic, imprinting not only the realm of human and organic life, but the physical and inorganic world. In other words, Jung had first viewed the archetype as an antimony between instinct and spirit; now he saw the psychoid archetype as a "bridge to matter in general," embracing the tension between spirit and matter. As he wrote in 1951, "The deeper layers of the psyche lose their individual uniqueness as they retreat farther and farther into darkness . . . becoming increasingly collective until they are universalized and extinguished by the body's materiality, i.e., in chemical substances . . . Hence 'at bottom' the psyche is simply 'world.'"[33] To this Jaffé adds the interpretation that once the unconscious content is apprehended by consciousness, the original parity of the opposites—the bipolar aspects of a single paradoxical archetype—retreats into a distance that consciousness can no longer reach; it is not even conceivable any more.[34] The archetype, then, is the stamp of wholeness on the psyche and the world of matter, divided into bipolar opposites only when it rises into consciousness.

Now arises the question: What is the origin of the archetype if the higher power that imprinted it is beyond human consciousness?

Spirit and matter, the psyche and the world of nature, are one. And what is that? Modern physicists, continually reducing matter to ever smaller units—atoms, electrons, protons, neutrons, and sub-atomic particles—have reached the conclusion that inanimate matter as such does not exist; all units, infinitesimally small as they may be, are forms of energy. This energy, beyond the scope of modern science to define, can be understood by the Eastern concept of *Chit*, as infinite Consciousness which finitizes itself in the universe of limited selves; limiting and defining itself both in matter and pragmatic consciousness in varying degrees. As previously explained, *Chit* (Consciousness),

---

[33] Collected Works, Vol. IX, par. 291.

[34] Jaffé.

with *Sat* (pure Being) and *Ananda* (Bliss), is regarded by the East as an attribute of the one eternal and universal Absolute or Irreducible Real, the alogical Godhead which the Maharshi called the Self and which we call God.

In his "Answer to Job," Jung seems to reaffirm the Eastern concept: "After all, we can imagine God as an eternally flowing current of vital energy that endlessly changes shape just as easily as we can imagine him as an eternally unmoved, unchangeable essence."[35]

This is a remarkable conclusion, coinciding as it seems with the East's concept of the Self which is infinite, static, and eternal, but which also finitizes itself in the limited world of shape and name while remaining itself unchanged. This, to me, is the closest Jung ever approached to the threshold of Eastern belief, but he does not cross it.

Jung's "Answer to Job," written when he was seventy-six years old and first published in 1952, is considered his most outstanding writing on the major religious problem of our time. All his life, Jung was concerned with the nature of God. Throughout his work, he does not view God in the aspect of an anthropomorphic divine being, as does orthodox Christianity. Instead, he regards God psychologically as a synonym for the unconscious, as an archetype. Hence he does not speak of God, the great unknowable mystery, but of the archetypal God-image. His intimations of God's duality, of a "good God" and a "terrible God" in one, first came in his vision of early boyhood. It was preceded by many older religions that affirmed God embodied both good and evil—a symbol of the primeval demi-urge who existed before the Beginning, who stands beyond the opposites, who is both a god and a devil.

In developing the theme that the archetypal God-image embraces the dual opposites of man himself, Jung lays bare our Achilles' heel, our ideal of righteousness. Bound by our frigid, moralistic Christian ethic, we conceive God as being wholly good, as should we who are created in His image. Hence we repress all those instincts incompatible with our moralistic

---

[35] Collected Works, Vol. XI, par. 555.

dogma, all the aspects of what we regard as evil within ourselves. As a result we are incomplete, deprived of the numinous
power of the divine in evil itself. This repression often results in
a neurosis that can be cured only by psychotherapy, which
releases the repressed contents of the unconscious into consciousness; in such wise Jung considered Freud's repression of
sexuality as a neurosis. Or else we project on others these
repressed inferior psychic elements, which Jung called the
"shadow."

His conclusion was that Individuation, then, is the process of
reconciling not only God and man, but the good and evil within
the archetypal God-image in man himself; and this can be
achieved only by consciousness. He makes it very clear in his
autobiography that he equates God and the unconscious when
he states, "Unconscious wholeness therefore seems to me the
true *spiritus rector* of all biological and psychic events. Here is a
principle which strives for total realization—which in man's case
signifies the attainment of total consciousness."[36] That is, God
needs man as much as man needs God.

This leads us to wonder if it is indeed possible for man to
alter that one universal consciousness beyond the reach of his
cerebral mind.

Jung, in his investigations of so many other fields, did not
directly tackle the problem of Time. This great mystery was
the primary concern of two of his noted contemporaries: the
Englishman J.W. Dunne, and P.D. Ouspensky, the Russian
exponent of Gurdjieff's teachings.

Dunne based his first book, *An Experiment With Time*,
published in 1927, on his thirty-year study of dreams. He was
convinced that our conception of time as linear, chronological,
was incomplete. There existed an eternal time which included
past, present, and future. He saw it as three-dimensional,
comprising a regressive series which he called Time 1, 2, and 3.
They were experienced by us as "observers" or "selves." Self 1,
because we are self-conscious, was always an object. Self 2, being
able to observe Self 1, was either object or subject. Self 3 was
never an object, for it was the ultimate observer.

---

[36] Jung, *Memories, Dreams, Reflections*, p. 324.

Ouspensky believed that Time had three dimensions beyond our three dimensions of space, which he equated with linear time. In his best-known book on the subject, *A New Model of the Universe*, published in 1922, he developed his theory mathematically and geometrically, rather than from dreams. The sixth dimension of Time was an aggregate of "all Times," imperceptible to our limited consciousness.

Both theories are hard to understand and more difficult to accept. Ouspensky was obsessed with his idea of "recurrence" and Dunne pushed his "regressive" series too far to follow. Nevertheless, they agree that the last of Time's dimensions, which Ouspensky calls the sixth, is rationally incomprehensible. Being eternal and indivisible, it can be experienced only by that ultimate observer or self. How closely this coincides with that universal consciousness, the one ultimate observer, which the Maharshi calls the Self.

The equation of the dimensions of Time with the dimensions of space is pertinent. According to Buddhism, as explained by Lama Anagarika Govinda, "This space, however, is not the external 'visible' space, in which things exist side by side, but a space of higher dimensions, which includes and goes beyond the three-dimensional one. In such a space, things do not exist as separate units but rather like the interrelated parts and functions of one organism, influencing and penetrating each other . . . a space filled with consciousness, a conscious space: the realization of cosmic consciousness."

To this eternal and universal consciousness, our dimensional and measurable time and space are but concepts of our limited rational minds. Their reality cannot be established by our astronomical measurements and probes of outer space, by a psychology that has not progressed into spirituality. Both time and space, as they appear to us, are illusions that can be dispelled only by our attainment of universal consciousness. This lies in the domain of what Freud called the "occult" and refused to enter, and the spiritual realization whose boundary Jung, in turn, never crossed.

Obviously, we can make no rational choice between the opposite views of the two spokesmen which are briefly outlined here. Beset by a multitude of Eastern teachings, and by the constant popular psychologizing of every aspect of our daily life, we are helplessly confused and desperately seeking a new goal for our aimless lives.

Blanket adoption by the West of any system of Eastern meta-physics—Brahmanism and Vedantism, Hinayamna and Mahaya-mna Buddhism, the Tantrism of India and Tibet, the Taoism of China, and the Zen of Japan—is of course impossible. Nor will the importation of Western sciences completely undermine the East's religious subculture. The nature and meaning of man, a universal and ages-long question, can be resolved only from a greater perspective which includes both views. In this future field of vision they may well appear to be complementary rather than contradictory. Reconciliation of the conscious and uncon-scious is indeed one of the great problems confronting mankind. But I believe it can't be fully achieved without reconciling the West's analytical mode of understanding with the East's syn-thetic process of meditative intuition.

This, as I've already suggested, is beginning to take place in this immeasurably old New World, the American arena between Europe and Asia. An increasing number of Western psychologists and physicists are discovering new depths and meanings in Eastern metaphysics, and many teachers of Eastern religious philosophies are adopting the principles of modern psychology.

Despite Jung's influence on so many of our lives, his work has many detractors and some of its weaknesses are growing apparent. For one thing, analytical psychology is virtually Jung's one-man achievement. Almost all its followers faithfully adhere to his pronouncements without deviation. It is appalling to read the papers of so many Jungian analysts and commentators who footnote almost every paragraph with a quotation from Jung, as if they had no original insights from the exploration of their own unconscious. Energetically revealing the "shadows" of their patients, of institutions, and nations, they ignore what well may be a collective "shadow" of Jungianism itself. As a result, Jungianism faces the prospect of being frozen into a rigid dogma as was Freudianism, a danger to which it is showing itself vulnerable.

Jung has increased the depth of our perception by adding the collective unconscious to Freud's personal unconscious, but beyond these must lie a numinous realm of spiritual totality which embraces and supersedes both. Not until a new discoverer can penetrate still deeper, as Jung advanced the pioneer work of Freud, will psychology progress farther. Western psychology then, as I see it, is not a conclusive answer. It is but one great step towards the East's mystical belief in one universal reality.

Albert Einstein, one of the West's greatest scientists, wrote: "The most beautiful and most profound emotion we can experience is the sensation of the mystical. It is the sower of all true science. . . . To know that what is impenetrable to us really exists, manifesting itself as the highest wisdom and the most radiant beauty which our dull faculties can comprehend only in primitive form—this knowledge, this feeling is at the center of true religiousness."

It is not surprising that the Jesuit priest Teilhard de Chardin has also said: "Mysticism remains the great science and great art, the only power capable of synthesizing the riches accumulated by other forms of activity."

Certainly no philosophy, no religion, no science, is permanently valid unless it embraces the complete spectrum of space, time, and life in all forms.

2

Sierra Madre Outposts

The religious-philosophical systems of ancient civilizations, as revealed by many scholars, were founded upon universal laws. They were concerned with man's inner being rather than his daily outer life. But nothing is permanently enduring; everything conforms to the cosmic law of perpetual change. Civilizations, like plants, animals, and man, have an organic life cycle of birth, death, and transformation. Yet mankind loses nothing which it has gained. Egypt today is not the Egypt of the past, but all that it achieved is still retained in the *akashic* record of esoteric theology, the indestructible memory bank which psychology calls the collective unconscious. Nor does modern Mesoamerica outwardly reflect the proud heritage of its Maya, Toltec, and Aztec past. It, too, has suffered a tragic death and is undergoing a transformation in its slow rebirth in modern times. In this new cycle, its goals are economic and social. They are impermanent but necessary steps toward realizing in full rational consciousness the truths of the unconscious past.

We know so little of the prehistoric past of our own America, I've often wondered if it contained a civilization as we today define it. The great Mound Builders network, with its thousands of earthen burial, effigy, and temple mounds, its populous cities, its exquisite art, spread across the whole eastern half of the

United States. In the Southwest the Pueblo complex shows in its ruins and in its still-existent architecture, social structure, and religious ceremonialism the perpetuated living values of the past. They both might be considered civilizations, if measured by their orientation to man's inner needs, rather than by our present secular standards. And both seem to reflect the influences of the great civilization of ancient Mesoamerica to the south.

What was it like, this vast motherland?

Perhaps it was this simple curiosity that impelled my first trip into Mexico years ago. I visited none of the majestic ruins of the once proud cities, knowing nothing about them. Instead, I traveled through a still ignored wilderness of desert and mountain, experiencing the heartbeat of the land and its people. How rewarding it was!

We, here today, depend too much upon our current maps and nationalistic histories to realize that our American Southwest owes it geographical and cultural allegiance to Mexico instead of to the far-off and foreign Atlantic shore settled by Anglo Pilgrims more than a century after Spanish roots had been implanted here. Sante Fe, New Mexico, is the oldest capital in the United States, and Tucson, Arizona, was the principal town in the Mexican province of Sonora long before our upstart Yankees baldfacedly stole the upper third of all Mexico. Centuries before Spanish and Mexican boundaries were established, the unbroken expanse of land was defined by Indian migration and trade routes between the prehistoric pueblos of Casas Grandes in Chihuahua and Pueblo Bonito in northwestern New Mexico. It is all one vast continental heartland, a common motherland of our ancestral myths, beliefs, and tongues.

It is traversed by the Sierra Madres, the "Mother Mountains," a continuation of the continental chain. There are two arms: the Sierra Madre Oriental on the east, and the Sierra Madre Occidental on the west, extending down through Chihuahua and Sonora to Durango and Guadalajara and Mexico City. This latter was the vast mountain wilderness that drew me to its heart.

So many years later, it may seem impossible to attempt to evoke the high feelings aroused when, alone on horseback long ago, I first confronted these mystical blue mountains floating on a sea of shimmering waves. Still, there are a few remembered campsites and outposts from that long journey.

As a brash young man, I was well equipped. I carried, strapped on my horse, a canvas duffle-bag filled with a change of clothing, a coffee pot and frying pan, and something to put in them. In my breast pocket was a two-bit, Spanish pocket dictionary. With me was a young boy I hired at the start as a guide. Neither then, nor in all the years afterward, did I carry a gun or a camera.

We made camp one night on the open desert, built a fire, cooked supper, and laid down to sleep. Sometime during the night, I awakened to see my companion sitting upright, eyes wide with fear, staring into the darkness beyond the perimeter of light. I became aware of a circle of horsemen surrounding us.

I rose, stirred up the fire. Upon it, I put the coffee pot and laid out our tin cups. In the flaring light of the flames, the leader of the horsemen dismounted and came to squat beside me. He was a big man, his shirt and weathered chaps black as his stallion. When the coffee was boiling, I poured him and myself a cup. He drank without speaking. Then I offered him a cigarette. When he had smoked it, he asked abruptly, "Where are you going?"

"To Mexico," I answered. "I like your country. I want to see it."

He kicked with his boot a small canvas bag beside the fire. "What's this?"

At that time, it was customary to change American dollars into Mexican silver pesos, and this canvas bag contained all the money I had brought with me. "This is the money I need to travel into Mexico," I answered forthrightly.

The *Jéfe* stood up, the firelight reflecting a sheen from the silver mountings on the gear of his black stallion. "*Pase*. As long as you're in my territory, I'll see you're not molested."

He mounted his stallion, and galloped away with his band of bandits.

Travel was not easy through the sierras. There were few ranchitos, sparse clumps of adobes or brush *jacales*, and they were far apart. The trails between them were not clearly marked, and difficult to follow. To guide me from one to another, I found a small boy or an older man, who could be spared more easily from their work in the family *milpas* of corn. Also, I found, they could be induced to talk—about the plants along the trail, to point out the sites of prehistoric ruins, about anything to break the hours of silence.

There was one drawback. According to tradition, a member of a community, one ranchito, never ventured beyond his own *tierra*, the earth to which he was bound. He had to go back when he reached its limit. So, I progressed slowly. Staying at one ranchito for a day, or several days, until another young boy or man could be induced to lead me to the next. Sometimes a horse would be provided, more often a burro. And sometimes I had to walk.

One ranchito I remember vividly. For several days, I lived in a one-room adobe with a large family until I could find someone to guide me farther. All its members slept on the dirt floor, wrapped in tattered serapes. One day, I returned to this adobe hut after searching for another boy. The woman of the house met me with tears of guilt and contrition. What had happened? During my absence, her small children had opened my canvas bag of silver pesos, rolling them across the dirt floor like cartwheels.

"Mother of God!" she wailed. "I picked them up, one by one. But I cannot count. Perhaps one is missing, and the Señor will think I have stolen it!"

How abjectly poor she was, like all the people in these rugged highlands. The men growing sparse *milpas* of corn on the rocky hillsides, the women grinding the kernels on a stone metate for tortillas which they cooked on a piece of tin laid over an open fire. This was their usual fare, with squash and beans, and on occasion a scrawny hen. The open bag of pesos on the floor was a fortune she had never seen before, and likely would never see again. A single stolen peso would have meant much to her, but her honesty meant more.

One mishap occurred during my journey. I was riding a scrawny mule, and mules are commonly believed to be more sure-footed than horses. On a narrow trail, however, my mule slipped. We plunged down a steep embankment into the rocky arroyo below, the mule falling partly on top of me. The boy with me managed to get the mule off. The mule stood unhurt, but trembling with fright. I lay on the ground unable to get up, my right hip wracked with pain.

Luckily, there was a solitary adobe not far down the arroyo. From it, my companion brought an old straggle-haired Indian woman. Between them, they dragged and carried me to a nearby mud pool, draining from a natural hot-water spring. The old woman wasted no time. She stripped off my clothes, dunked me in the pool to soak, then smeared my hip and legs with hot mud to dry for an hour or two. She then took me into her adobe hut to sleep. For a couple of days, she repeated her treatments: immersing me in the pool, smearing me with mud-packs, giving me herb tea to drink, and feeding me soup, tortillas, and beans until I was able to continue my journey.

Evidently, the accident had dislocated something in my hip joint. Although it didn't bother me too much, the injury remained with me always as a souvenir. Turning over in bed or in the bathtub, the hip seemed suddenly to slip out of joint. Often this occurred when I was walking, my companions being shocked by the strange clicking noise. I would go then to a chiropractor who, yanking my leg, would pull the joint into line. Eventually, the muscles compensated, or adjusted, although my right leg became a trifle shorter than my left. Not until many years later did the old injury catch up with me, manifesting in a slight lameness.

Train travel was also arduous down the west coast. This last "Far West" was a narrow shelf between the wall of the Sierra and the Pacific. It was cut by innumerable rivers like the Yaqui and Mayo, and flooded half the time by swamps and savannas often impassable by meandering dirt roads. The railroad line ran through it from north to south, the train running two or three times a week. The train, which I took at Nogales in 1931, comprised a Pullman car at the rear, a dining car for through passengers to Mexico City, and two second-class coaches whose wooden benches ran lengthwise, the aisles crowded with people, dogs, chickens, a pig or two, and innumerable boxes, crates, and bolsas of woven hemp. Ahead of this human cargo, the train carried a baggage car and a flat car. The unloading and reloading of the baggage car at every remote station necessitated a stop of several hours. These stops served as our mealtimes. Ocote torches and small bonfires lit up the scene. Vendors of meat, beans, and tortillas squatting over their charcoal brasiers, serape sellers parading up and down with their distinctive white, blue, and black Mayo blankets.

The flat car in front was loaded with Mexican soldiers, for there had been another Yaqui uprising and more trouble was expected. These *soldados* contributed little to the feeling of safety they were expected to insure. Most of them were barefoot. Few of them had uniform coats or blouses, and the buttons of these were missing—torn off to exchange for tortillas, revealing naked brown torsos. Swaggering up and down the length of the coaches, they appeared to be no more than backdrop characters in a comic opera.

At the box-car station of Corral, I transferred to a local train that once a week chugged ninety-seven kilometers up along the tortuous Yaqui River into the heart of the rebelling Yaquis. Everyone protested my foolhardiness, but remembering the friendliness of the Yaquis I had previously known, I had no qualms. The train comprised a box car, a flat, and a coach for our seven passengers. At Tonichi, the end of the line, the train stopped on a turn-table. The few of us on board were ferried across the brown, swollen river to the ancient town on its high bluff, marked by a great church. Here a friendly Yaqui took me into his home to stay for a memorable week.

It was my intention to cross over the sierras from Sonora into Chihuahua. Fortunately, I met a small group of friendly Yaquis who promised to supply horses and guide me if I would obtain for them a supply of 30-30-calibre rifle shells. The government had prohibited the sale of arms and ammunition to Yaquis, although they could be bought by an American for hunting. On this pretext, I was able to buy a small supply of shells. We started out. Why at night these Yaquis didn't murder me while I was sleeping, and appropriate the rifle shells, I don't know. But friendly and courteous, they accepted the shells I doled out to them daily for their wages and use of their horses. Passing through Bacanora—a pueblocito that gave its name to a distinctive, brutal drink known throughout these highlands—we finally reached Sahuaripa fronting the crest of the sierras. Here my Yaqui friends persuaded me to give up my trip. Crossing the divide into Chihuahua would take a well-equipped pack train of many men and animals. So I returned to Corral to wait for the next main-line train south.

In Mexico City, I wanted to visit the historic Aztec village of Tepotztlan, far south. To reach it from Cuernavaca would require a long horseback ride. I was advised to take a train from Mexico City to El Parque in the mountains above Tepotztlan. This I did. El Parque was a flag-stop to pick up charcoal prepared by the Indians below. The station comprised only a box-car and a shed to protect the charcoal from the driving rain. It was late afternoon, and the place was deserted, save for a single Indian with a burro haltered with a piece of rope. With my duffle-bag on its back, we descended the precipitous cliff wall on foot for two hours to the village below.

Tepotztlan was dark when we arrived, and I paid my companion seventy-five cents for conducting me. There was no hotel, or *casa de huespedes*, where I could obtain food or lodging, so he took me to his one-room hut. It was crowded with his wife and children, several chickens, and a roaming pig. But here on the floor, I was welcome to wrap up in my serape. Hardly had I lain down before the señora objected; she seemed as circumspect and socially conscious as a New England hostess. Her humble home was not suitable for a visiting Imperialisimo Yanqui. So, she drove her husband and me across the dark plaza to a great building more suitable as a *casa de huespedes*.

The woman who let us in said there was only one available room across the patio. It was an immense room with a fifteen-foot-high ceiling, used as a corn storage room. It had to be emptied of its huge mountain of corn, the floor swept and washed. Then a mammoth Spanish bedstead was brought in, and covered with a petate to lie upon, and a serape to cover me. A candle was lit, and a book of prayers printed in Spanish was spread out in the light. Only then, long after midnight, was the room opened for me as an honored guest.

The locations and the names—if they had any—of all these pueblocitos, tiny ranchitos, railroad way stations, and camp-sites, I don't remember. They all resolve into a kaleidoscopic picture with a backdrop of mysterious blue picachos, abysmal canyons and gorges, and the vivid faces and hands illumined by firelight. How courteous and generous were these few people scattered throughout the sierras. They shared sleeping room on their dirt floors, mended my torn serape, gave me their tortillas and beans, their friendship.

Many years later, I drove down to the sierra wilderness of Chihuahua with Brice Sewell, an Indian trader, and Jose Abeyta, the aging Indian *cacique* of San Juan Pueblo in New Mexico. We drove west of Chihuahua City to the end of the road at the 300-year-old town of Guerrero. There we obtained the services of Umberto Frias, a young truck driver, to drive us farther into the sierras. We needed him. The road, if such it could be called, was unmarked, crossing river fords, and climbing the seemingly impassable and interminable mountain ranges. In low gear, double-clutching to inch the axles over high rocky centers, Umberto reached the crest of one range only to confront another. Fording streams and rivers demanded an agony of effort. The car would sink in icy water, requiring all of us to strip off our pants and shoes, jack up the car under water, and then pry it out with poles. Not until we crossed the Continental Divide did we see any sign of life, save an infrequent *jacal* fronting a *milpa* of squaw corn. This was the crest of the Sierra Madre, almost opposite Sahuaripa, which I had wanted to cross years before. Its high forested ranges, rocky gorges, and deep canyons would have been impassable for us on horseback without adequate supplies.

Just below the Divide lay Bacoyna, a frontier settlement where we siphoned gas from a huge storage tank and ate tortillas, beans, and eggs in an adobe where chickens ran across the floor. We might have been back home in the Navajo and Hopi country of a century ago.

Late that afternoon, we reached Sisoguichi, a Jesuit mission established here in the wilderness heartland of some sixty thousand Tarahumaras, the most remote and primitive tribe left in Mexico. Ours was the first passenger car to enter Sisoguichi, and the eighty-five-mile drive had taken us eleven hours. There was no room in the mission compound to accommodate us, but a hospitable Tarahumara woman outside gave us a supper of more tortillas, beans, and eggs, and a room in which to spread our sleeping bags. Here we helplessly gave ourselves up to the swarm of fleas.

It had been our hope to drive to Creel, and thence to the brink of the great maze of five canyons collectively known as the Barranca de Cobre, deeper and longer than the mile-deep and 283-mile-long Grand Canyon of the Colorado. But the indiscernible, tortuous road bestrewn with rocks and boulders was impassable. Wearily, we turned back, hoping to reach Guerrero before the car burned out. Not until another few years later did I finally descend into the Barranca by muleback.

The presence of Jose Abeyta with his long hairbraids and little medicine pouch of buckskin worn at his breast, however, opened a door to the Tarahumaras for us. Wary of the mission padres, they told us of their people's customs, beliefs, and ceremonies, and of their ancestral home along the Rio Papigochic near Guerrero where we would find their ancient inscriptions on the cliff walls.

We arrived, at last, safely back at Guerrero to meet a treasured friend of mine, Guillermo Gonzales. He was a descendant of the immensely wealthy and aristocratic Amaya family, which once owned the great hacienda near Santo Tomas some miles away. Driving us there, he proudly showed us the ruins of the private Amaya chapel, known as the Amaya Cathedral or the Templo de Nuestra Señora de Guadalupe, which had been built by Sr. D. José Francisco Amaya before his death in 1873. How ghastly was the ruin! The single bell tower of adobe bricks still rose above the pink stone facade. But the twelve-foot-high carved doors sagged on their hand-wrought iron hinges. Inside, the wall murals of angels with blue wings surrounded by white doves were still visible but falling down in huge chunks. The crypt in which Sr. Amaya and his wife had been buried had been built of Italian Carrera marble brought by muleback from Vera Cruz. Their remains had been moved to the Santo Tomas cemetery, and the tomb was now a gaping hole. The sacristy was littered with other holes dug by treasure hunters; and through the gaping hand-carved doors wandered pigs, rooting up the floor.

The Mexican Revolution, during which all the Amaya land had been confiscated and the chapel destroyed, was a fact no one could deny. On the way back, we all drank to it with a crowd of campesinos at a country cantina.

Next day, Guillermo drove us to the distant Rio Papigochic where it made a great curve around a cliff wall. This, as we had been told in Sisoguichi, had been the ancestral home of the Tarahumaras before they retreated to their remote mountain barrancas—Citahuichic, the ancient "Place of Reunion." The faces of the cliffs and boulders along the bank of the river were engraved with carven petroglyphs and symbols. We were all fascinated, especially José, who made a number of drawings of them.

Then, Guillermo pointed out a ranch down-river which he thought might interest us. My first look at it recalled a strange story told me years previously by an elderly German in Taos. He had met there, when young, a poor German immigrant, who through an intimate association with Pancho Villa, the Mexican revolutionist, had become mysteriously rich. Establishing a great ranch there, he had become even more rich. For in the sierras above, he had discovered a rich lode of gold. The location, which he kept secret, was too remote and inaccessible for him to pack out the ore by muleback. So he bought a plane to bring it out.

Such stories of secret gold bodies and hidden treasures one can hear anywhere in Mexico. There was, in fact, a mountain range not far off which had a curious formation known as *El Leon de Minaca*. This "lion" reputedly guarded a great treasure buried by early Spaniards during an Indian uprising and which had not yet been found. I discounted completely the story told me in Taos until I saw the great ranch house and happened to remember the name of Heimpel, its fabulous owner. The world is a small place after all, as someone observed long ago, and eventually its places and persons somehow connect in our minds.

This Rancho de San Pedro confirmed everything I'd heard about it. The immense hacienda was unbelievable—a German-style monstrosity of poor taste, surrounded by 4,188 *hectares* (about 10,000 acres) of land. On this were grazed large herds of cattle, and grown corn and wheat. The present owner, Ricardo Heimpel, son of the founder, lived in Chihuahua with his family, making frequent trips to the ranch. Luckily, he was there when we arrived. He showed us a private bull ring and the remains of his father's plane and the rusted machinery used to refine the ore. Where the secret gold lode in the sierras was, he did not know. Then he conducted us through the great house, painted white with a garish green trim. The billiard room was seventy-five feet long, containing a fountain in the center. Mounted on the walls were the horns of more than thirteen hundred deer and antelope. The immense dining room was hung with dozens of signed photographs of Francisco Villa and his wife Luz, and plastered with Villa bank notes. There were countless other rooms.

How this great hacienda came into being, he then explained. His father, Gerardo Heimpel, had arrived in Mexico as a poor German immigrant in 1902, and settled in Chihuahua to make his living by small trade. One night, a neighboring woman brought him a gold bar for which she wanted its equivalent in money. She refused to tell him where it had come from, and said she had been instructed not to take it to a bank. Heimpel gave her the exchange, promising to tell no one of the transaction. A few nights later, she brought over Francisco Villa. He had been short-changed by other go-betweens before, and was impressed by Heimpel's honesty. They became close friends. As the Mexican Revolution got under way, Villa appointed Heimpel as the purchasing agent for all the arms to supply his Dorados, his elite troops.

Heimpel imported the rifles from Germany. The shipments were of course known to the federal government, which also bought rifles. All the Federalistas' rifles were numbered. Those supplied the Villistas were without numbers, so that the government could not learn how many were being supplied to the revolutionists.

El Rancho de San Pedro, which Heimpel established as his headquarters, became for a time Villa's base of operations. Here, remote in a veritable wilderness, he quartered his carefully picked Dorados who supplied themselves with meat from hundreds of deer and antelope, hanging their horns in the immense billiard room. Here, too, Villa hid to recuperate after the only time he was shot.

The revolution required a lot of money. Villa, desperate to pay his troops, began to print his own paper banknotes and named Heimpel as his treasurer. The currency was commonly accepted by people in the region as payment for horses, hay, and provisions. Printing and storing of it at the ranch became a major task.

Ricardo Heimpel had many amusing stories to tell as he conducted us through the immense ranch house. The great dining room was papered with $14 million in Villa banknotes. In a private office were stacked uncounted millions more on the floor. When, as a boy, he had committed an inexcusable prank, his punishment was to count it; $7 million was the limit of his patience. Beyond this *oficina* were other secret rooms and closets filled from floor to ceiling with more stacks of banknotes.

Looking at these worthless millions, I remembered my few silver pesos a poor hill woman had wept over, believing her children had lost some. I was reminded, too, of the continuous cycles of war, revolution, and inflation bankrupting governments the world over, making their currency worthless. Could it be, I wondered, that the only real medium of exchange was an ear of grain, and the one enduring value was the patch of living land that gave it birth?

This hard fact the tribes of Indian America have always known. It reflects their deep reverence for their Mother Earth. And, of course, it was the cause for the revolution in Mexico.

The significant "revolution" was not the political revolt against Spain in 1810 which achieved Mexico's independence. It was the revolt in 1910 by the preponderant Indian peoples against White European control.

"Land and Liberty!" Liberty from absentee landlords, the domination of European culture, the tyranny of American "dollar diplomacy." Restoration to the eighty-percent Indian population of the land held by feudal *hacendados*, the Church, and United States industrialists. Throughout all Mexico this grass-roots revolution erupted under Villa in the north, Zapata in the south, and Felipe Carillo Puerto in Yucatán. Under these great revolutionaries, Porfirio Diaz was driven out, Huerta fled, Carranza was killed, and the country was swept by one of the bloodiest revolutions in history. It was followed by the agrarian reforms of Indian presidents Calles and Cardenas, and the renaissance of Indian art by Diego Rivera, Orozco, Goita, and Sigueiros. How wonderful and exciting were these results of the revolution and the awakened pride of the whole country in its natural heritage.

How much has changed in the half-century since then! The American tide of progress has swept down the West Coast. Guaymas and Mazatlán are beset by so many huge luxury hotels and modern resort motels that they resemble the famous Strip of Las Vegas. Small towns and villages I once had known have grown into large commercial or industrial centers; the dirt roads are now paved highways swarming with mammoth semi-trucks. Mexico City with ten million population is fast growing into what may become the largest city in North America. Into it are pouring hordes of people from the countryside, people displaced from their land by agri-business and multi-national development corporations. Unable to find jobs, thousands of them are illegally migrating as "wetbacks" into the United States.

Only throughout southern Mexico and the highlands of Guatemala does one see a land and people which have not yet been engulfed by modern civilization. The people are preponderantly barefoot Indians, still tilling the land by hand or by oxen, living in scattered adobe or thatched huts surrounding villages in which they mass on market days.

One sees them best in the mountain village of Chichicastenango in Guatemala. Its immense plaza is crowded with thousands of Indians from the mountains and hamlets, carrying on their bent backs loads of fruit and vegetables, firewood, clay pottery, textiles, even pine tables and chairs. All wear their native dress, whose variations designate their own villages. From the steps of the great church of Santo Tomás rise clouds of copal smoke, the sweet-smelling resin which the people burn to accompany their prayers. And inside, the bare interior is filled with more barefoot worshippers kneeling on a floor strewn with wildflower and rose petals, burning candles and more copal.

Chichicastenango on *el día de la plaza* is justly famous and increasingly popular. As tourist brochures state, no other scene in Mesoamerica is so colorful and exciting. One seems transported back to the time of the ancient Mayas.

But beyond its colorful aspect, one senses a deeper reality: the extreme poverty and abject humility of the people. Here in Chichicastenango originated the *Popul Vuh*, the sacred book of the Quiché Maya, the oldest book of the New World. Few of the people today know of its existence, little of the old Mayan gods to whom they pray, nor of the new Christian gods enshrined in the church. They are exiles caught between two worlds. The revolution in Mexico in 1910, with its slogan of "Land and Liberty," meant nothing to them. Under their own dictatorial government, there was no hope of gaining either. So in abject poverty and humility, they endure a life that seems without hope or redemption, still rooted in their enduring, maternal earth. Yet, like other seemingly stagnant pools of humanity, they are moving on the upward climb to rational consciousness. It is the long evolutionary road through many phases taken by all mankind.

Around the globe the Mexican Revolution of 1910 was repeated in China in 1949. The immediate causes seem to have been the same. Land and Liberty! Its meaning may lie deeper; for it resulted, as will be sketched later, in a pattern of life so new and different that it confused the world. Yet it, too, did not last. The inexorable world-wide tide of change caught up with it in 1979. What sweeping changes it will make in the lives of one billion Chinese people, one-fourth of the world's population, no one knows, but certainly the changes will affect us all, East and West alike.

3

The East is Red

China's color in the world spectrum always has been red. Brilliant red as the lacquer-painted pavilions of old; the tissue-wrapped packages of firecrackers we children used to buy for the Fourth of July; and the gorgeous silk streamers waved by crowds massed in the great T'ien An Men Square in modern Peking. Not surprisingly, the title of China's most popular song is "The East Is Red."

China, for me, had always lurked somewhere in that nebulous realm between fact and fancy. A far-off country of heathens wearing pigtails, for whose necessary conversion we dropped pennies in Church missionary boxes. A barbaric land of dread Communists who constituted a threat to all the free and enlightened nations of the world.

What China was actually like, I didn't know until 1976 when I made a month's trip through its mainland in a tour of twenty persons conducted by the U.S.–China Peoples Friendship Association. We traveled from Hong Kong and Kowloon in the south, west to Canton and Kweilin, north in the interior to Peking, and down to Shanghai on the coast. Our itinerary was laid out by China's International Travel Service which supplied three interpreters who accompanied us during the whole trip. At every city where we stopped, a government bus took us out to various sites in the countryside. These included many historic and scenic areas: the Great Wall, the Ming Tombs, the Forbidden City, and by boat up the indescribably beautiful Likiang River winding down to fabled Kweilin between hundreds of sharp-pointed "karst" mountain pinnacles. These views of the past were but icing on the cake. The living present was of more concern: communes, primary and middle schools and universities, hospitals and health clinics, factories, housing developments, stores.

Despite contrasts and contradictions, China gave me a conscious feeling of familiarity, admiration, and an enlarged perspective that greatly enriched my life. Yet the trip evoked a strange, unconscious, and negative reaction when I returned home.

I arrived here with a deep chest cold and cough, only to discover there was no running water in my closed-up house; there had been another electric power failure which had jimmied the water pump. It was two days before I could secure plumbers to restore the water system.

For several days I stayed in bed, completely drained of energy. This physiological discomfort was accompanied by an even worse psychological distress. My own home and its long-familiar surroundings, even the two great mountain peaks—El Cuchillo and the Sacred Mountain—seemed out of focus, without meaning. My maladjustment manifested itself in recurring dreams and nightmares, in which I was surrounded by crowds of Chinese people. Even my bed was so full of people I couldn't turn over. This distressing dream-state showed me how powerfully the psychic influence of a new continent, with its own spirit-of-place, can affect one.

A month later, I related these dreams and nightmares to two Jungian psychologists visiting me from Connecticut. Their own interpretation was pertinent and revealing: the collectivism of New China had so crowded my own individualism I could not turn over in bed.

The word *fanshen*, "turn over," literally means in Chinese "to turn over the body," according to the book *Fanshen* by William Hinton. It meant to millions of landless peasants to stand up, to throw off the yoke of poverty, to become self-reliant with the advent of "Liberation." Hence each village, as it adopted Chinese communism, "turned over," and *fanshen* became the key word in the Revolution.

Apparently then, my nightmarish dreams warned me through the unconscious that I, with my lifelong orientation to individualism, was not yet ready to accept for myself the collectivism of China, however much I consciously admired it.

And this, I think, had been the unconscious reaction of most of us in the Western world to the new People's Republic of China. Our blurred image was still that evoked by McCarthyism: a communist nation intent on enslaving the whole world. To combat this threat, the United States supplied more than $2 billion in military equipment to the Chiang Kai-shek regime before it was driven from the mainland of China to the offshore island of Taiwan. In 1972, President Nixon and Premier Chou En-lai issued the joint Shanghai Communiqué affirming that Taiwan was an inseparable part of China, and that resolution of the Taiwan problem was the internal affair of China, in which no other country had the right to interfere.

Yet, since then, we had poured $1.1 billion more into the effort to maintain the Kuomintang, or Nationalist government. Five new Kuomintang consulates had been opened in the United States, but we still did not have an embassy in the great mainland country of 800 million people.

This was the current United States–China relationship in 1976. It has changed drastically since then. But the following pages, taken from my notes, record my impressions of China as I saw it then.

A vast beautiful land. What struck me immediately was the supreme calm of the landscape everywhere. How strange it was that, after three thousand years of war, internal revolution, rape by foreign powers, the struggle to evict the Chiang Kai-shek forces and Japanese occupation troops, followed by China's revolution, the face of the land still maintained its ageless serenity. It was the same look seen on the placid face of the people. One wondered if the calm of the ancient landscape steadied the people throughout all their bloody human storms, or whether their own imperturbability of soul was reflected by the land itself.

Still, one sensed the everpresent, unseen Dragon of China, whose power flows deep underneath the soil in currents of invisible energy called *lung-mei*, "Paths of the Dragon," once divined by ancient geomancers. One felt the subterranean old Dragon exerting beneath the calm surface an inner power being transmuted into exterior realities.

For hours at a time, we could see from out the train windows great expanses of green rice and wheat tilled by barefoot peasants and water-buffalo, the fields stretching away to mountain foothills themselves terraced for crops. The pinkish dirt roads were unfenced, without signs or billboards. Most of the highways were planted with trees on each side; tree planting was a major government program. How wonderful it was to see this vast ancient land unobstructed by Coca Cola billboards!

Tiny, primitive villages of adobe dwellings appeared, as if transported bodily by a magic carpet from New Mexico or Old Mexico. The great renowned rivers of China unwound one after another, wide brown thoroughfares since antiquity, still carrying traditional junks and sampans and also modern steamships. And on their banks were huge modern cities with populations up to ten millions or more.

There were no privately owned automobiles. The people rode bicycles in silent swarms, flocks, herds on every highway, in every street. Men and women alike wore the same dull blue cotton jackets and trousers. And everyone worked, the women as well as the men driving tractors in the fields, operating lathes in factories, as well as rearing children. All manifested an air of equality with the men without the need for a Women's Liberation Movement, after centuries of having their feet bound and unable to walk, being kept at home as virtual slaves of their fathers, husbands, and landlord masters. We were told there were no beggars, no prostitutes, no drug addicts, no alcoholics.

And the children. One was wholly captivated by the children. Tiny tots lined up, clapping hands to welcome us into the courtyard of the Seven Star Pink Kindergarten in Kweilin, then giving us a program of dance and songs. And again in Peking, at the kindergarten school of a heavy-duty machine plant for babes up to six years old while their mothers were working. In every school, their vitality was impressive. And significantly, all children were being taught English in the third grade.

The old Dragon had uprooted the bones of venerable ancestors to make room for living rice, but it had not abolished the ancient custom of drinking tea. Everywhere we went, tea was served. On trains, in communes, factories, schools, hospitals. Arriving after midnight at Wuhan, we were conducted into the railroad station and served tea. This was followed by another serving of tea when we arrived at the hotel. Next day, we were taken to the spectacular bridge across the nearly mile-wide Yangtze River, the longest main street in China. In a room within one mighty pier, tea was served us again. Even when we were given a ride on Peking's new subway system, the terminal was set with a white tablecloth and we were served tea. Tea—black, green, or red. Always served Chinese-style, without teapots. A spot of tea was simply placed in a large cup into which was poured boiling water, then covered with a porcelain lid. How I loved those great teacups! They were placed in every hotel room, along with a large thermos jug of hot water, so we could make our own.

The regimentation of the people was obvious. The average Chinese had no freedom of movement and little to say about determining his daily life. General living conditions were uniformly low by our standards (which I will sketch later). Yet China did not appear to be the "Slave State" so often pictured. The Chinese smile, courtesy, and friendliness were shown us by crowds everywhere. The people did not betray the stresses and strains of combative competition, the perpetual worry and anxiety reflected in the faces of people on every street corner in the United States.

There seemed to be ample reason for this. Anyone who had known or read of their tragic life before the revolution—slavery by warlords and landowners, abject poverty, widespread starvation forcing sale of children and drowning of new-born babies—could not fail to be impressed by what they had gained since liberation in 1949. Brush shelters along the rivers and shacks

in city ghettos were being replaced by modern housing developments. Work, clothing, schooling, medical care, and most
important, food have been provided.

There may be another, psychological reason. China suggested
what the United States must have been like when the first
thirteen colonies "liberated" themselves from Great Britain in
1776 and unified themselves as a separate nation. The new
People's Republic of China unified twenty-two provinces, five
autonomous regions, and fifty-four nationalities. There was a
feeling of national unity, a sense of direction, which we have
lost.

The unification of China, and its miraculous transformation
in a scant twenty-seven years, was the primary achievement of
one man, the greatest revolutionary of modern times, a ruthless
realist, an almost mystical visionary, a poet, a master of military
strategy, and a consummate politician—Mao Tse-tung. Virtually
deified throughout China, generally feared, hated, and often
reviled in Europe and America, Mao was regarded more as a
symbol than a man. Little was popularly known about him, and
stories of his contradictory character didn't help.

He had died on September 9, just a month before our party
arrived in China. The official mourning period was over, but
huge posters of him were plastered everywhere—on the walls of
railroad stations and airports, in all public buildings, offices,
homes, and on the streets. One saw pictured his sturdy body,
large balding head, and broad-cheeked face, and still wondered
what manner of man he was.

A fuller picture of his life emerged as we were taken to various
places where he had lived, studied, and developed plans for the
Revolution.

Mao was born in 1893 in Hsao-shan, Hunan Province, a lovely
mountain village some two or three hours drive east of Chang-sa.
According to the Party line, Mao's father was a humble peasant.
Actually, he was a landowner and prosperous grain merchant.
Mao's birthplace, a large, sturdy adobe with tiled roof, reminded
me of a Spanish-Colonial hacienda in Mexico. It comprised a
living room, a dining room in whose ceiling I noticed a handmade nest for swallows, several bedrooms, a kitchen, a tool
room, storage room, a milling room containing a foot-controlled

machine for grinding rice, and another for separating the grain from the chaff. How commodious it was!

There was no doubt it had been restored to serve as a national shrine now visited by a million-and-a-half pilgrims each year. On the day we were there, a line of people two blocks long were waiting to file through it.

Here, Mao spent his early childhood. His father believed that five years in primary school were enough for his son. But Mao, when thirteen years old, ran away to Chang-sa to study for twelve years. He then went to Peking where he married, became a Communist, and in 1921 was selected as one of a dozen delegates to the First Congress of the Communist Party.

For the next three years he lived in Chang-sa conducting revolutionary activities at the First Normal School, near Clear Water Pond. Here one could still see the dark and dreary bedrooms, living and work rooms, hung with family photographs.

In 1924, he moved to Canton, converting a Ming Dynasty Confucian temple into the Nationalist Peasant Movement Institute. The architecture and courtyard were still beautiful; but the rooms in which he lived, worked, and taught were furnished with crude, Spartan simplicity.

A few years later, the newly organized Kuomintang, or Nationalist army, began to destroy urban Communist centers. Mao built up an army of peasants in the remote mountains of south-central China. Then began the long, bloody warfare between the two forces. In these bitter years Mao's first wife and sister were captured and beheaded by Kuomintang troops, though he escaped. He married again, his second wife bearing him five children, and a third time, in his middle age, to a young actress.

The Long March in 1934–35 is now legendary. Mao's Red Army, fighting all the way, marched two thousand miles north to Yenan. Of the estimated three hundred thousand ill-clad and under-fed men, less than thirty thousand survived. But Mao had won the loyalty of the people; peasants everywhere organized to support him.

Fourteen more years of struggle followed: the bloody Civil War to drive Chiang Kai-shek's forces to the island of Taiwan, and the War of Resistance against Japan, resulting in the expulsion of all Japanese troops. At last, in 1949, the Army of Liberation marched victoriously into Peking, and on October first proclaimed the united People's Republic of China under Mao's undisputed leadership.

The visual record of Mao's life, the history of the Revolution, and the creation of the People's Republic of China, were recorded in the great museum in Mao's native village of Hsao-shan. Eight huge rooms filled with large photos of him from a smooth-faced youngster and a worried guerilla leader up to his aging years. With them were those of all his family, friends, and associates, as well as scrolls, plaques, sculptures, maps, firearms, and handmade weapons. All complete with dates, statistics, and descriptive texts.

This mass of material gave me a feeling of immediacy of him as an actual man, but he still remained an enigma. The facts about his outer life did not explain his curious obsession in early childhood with the plight of the peasants. Nor did they reconcile the contradictory aspects of his controversial character.

Dictator or demigod, the impress of his thought and will was reflected in every aspect of life throughout China. The rural peasant was the common denominator, the foundation of the nation, in contrast to the urban industrial worker of the Soviet Union. This difference was the reason for the celebrated break in 1961 between China and Russia, both founded on Marxist-Leninist ideology. For in Russia, with its emphasis on industrialization, there emerged a privileged and ruling elite avid for wealth and power which in effect changed Russia from a socialist to a capitalist country. Whereas China under Mao Tse-tung stubbornly adhered to the policy of utilizing the efforts of peasant, trained worker, and intellectual alike. There were no incentives for accumulating personal possessions and gaining individual recognition. All worked only "for the people," a key slogan. And everyone worked.

About eighty percent of China's vast population lived in the countryside, and on its hundreds of communes depended the major task of developing the country. The large one we visited east of Canton comprised 4,000 *hectares* growing rice, wheat, peanuts, sugar cane, and vegetables, and producing 60,000 pigs a year. The commune supported 68,800 peasants living in

13,000 houses—virtually a city. Most houses comprised three rooms, comfortable but austerely utilitarian. Workers were paid on a work-point system conforming to the principle of "from each according to his ability, to each according to his work." The workers averaged 254 *yuan* (about $127) a year. They were allotted grain, furnished with medical care and schooling for their children.

Each commune determined its own needs and originated a development project which was approved by its Revolutionary and Party Committees. The brigades and teams then carried out the work. They had—like the oft-quoted example of Taichai in Shansi province—converted barren hills into fertile fields, dug irrigation ditches by hand, built aqueducts, canals, bridges, and power plants.

Emphasizing that the national economy was keyed to agriculture, "May 7 Cadre Schools," called "reform labor concentration camps" by our American press, had been established. The Chinese used the word "cadre" to designate any person holding an administrative post in the country. In the Cadre Schools, such persons in government, industry, and education spent six months every five years doing manual work with the peasants by day and studying at night the Marxist-Leninist-Mao doctrine. The one near Wuhan we visited had some five hundred intellectuals and officials being re-educated in socialism—"retaining the sweat of hard work but washing away bourgeois dirt." They included directors of factories, principals of schools, public administrators, and the writer of a history of China.

Light industry was a secondary, supporting factor to agriculture. Farm equipment, tractors, plows, tools were desperately needed to replace the labor of peasants tilling the fields and picking cotton by hand. Heavy industry followed in importance. Industrialization, now centered in large cities, posed a severe problem of pollution. Canton, Kweilin, Chang-sa, Wuhan, Peking, and Shanghai were blanketed with smoke. Even from our fifteenth-story balcony in the modern, luxurious Peking Hotel, sight of the rising sun was obscured by a gray curtain. Yet no steps had been taken to solve this growing problem.

Life in the city was austere as in the country. Shanghai with a population of nearly eleven million was a major industrial center containing one-and-a-half million workers. The city was divided into barrios or neighborhoods, each supervised by a Neighborhood Revolutionary Committee whose members were chosen from the community. At higher levels were the District Revolutionary Committee, the Shanghai Revolutionary Committee, and the Party Committee. The highest authority was the Central Committee of the Communist Party of eight million members. Plans for local projects were referred to a higher committee which passed down suggestions for discussion. The result was then sent up to higher authorities for approval. The emphasis was on full discussion and participation of the workers in planning and management, as in the communes.

The Supai neighborhood was formerly waste land. Now it supported 56,000 population, with 13,200 families housed in huge, modern apartments. One apartment was occupied by a family of four, all working, and receiving a total income of 270 *yuan* monthly ($135). They paid only 24 *yuan* rental a month, and food averaged about 100 *yuan*.

Living conditions in Peking were comparable. The "Temple of the Moon" Neighborhood Revolutionary Committee covered 110,000 population comprising 24,000 households. One apartment of four rooms accommodated a couple and four children, two of them working. Their total income was 170 *yuan* a month, allowing them to go to a movie at a cost from 5 to 20 *yuan*, and to buy a radio for 80 *yuan*.

In a second apartment of two rooms lived a sewing woman retired at seventy percent of her salary (38 *yuan*), her husband, who worked in a meat factory, and one of their five children. Their total income was 130 *yuan* a month. Rental of their two rooms cost 8 *yuan*, electricity and water 2 *yuan*, and food about 20 *yuan* per person per month. Hence, their combined living expenses amounted to about 100 *yuan*, permitting them to save 30 *yuan*.

All these housing developments were huge, modern, and comfortable, with gas and running water in every apartment, but depressingly utilitarian. Save for the ever-present photograph of Mao, there were no pictures on the walls, no calendar prints such as enliven the simplest adobe huts in our own Southwest, no books, not even a geranium potted in a tin can at the window.

The great hospitals further illustrated how China, a Third World country, was trying to pull itself up by the bootstraps. The 500-bed general hospital at Canton, affiliated with the Sun Yat Sen Medical College, served the area for treatment of patients, research, and teaching. About 15 percent of the personnel trained peasants, workers, and soldiers at the grassroots level to go out into the country where no doctors are available. There were 1,300,000 of these "barefoot doctors," so called because the first young people with only a few months' medical training worked barefoot in remote villages and paddy fields, treating minor ailments and giving immunizations. In the larger 800-bed Wuhan Medical College Hospital 40 percent of its staff of 1,100 doctors and medical workers had been barefoot doctors, and all doctors were required to spend time in the country as barefoot doctors themselves, combining theory and practice.

Therapeutic acupuncture was commonly used for such ailments as thrombosis, rheumatic heart, and rheumatism. We saw rows of patients lying fully dressed on cots, pants and sleeves rolled up, to reveal the needles inserted in their legs and arms. We witnessed two acupuncture anaesthesia operations for thyroid tumors in the throat, the patients being conscious throughout, and one for a brain tumor. Save for a preliminary mild sedation, no anaesthetic was given the latter patient before the acupuncture needles were inserted in leg, arm, and thumb, and electrically vibrated for about fifteen minutes. The medical doctors in our group were surprised at seeing the surgeons sawing through the skull by hand; in the United States this would have been accomplished electrically in a moment. Nevertheless, they were impressed by the skill of the surgeons. The patient, a young woman of twenty-three, was conscious throughout the ordeal. We were happy to learn that her egg-sized tumor was benign and that she would recover within a week. The expense of her operation was, of course, borne by the government.

Instruction on family planning was given in all health clinics. In order to lower the two-percent birth rate of China's enormous population, the government actively discouraged a woman from marrying until she was 25, and a man until he was 28, and recommended that they limit their family to two children. Contraceptives were given free to married women, none to single women. Large charts on the wall listed the many methods used and the numbers issued. Abortions were also given. Pre-marital sex was said to be uncommon, and inhibition of the sex instinct assertedly resulted in no neurotic tendencies. The reason given was that sex was not given the widely-advertised, prominent role it plays in the United States.

The great advances made in providing the huge population with food, housing, clothing, schooling, and medical care had not yet been extended to other fields.

In the Revolutionary Committee's Arts and Crafts School outside Shanghai 380 students were being trained in jade, wood, and ivory carving, needlework, embroidery, tapestry, and furniture-making. The jade carving especially was superb, but the subjects were quite different from the ancient motifs of flowers, dragons, pavilions, and the phoenix. One piece depicted a worker climbing a telephone pole to make repairs. The subject and the exquisite jade from which it was being carved seemed a bit incongruous. When questioned about this, the teacher replied that when politics change, art should change. Socialist art was meant to serve the people, not an elite minority, thus portraying their life, the revolutionary movement. It preserved the essence, discarding the decadent values of an outmoded system.

The main purpose of the school, he explained, was to train students in the development of social consciousness. To this end, talented young people about the age of eighteen were selected and admitted to the school, where for five years they studied the Marx-Mao doctrine and the history and theory of art, combined with practical work and physical labor. They then became teachers or were assigned another work.

Notable art was still being produced, like the exquisite silks woven in Kweilin, but only for export. There were no free and independent professional artists—composers, writers, painters, sculptors—as there are in America. All were restricted to expressing the political ideology.

In education, as in art, political dedication was paramount. Much as I admired the kindergarten schools, the five-year primary schools, and the five-year middle schools, I was disconcerted by the process by which graduating students were admitted to colleges and universities. A middle-school graduate must serve two years in a commune, factory, or the army before he applied for admission to a university. His application must first be recommended by the "masses," the peasants, workers, or soldiers with whom he had been living, and then approved by the local revolutionary committee. The decision to admit him was not made on the basis of his scholastic qualifications, but on his "political consciousness"—whether he was completely dedicated to working "for the people" rather than his own interests, and advancing the cause of socialism. The brighter students who were often eliminated in favor of those who expressed a firmer belief in the ideology were then assigned to the peasants, the industrial workers, or the army. The purpose of this process was to prevent the emergence of an intellectual elite, and to promote the gradual cultural development of the masses.

How valid was this to the individual? One answer was given us when we visited Hunan University outside of Wuhan. The many buildings were situated on top of a hill, reached by a steep climb up four flights of stone stairs. Washed by rain, their Chinese-style sloping roofs of jade-green and red tiles glistened with color. We attended several classes, and were then given a briefing by members of the faculty.

The sixty-year-old university, we were told, now had twelve hundred teachers and maintained eight departments, two branch schools, and three agricultural farms, and tied in with a hundred communes. Class work was alternated with field work, following an "open door" policy of work, study, and teaching. Every male professor spent six months every five years in a May 7 Cadre School renewing his relationship with the land and the peasants.

It was a cold, rainy afternoon. The talks were dull, and the tea was cold. Then came the most emotional impact I received in China. A teacher was called upon to speak. She was a Chinese woman about sixty years old, who had been educated in a missionary college and then sent to Columbia University in New York for three years. Here she became familiar with American literature classics, and especially loved Mark Twain's *Huckle-*

berry Finn. Shortly after Liberation in 1949, she had returned to China to teach at Hunan University.

Mao Tse-tung's communism confused her and posed a psychological problem. She could not accept it at first. All her friends and the Party leaders, rather than condemning her, were patient and understanding. They gradually taught her the doctrine of Maoistic socialism. Her final acceptance of the need for submerging her individual egoistic self in the greater life of all the people must have been a difficult experience to live through.

Her moving testimonial, equivalent to the confession of a religious conversion, affected all of us. Many of our group recorded her on tapes, interviewed and photographed her. I myself did not bother to record all the dates and details. I didn't even record her name. For it seemed to me that she was anonymously speaking for all people everywhere who will in time supersede class, national, and racial differences as members of one united brotherhood of man. Her sad, tragic face still haunts me. It mirrored the struggle of one who consciously dedicated herself to this greater role.

Her testimonial raised the question of religion in China. The stock answer to every question about religion was that every Chinese was free to choose any religion, but he was also free to choose none. The government, however, had expropriated all property owned by religious denominations. We were told that while a few small groups met in private homes, there were no missionary Christian churches, no Buddhist and Confucius temples, no Taoist shrines. They had been converted into schools, utility buildings, museums, or historical sites. Hence there was no common orthodox religion. Its place had been supplanted by Maoistic communism.

Mao himself was practically deified. Photographs of him were everywhere—in homes, public buildings, and on the streets; and the Little Red Book of his sayings was studied and quoted assiduously as a Bible. It was impossible to believe that 800 million Chinese were as wholly dedicated as the sensitive woman teacher mentioned above. It seemed more reasonable to assume they accepted Maoism as a regimented people under strict government control. But if only a small percentage of them were dedicated to higher principles, how much they were accomplishing.

L.S. Stavrianos in his book *The Promise of the Coming Dark Ages* quoted a Jesuit priest as saying that "Maoism presents the theologian with a baffling problem: how to account for so numerous a people engaging in such a widespread practice of virtues which in the West have been traditionally associated with religious belief and practice." Chinese religious philosophy has a long history. It produced as early as the eighth century the great *I Ching* or *Book of Changes*; the *Chin Ten Chiao*, the *Book of Life*, now known as the *Secret of the Golden Flower*, and the *Tao Te Ching*, the mystical teachings of Lao Tzu. Hence it seemed inconceivable that the soil and soul of China should now have become too barren to produce another shoot, another flower. If Maoism was indeed such, did it reflect any elements of the religions China had known in the past?

Confucianism was presently condemned on the grounds that it upheld the feudalistic dominance of a bureaucratic elite, with its reliance on rational knowledge and rigid social structure. Buddhism, introduced into China during the first century, was equally rejected, but it may have had a firmer archetypal hold. One of its oldest doctrines is that an enlightened Buddhist vows not to achieve Buddhahood and final release into Nirvana until all other human beings are freed from the Wheel of Life. To this end, he returns through countless reincarnations as a Bodhisattva in order to guide others on the Noble Eight-Fold Path. So too does Christianity, later introduced, embrace the ideal of the brotherhood of all mankind. Taoism, China's oldest religion, was based on the ultimate, undefinable reality, Tao, the "Way" of all the cosmic forces of the universe, in heaven as on earth. Its intuitive wisdom derived from observation of the cyclical changes and transformations of nature. On a temporal level, Red China had abolished all these religions, yet archetypal concepts and unconscious influences may have persisted.

The age-old endeavor of all world religions has been to change the world and man. The high aim of Mao seems to have coincided with this goal. "History has set us a great task," he said, "not only to know the world, but to transform it."

But man alone cannot contrive these collective transformations by the exercise of temporal power. Some transcendental influence from higher powers that direct the evolution of all life must dictate these disruptive changes in the earth itself and in the spirit of man. Only then do his inner realities manifest themselves in a new order of intelligence, new religious forms and social structures. This has happened over and over again in successive civilizations throughout world history. And this may be the real meaning of all revolutions, of evolution itself, the continuous evolution of consciousness. We might believe, then, that this great change in the life of the Chinese people may have indicated a much higher goal than that of a solely materialistic philosophy.

This is why it was so arresting to read the comments of Henry Kissinger on his last interview with Mao. The aging Chairman, an admitted atheist, projected no material vision of China's future, but asserted that he had created "a new world," a "spiritual thing." Increasingly, he spoke of "being called by God" to his great mission.

However the reference may be interpreted, the transcendental powers of destiny had tapped him on the shoulder for his great role.

As I have already mentioned, Mao died on September 9, 1976, hardly a month before our party arrived in China. Everywhere we went there was an air of subdued tension, rumors of a plot to seize power, and of the selection of a new Party chairman. In Wuhan, the streets were crowded with processions carrying red silk banners and portraits of Mao, with an occasional poster of Hua Kuo-feng, premier and first vice-chairman of the Communist Party. The scuttlebutt was that he was to be appointed Mao's successor. This was not confirmed by our interpreters, but clearly something was in the wind.

Excitement was at peak when we arrived in Peking at six o'clock on the morning of October 24th. After breakfast, we were hurried to the lovely Summer Palace of the Empress Dowager, deposed during the Boxer Rebellion. On the drive back to the city, there was no denying that a momentous occasion was imminent. The highways and tributary roads were filled with marching columns four-abreast, carrying large posters of Mao and Hua Kuo-feng, waving red banners, beating drums and clashing cymbals. It was then that our official interpreters confirmed the rumors of the selection of Hua Kuo-feng. The public announcement was to be made that afternoon, and our group was invited to attend it.

By official directive, our bus was admitted into a reserved parking place, and we were conducted to standing room below the Gate of Heavenly Peace overlooking the great T'ien An Men Square, which may be the largest in the world. Two other visiting groups joined us, French and British. The square below was packed solid with a crowd estimated to be from a million to a million-and-a-half people. All listened in silence, in a chill wind, to two hours of speeches from five officials on the reviewing balcony. Each speech was unutterably dull: repetitious reviews of the Party line, followed by accusations against the "Gang of Four" revisionists who had tried to usurp the power of the Party, and ending with diatribes against the two chief enemies of China—the militaristic Soviet Union and the imperialistic United States. Mimeographed copies of the speeches translated into English had been distributed to us; and a Chinese beside me insisted on reading each to me out loud, line by line. He assured me that Chinese opposition to the capitalistic and imperialistic United States was directed solely to the federal government, not to the American people. Hua Kuo-feng then spoke as the new Chairman.

This was a signal occasion in China's long history, and we were fortunate to attend. I had never seen so impressive a sight as this vast, packed mass of humanity. Who could consciously assess the emotional impact of a million or more people so orderly, patient, and silent? Or deny the visual impact of their thousands of waving red silk banners? Surely some of this vast multitude I carried home to plague me in my dreams and to crowd me in my bed.

The revisionist "Gang of Four" included Mao's widow, Chiang Ching. Their power base had been Shanghai. When we arrived there a week later, the immense industrial city of almost eleven million people seemed so volatile I hesitated to light a match for fear the whole city would explode. Popular resentment against the Gang of Four was in full blossom. Day and night endless columns of marchers paraded through the streets waving red banners, carrying posters, beating drums and cymbals. On every corner throngs of workers stood staring at caricature drawings of each of the four posted on the walls. Those of Madame Chiang Ching were especially vindictive. They portrayed her as the Empress Dowager of the old regime, a harlot, and an American capitalist in high button shoes wielding a long cigarette holder.

Evidently, there was much truth in them. A third-rate actress whom Mao married when she was 24 (and he 54), she rose to prominence and power during the Cultural Revolution in the 1960s when she dictated proletarian art forms on the stage and screen. Personally, however, she was reported to have had a decided love of bourgeois American films, especially those of Greta Garbo, Chaplin, and violent Westerns. These, she asserted, should be reserved only for private showing to privileged leaders like herself, but not to the ignorant masses. The differentiation of herself from the people was of course contrary to Maoism, and was soon detected by the general population. Widely disliked, she was regarded as an ambitious, power-hungry, modern Empress. Hence her move toward power with her three Shanghai revisionists, upon the death of Mao, was viewed throughout China as a betrayal of Maoism. Now they had been ousted from the Party and were under house arrest, and Hua Kuo-feng had been selected as the new leader of China.

Stavrianos, already quoted, believed that "the present decline of Western civilization is creating the matrix for another sort of rebirth in which Third World countries may soon take the lead"; and suggested that "if Maoism prevails, China will profoundly influence future global trends, not as a blueprint for others to copy but as a precedent indicating what is possible for human society."

The negative American view of New China as a "Slave State" was countered by the Chinese view that the United States more closely occupied that role. Our people were dominated by corporate finance which manipulated all the country's wealth and its organs of opinion. Multi-national corporations created consumer demand through aggressive sales promotion in all media, constantly speeding up the manufacture of material goods, and ever-increasing our passive peonage to "things." The unremitting drive to increase production necessitated the exploitation of natural resources in the underdeveloped Third World countries. And this, the Chinese believed, had now resulted in the capitalism of the United States emerging into imperialism, the stage in which it was endeavoring to dominate the economic life of the world.

It seems certain that any expansionist drive by one nation toward consuming the natural resources of others is doomed to eventual failure. It is as disastrous to the consuming power as it is to the undeveloped countries drained of their means of growth. We are already becoming uneasily aware that Western civilization, with its unrestrained greed for personal power and material possessions, has almost run its course. A gluttonous society choking itself to death on its own refuse, it offers the world no new hope for the future.

New China may indeed have posed an example for all undeveloped Third World countries, and shown to the Free World countries, with their unbridled self-interest, that a better utilization of the world's wealth for the common good of all peoples lies in the future of mankind.

This was my reaction to China in the fall of 1976. It resulted, of course, from a favorable picture given us by our official tour guides, eliminating the dire poverty of remote villages, withholding from us signs of underground unrest, news of sporadic revolts put down by the Red Guards, and denying reports of torture of groups of dissidents. Despite doubts and criticism, I think my overall favorable impressions were shared by other members of our group, which included prominent economists, university professors, psychologists and medical doctors, and a member of the World Bank. They all expressed admiration and a lift of spirit from the wholly new and different lifestyle they had seen. Whether it was wholly enforced, or could endure as an organic growth, it presented a new ideal for the aspiration of all peoples.

How different is the picture today! Only the inexorable law of change asserted in China's own ancient *I Ching*, the *Book of Changes*, can account for her sudden change of polarity. For on January 1, 1979, diplomatic relations between China and the

United States were established after three decades of estrangement.

With this emergence from isolation and self-sufficiency, China opened herself to world trade in goods and ideas. This "Great Leap Outward," or the "New Long March" to propel China into the modern world by the year 2000, has been undertaken under the slogan of "Four Modernizations"—of agriculture, industry, science and technology, and defense. Trade agreements have been made with the United States and other countries. Restrictions on foreign books, films, and tourist travel have been lifted. Hua Kuo-feng has been replaced. Renunciation of Mao's doctrine is under way, and Mao Tse-tung himself is undergoing a period of debunking. This loosening of governmental control seems constructive. For as the vast human resources of China are developed along with her natural resources, there are certain to emerge individuals with cultural and spiritual values unrecognized and not permitted expression under Maoism.

Nevertheless, there are many grievous questions lurking behind this pretty picture. Is China too about to be engulfed in the world-encompassing materialism? Will chains of modern resort hotels for tourists, highway billboards, Wild West movies, hot dogs and TV dinners, and panty hose change the people? The civilization of China is so ancient, has undergone so many cycles of change, one wonders if the present about-face will be as complete as it seems. Or whether China will in time outgrow this phase as it has outgrown Maoism, and assert in a new form the fundamental aspirations of all humanity.

My mountain slopes mirror these reflections today. The blood-red sunset glow on El Cuchillo and the Sacred Mountain seems to merge into the sunrise red of New China. And in the effulgent light of a fading era, it seems to me that both China and our America today are entering still another great evolutionary transition ultimately beyond human control. As these followed one another in the long past, new civilizations rose out of old ones, and man's own consciousness expanded to a greater awareness of his role in the universe.

We are already feeling the tug of an invisible tide of change moving away from the superficial divisions which separate classes, nations, and races; moving towards their eventual fusion into one cohesive pattern. This change in direction we sense in our uneasy hearts and worried minds as we recognize more clearly the role China is beginning to play in the world at large.

4

America: A Footnote

Whatever can be said about Western civilization is no more than a footnote in the countless volumes expounding, pro and con, its confusing nature and unpredictable future. By Western civilization we mean, of course, its full flower and greatest power, our America, the United States.

The nature of the world and man as perceived by the great civilizations of the past in Egypt, India, Tibet, China, and Mexico have already been briefly outlined. What impresses us is the similarity of their views. All assert the inherent wholeness of man and his oneness with the universe. Their religious-philosophical systems, primary as some of them might appear or as developed into a comprehensive "sacred science" far beyond the purely mechanistic sciences of today, were based upon universal laws. They were concerned with the development of man's inner being rather than his outer daily life.

Modern spokesmen adhere to the same belief—Schwaller de Lubicz, Jung, Wilhelm, Evans-Wentz, Wachsmuth, Gurdjieff, Ouspensky, and Collin, all the many others I have quoted. They are a small minority, indeed, whose quiet voices are generally ignored. As is their conviction that man replicates the structure and functions of the universe, is susceptible to the cosmic laws that govern the rhythms of nature and the movements of the heavenly bodies, and so inherently reflects the harmonic unity of the universal whole.

In direct opposition is the dogmatic view predominant throughout our materialistic and rationalistic Western civilization whose tentacles are enwrapping the entire globe. It asserts the obsessive belief in economic progress, whose sole objective is to continually increase the Gross National Product. This reflects the assumption that man alone is the arbiter of his destiny, and that modern Western society is the culmination of all his past achievements.

We cannot indict this ruling assumption and its outmoded values without acknowledging the remarkable accomplishments of our highly developed rational consciousness and the technological achievements of modern science. They have served the real purpose of enabling us to comprehend more fully the intuitive truths gained in the past and to envision those areas to be explored in the future.

Modern Western physics is investigating the interrelationships between all constituents of matter. It has abandoned the mechanistic view that matter is comprised of independent "building blocks" of nature—molecules, atoms, electrons, protons, and other sub-atomic particles too infinitesimally small to be observed. As material entities, they do not exist; they are forms of energy. The great physicist Niels Bohr is often quoted as saying, "Isolated particles are abstractions, their properties being definable only through their interaction with other systems." All that is known about them is achieved by projecting them at extremely high speeds in a high-energy particle accelerator to a target area or "bubble chamber." Here they collide with other particles, leaving tracks which are photographed. The properties of the particles are then deduced from a mathematical analysis with the help of computers.

These invisible sub-atomic particles have been said to be only products of theoretical reasoning; and that the physicist's view of nature is not that of nature itself, but merely constructed from his own human postulations. The physicist conducting the experiment is not detached from the "objects" he observes; his own consciousness is involved as a participant rather than as an objective observer. All barriers between the observer and the observed, subject and object, are extinguished. The known and unknown, and the very process of knowing, are fused into one undifferentiated whole. This calls to mind the *I Ching*'s oracular readings which result when one throws coins to obtain a hexagram. For in the very act of throwing the coins, there is interjected the psychical state of the questioner which coincides with the physical events outlined by the text.

In light of the scientific concept of our participation in all the phenomena of the world of matter, the complete universe appears to be formed not of separate entities, but is a web of relationships between interconnected parts of a unified whole. Such a concept coincides with the premise of Eastern metaphysics that all things perceived by the senses are but different manifestations of the one universal and eternal Absolute, the Irreducible Real. And this seems to be the one great pattern of the universe—the inter-connectedness of all living systems from the world of man to those of the planets and stars in outer space.

Psychology as an applied science is the product of Western civilization. It is revealing the relationship between matter and the human psyche. Jung, as we recall, had first defined as "archetypes," his own term, the primordial images that have existed in man's collective unconscious since earliest times. Later he defined them as "psychoid archetypes," being both psychic and non-psychic, imprinting not only human and organic life but that of the physical and inorganic world—a bridge connecting spirit and matter. From this he developed his theory of synchronicity: that archetypal energy was manifested in the causally unconnected coincidence of a psychic state and a physical event. Here again we see the energy of the archetype stamping its imprint of wholeness on the spirit of man and on the world of matter. The human psyche and the world of nature appear to be one.

Yet psychology has its limits. It regards gods, spirits, ghosts, and other materializations as mental phenomena projected by the unconscious. The metaphysical East, on the contrary, accepts them as real phenomena appearing to the *sangsaric*, or limited, mind perceiving them.

Another bone of contention between the metaphysical East and the pragmatic West is the stubborn problem of reincarnation. Orthodox Christianity rejects the idea, and Jung himself could not accept it. The Maharshi, already quoted, stated that he had been able to achieve Self-Realization here and now because of his efforts during previous incarnations. He subscribed to the doctrine of reincarnation to the extent that karma, the influence of past lives, is engendered by the Doer. That Doer, however, is the Ego which belongs to the lower plane. Its reincarnations are merely superimpositions which may be transcended by Self-Realization. Hence his characteristic and seemingly contradictory assertion that there is no reincarnation because there is no Ego; there is only the Self. So realize the Self and be done.

Yet today there is an ever-increasing number of people in all walks of life becoming convinced of the existence of a vast Other-World beyond that perceived by our physical senses; and another-dimensional Time in which we coincidentally exist. Psychics and mediums are giving accounts of this realm. Living persons present testimony of their previous incarnations. There are authenticated instances of hypnotic regressions to the prenatal state, a hundred other aspects of the paranormal life we lead beyond our sensory existence.

All these phenomena are no longer ridiculed as belonging to the domain of the occult. Investigations of extrasensory perception, psychokinesis, life after death, and out-of-body experiences are being conducted by governmental agencies, universities, institutions, and individuals which include scientists in many fields. Parapsychology now appears to be at the same stage where Freudian psychology was soon after its inception, and there seems little doubt it is emerging as the new pioneering field of the future. The common denominator of all its categories is the premise of the extended interrelationship between spirit and matter, the living and the dead, and chronological and eternal time.

All these modern scientific advances confirm the belief of ancient civilizations in the inherent wholeness of man and his harmonic relationship with the entire universe. Comprehension of them is largely confined to scientific and academic fields. They exert no influence at all upon the arbitrary and all-powerful forces of federal government, multi-national, military, political, and public media agencies that dictate the course of present Western civilization and the daily life of the general public. Their destructive system of rule seems to be guided by a linear view of time and history, and the assumption that the world is wholly material.

Let us take a close look at these two notions.

Time itself, as we have learned, is not a linear progression of past, present, and future. It is a rounded whole embracing at every moment all the subdivisions of our rationally conceived linear time. The ancient symbol of the Uroboros—a snake biting its own tail—represents the complete circle embracing all time and space, linking the Beginning and the End. All life reflects Time's circular nature and cyclic periodicity: the stars wheeling in their orbits, the succession of seasons and zodiacal ages, the birth, death, and transformation of the earth and all living entities; even civilizations are subject to this organic cycle.

So it is with human history. It does not comprise a straight-line evolution from prehistoric societies up through primitive cultures to the proud apogee of twentieth-century Western civilization. As we have observed, previous civilizations achieved heights of conception and purpose we have not attained. Our Empire State Building cannot be compared to the divinely inspired Great Pyramid of Egypt and the Pyramid of the Sun in Mexico. Our colossal Rose Bowl stadium and others are but commercial sports arenas that bear no relation to the great ball courts of Mesoamerica whose games carried out a religious function. Nor have we achieved a religious philosophy to match those of ancient Egypt, India, Tibet, and China.

Our narrow secular view of history is upheld by orthodox Christianity which measures mankind's life on a linear time-scale from the advent of Christ to an eventual apocalypse, the Second Coming. Ignoring the cosmic cycles of birth, death, and transformation of all living entities in nature, and negating the belief in reincarnation for man himself, it limits him to one, short, worldly lifespan, and to an eternity in an imagined heaven or hell.

Yet throughout the centuries has run an underground stream of consciousness transcending this linear view. Nourished by Hindu and Tibetan yogis, Chinese Taoists, Gnostics, Cabalists, Sufis, Rosicrucians, and a handful of Christian mystics, it has kept alive the ancient hermetic teachings.

It is useless for idealists to entertain the illusion that we can replace the concepts governing our present life by the teachings of the past. Our all-devouring Western society cannot, willy-nilly, do an about-face. It has gone too far down its linear-historical, one-way road to turn back.

The other main reason for our inability to change horses in mid-stream, as I see it, is our prevailing stage of consciousness which regards the world as only materially real. Man's consciousness always determines the way he sees it. Alter this and the world changes. Its very planetary shape has changed with man's evolving consciousness; it has been seen as flat, four-square, round, elliptical; as the hub of a circular universe, and lately as an infinitesimal speck in one of numberless galaxies.

Whatever it is, the world as we see it is materially real as the earth underfoot. Its actual weight in tons has been calculated to twenty-two figures, and photographs have been taken of a sub-atomic particle with a diameter of about four-billionths of an inch. Interplanetary space is measured in millions of miles and light-years; time is broken down into millionths of a second, into "shakes." These macro and micro units of measurement have reached the absurdity of the "googol," the number 1 followed by 100 zeros.

But the world as seen by Eastern metaphysics may also be insubstantial and unreal, the construct of our limited consciousness. If this is true, how then will the world appear when our consciousness expands to reveal another view? Will it seem to us that, like children, we were but trying to measure and explore an evanescent soap bubble? The landing on the moon of an astronaut carrying his golf clubs only increased our technological knowledge and evinced our intention to extend our domination to such celestial bodies at the expense of millions of starving people on our own planet. It did nothing to expand our own limited consciousness, and this function seems to be the only valid measure of all human accomplishments. Of what use the probing of still farther interstellar space by cumbersome mechanical hardware for months or years on end, when even the greatest, immeasurable distances can be spanned instantaneously by a thought?

So it is with time. By a dream, a vision, a paranormal experience, we can supersede the linear limits of our presently conceived past, present, and future. How is this possible if time and space are dimensional fields as we now believe them to be? What if they are but manifestations of one universal Consciousness? It would be easier to bridge them within ourselves rather than projecting them outside.

Granting equal validity to both the materialistic and metaphysical views, how then can the world exist as materially real and insubstantially unreal at the same time? Only consciousness determines the way we see it. And there is a great difference between the Eastern and Western concepts of consciousness.

The Tantric teachings of India and Tibet assert there is but one unlimited, universal Consciousness, dissociated from mind and matter. Human consciousness, on the contrary, is associated with the psycho-physical body, being the thinking faculty of the limited mind. What it observes constitutes only the objects we perceive through the physical senses and their extensions as microscopes and telescopes—a small fact-section of the whole spectrum of life. The mind is not an objective observer at all. Because what we call consciousness is really unconscious, for it in turn is the object of the one ultimate observer, the cosmic Consciousness.

Now to this infinite, eternal, and only objective Consciousness is ascribed the power to *Be* and to *Become*. It finitizes itself in the world of shape, name, and form while remaining itself unchanged. This power to evolve in the material world and to involve it again, seems alogical to our pragmatic Western mind. Yet it explains the Eastern belief that a finite stone is also infinite Consciousness limiting and defining itself in matter, just as it limits and defines itself in our pragmatic consciousness.

The smallest particle of organic and inorganic matter also embodies infinite Consciousness and its power to *Become*, as shown by the potency of the living germ and cell to expand and multiply, and by the immense power of the material atom when released.

This Tantric explanation of our limited human consciousness seems too philosophically obtuse to be swallowed by our technological, progress-oriented Western leaders, so allergic to Eastern metaphysics. Moreover, modern analytical psychology positively denies the existence of any such Cosmic Consciousness or Universal Mind beyond our limited human mind.

Robert Ornstein, however, recently has offered a more acceptable neuro-physiological explanation of why we think the way we do. He postulates two different functions of the human brain. The left cerebral hemisphere controls the right side of the physical body and our rational thought, which is geared to linear time. The right cerebral hemisphere is connected with the left side of the body and controls the intuitive process, reflecting our holistic orientation in space and time.

What has taken place during Western civilization's rise to world supremacy, he believes, is that we have increasingly relied upon the rational thinking function of the brain's left hemisphere to the extent that we are dominated by its concern with the material aspects of the world. Ours is an intellectual, right-handed culture almost totally repressing the modes of consciousness reflecting intuitive and spiritual perceptions.

This physiological split-brain theory seems paralleled by the psychological postulation that man's duality is caused by the split between the unconscious and the conscious. Both of them are based upon the premise that consciousness is associated with the psycho-physical body, in contrast to the Tantric belief that the mind and its limited consciousness interposes a veil between our innate perception and universal consciousness.

The duality is illustrated on a universal scale by the ancient Chinese symbol, the *t'ai-chi*. Its two halves enclosed within a circle, the Yin and Yang, represent the opposite polarities of all life, male and female, light and dark, winter and summer, etc. That these opposites are complementary and reconcilable is indicated by a Yang spot in the Yin half of the symbol, and a

Yin spot within the Yang half. For as the ancient *I Ching* asserts, each polarity eventually changes into its opposite. The enclosing circle is the Uroboros, embracing all time and space, linking the Beginning and the End. And this affirms the circular, cyclical nature of time itself.

The evolutionary expansion of human consciousness thus appears to follow the organic pattern of all Creation. It does not take place gradually, but in cycles of birth, death, and transformation. And our periodic enlargements of consciousness coincide with the cyclic changes dictated by the one cosmic power that governs the indivisible life of all mankind, all nature, the universe itself.

This transcendent power is beyond our comprehension, and beyond our control. Under it, former, secular, linear civilizations have flowered and died. Others have bequeathed to us through their enduring monuments and hermetic records their greater degree of spiritual awareness. Today, in turn, our Western society is suffering the end of its materialistic world dominance at the close of both the present zodiacal age and precessional period. But the future is not as dark as the Maya and Hopi Prophecy predict; despite catastrophes, mankind endures. For this most pivotal hour of change since the beginning of the Christian era marks not only the death, but the transformative rebirth of our current limited beliefs. It will not come overnight nor even in a tragic century. Yet the change is already under way. We can sense its underground movements breaking surface in paranormal experiences of every kind, the receptivity of formal sciences to ancient doctrines, in the political and social revolutions throughout the world. Something of deep import is happening which heralds, if we heed the transformative changes now taking place, a new stage of our ever-expanding consciousness.